# Constructing the New Consumer Society

Edited by

## Pekka Sulkunen
*Senior Research Fellow, Social Research Unit of Alcohol Studies*
*University of Helsinki, Finland*

## John Holmwood
*Reader, Department of Sociology, University of Edinburgh*

## Hilary Radner
*Associate Professor, Department of Communication and Theater*
*University of Notre Dame, Indiana*

and

## Gerhard Schulze
*Professor, Fakultät Sozial-und Wirtschaftswissenschaften*
*Otto-Friedrich-Universität, Bamberg*

Foreword by Erik Allardt

Consultant Editor: Jo Campling

First published 1997 by
**MACMILLAN PRESS LTD**
Houndmills, Basingstoke, Hampshire RG21 6XS
and London
Companies and representatives
throughout the world

ISBN 0–333–63131–5 hardcover
ISBN 0–333–63132–3 paperback

A catalogue record for this book is available
from the British Library.

10   9   8   7   6   5   4   3   2   1
06  05  04  03  02  01  00  99  98  97

Printed and bound in Great Britain by
Antony Rowe Ltd, Chippenham, Wiltshire

---

Published in the United States of America 1997 by
ST. MARTIN'S PRESS, INC.,
Scholarly and Reference Division
175 Fifth Avenue, New York, N.Y. 10010

ISBN 0–312–15944–7

# Contents

# Foreword

In contemporary affluent societies, recent decades have brought forth radical social transformations including profound changes in the everyday life of citizens. The East European revolution, the weakening of class politics, the increasing importance of interaction patterns of an expressive nature at the expense of the influence of nationwide organisations, the simultaneous rise of both international and local networks, and so on, have created new social contexts. In these circumstances, it is not surprising that there is now an intensive search under way in the social sciences to identify the dominant logic of our times and for new visions about our future. The writers gathered in this book, *Constructing the New Consumer Society*, are fully engaged with this task. They represent different and sometimes contradictory points of view, but the thrust of their arguments is that the breakdown of traditional barriers and structures requires social scientists to focus on the motives and grounds for individual decisions much more thoroughly than has been the case previously.

One of the most promising developments is their vision of a *new consumer society* and of the emergence of social codes emphasising consumer preferences, visual stimuli and the moral right to search for Dionysian experiences. In 1950, David Riesman and his associates in their book, *The Lonely Crowd*, presented the first influential description of the change from a society centred on production to one centred on consumption. They focused on the American middle class, describing how the type of social character dominant in nineteenth-century society was being replaced by a new type oriented to consumption, sociability and pleasure. According to the writers of *Constructing the New Consumer Society*, this orientation is now more total, both in terms of the number of people involved and in terms of the realms of life affected. They present a rich and wide range of ways in which this is so, and provide an excellent realisation of Pekka Sulkunen's declaration in his introductory essay that consumption, in a theoretical sense, is very much more than the mere acquisition and depletion of goods.

The new consumer society is constituted by many different characteristics and dimensions, and this book represents a number of different points of departure. It is a truly impressive collection of essays presenting original and even profound views about the social character and game in today's developed societies. There are essays discussing new emphases on sensuality, visualisations, bodily experiences, symbolisation of life-styles, as well as analyses of the new social bonds, new social contracts, forms of moral discourse, rationalities and new tokens of citizenship. There is a common core despite their different viewpoints. All the authors are keen both to observe latent features of contemporary societies and to search for what is new in the forms and logic of consumption. The heterogeneity of viewpoints, however, contributes to its readability and, appropriately, its pleasures. Naturally, there are issues which are left open and unanswered, but the book is a treasure for all who strive to comprehend what present societal change is about and who are themselves searching for new ways of understanding the society of today.

ERIK ALLARDT
*Professor, Member of the Academy of Finland*

# Notes on the Contributors

**Pasi Falk** is a Senior Research Fellow and Docent at the Department of Sociology, University of Helsinki, Finland. He is the author of *The Consuming Body* and has published widely on sociological theory and on the sociology of consumption.

**Denise A. Herd** is Associate Professor of Sociology at the University of California, Berkeley, USA. She has published on alcohol use, culture and race in American society.

**John Holmwood** is Reader in Sociology at the University of Edinburgh, Scotland. He is the author of *Explanation and Social Theory* (with A. Stewart) and *Founding Sociology? Talcott Parsons and the Idea of General Theory*. His research interests are in sociological theory and issues of inequality and welfare in modern societies.

**Kaj Ilmonen** is Professor of Sociology at the University of Jyväskylä, Finland. His publications are on the sociology of food consumption, on social movements and on social theory.

**Thor Øivind Jensen** is Associate Professor at the Department of Administration and Organization Theory at the University of Bergen, Norway. His published work is mainly on citizenship and the welfare state.

**Sytze Kingma** is Research Fellow at the Universities of Tilburg and Amsterdam and teaches sociology at the Tilburg Academy of Architecture, The Netherlands. His research interests are in matters of consumptive pleasure.

**Unni Kjærnes** is Research Fellow at the National Institute for Consumer Research, Norway. Her publications include studies in the sociology of nutrition, with particular interest in food policy.

**Michel Maffesoli** is Professor of Sociology at the Sorbonne, Paris, France. His research covers a wide range of topics in sociological theory and in postmodern culture. Two of his books have been published in English translations: *The Shadow of Dionysus: A Contribution to the Sociology of the Orgy* and *The Time of the Tribes: The Decline of Individualism in Mass Societies.*

**Justin O'Connor** is Senior Research Fellow at the Manchester Institute for Popular Culture at the Manchester Metropolitan University, England. He has published on cultural theory and cultural policy.

**Hilary Radner** is Associate Professor in the Department of Film, Television and Communication at the University of Notre Dame, Indiana, USA. She is the author of *Shopping Around: Feminine Culture and the Pursuit of Pleasure,* and co-editor of *Film Theory Goes to the Movies*

**Gerhard Schulze** is Professor in the Fakultät Sozial- und Wirtschaftswissenschaften of Otto-Friedrich Universität, Bamberg, Germany. He is the author of *Experience Society* and several other works on cultural consumption.

**Peter Simmons** is Research Fellow at the Centre for the Study of Environmental Change, Lancaster University, England. He has contributed to books and journals on 'green' consumption and environmental issues.

**Eivind Stø** is Head of Research, Social Sciences, at the National Institute for Consumer Research in Norway. He has published articles on consumer policy, advertising and consumer satisfaction, dissatisfaction and complaints.

**Pekka Sulkunen** is a Senior Research Fellow at the Social Research Institute of Alcohol Studies and Docent of Sociology at the University of Helsinki, Finland. He is the author of *The European New Middle Class: Individuality and Tribalism in Mass Society* and other books and articles on consumption, contemporary society and social theory.

**Gary Wickham** is Chair of the Sociology Programme at the School of Social Sciences, Murdoch University, Perth, Western Australia. He is the author of *Foucault and Law: Towards a Sociology of Law as Governance* (with A. Hunt) and articles on social theory and on the sociology of law.

**Derek Wynne** is Co-Director of the Manchester Institute for Popular Culture at the Manchester Metropolitan University, England. He is the editor of the *The Culture Industry* and the author of publications in the area of cultural sociology. His research interests are in cultural change and the new middle class.

# 1 Introduction: The New Consumer Society– Rethinking the Social Bond

Pekka Sulkunen

For much of this century, the idea of a 'consumer society', popular in journalistic and ideological discourse, has been an object of sociological criticism. Consumerism as an ideology has been seen as displacing class awareness by promulgating an illusion of united interests of consumers instead of recognising conflicting interests in the sphere of production and distribution. Or it has fallaciously limited the conflict to the protection of consumer interests against excessive profiteering by producers of consumer goods.

Mass consumption has been seen as a relatively marginal 'other' of production, as compared to the basic structures of society such as social class, religion or the institutions of the market, the state or the family. Or it has been looked at from a critical perspective, either as an ideological apparatus or from the point of view of the satisfaction of 'real' needs of reproduction. These arguments imply a moral normative judgement on the value of what is consumed, how and by whom. But the normative nature of such criticisms has been disguised by the fact that they have rested on a widely accepted moral foundation – the ethos of a producing, programming and progressing society.

Now it seems that production has lost its central role in organising social theory, and this has had a splintering effect on sociological visions of the social bond, and consequently on social criticism. Public debate on social policy and the role of the state in a market society has been reshaped along these lines. In the 1980s a new sociological literature on consumption began to appear on themes such as taste and style, fashion, shopping, collecting, the use of cultural products and the media, various kinds of addictions and so on. They soon caught the attention also of social theorists, often in the context of the debate on postmodern society.

Consumption, in a theoretical sense, means much more than the acquisition and depletion of commodities. As compared to production, which implies a plan, deferral of gratification, integrated social order and coordinated action, the logic of consumption collates action and its purpose in the here and now. Instead of conflicts over the distribution of products and the burden of producing them, the new consumer society gives primacy to conflicts over individual freedom against control. Instead of questions about expressed ideals of progress and efficacy, the new consumer society is concerned about unintended consequences and latent motives, desires and functions of individual behaviour. In other words, looking at contemporary advanced societies as societies of consumption marks a change in perspective that cannot be reduced simply to a change in moral dispositions of sociologists. That, too, may be involved, but it is of much greater importance – and interest – that the change in focus of sociological research and theorising may allow us to see our contemporary reality in a different light, drawing our attention to observations that may be familiar to us but go unnoticed until they are interpreted in a general context of the operation of our social system as a whole.

The chapters in this volume explore the possibilities of this vision, both on the level of general theory and in studies of concrete cases that all somehow reflect the new importance of consumption as the structuring principle of our societies. The volume is hypothetical and exploratory in the sense that it raises issues and points out problems but does not attempt to develop a coherent and closed system of concepts and interpretations. The authors are often, if not in disagreement, looking at the new consumer society from different points of view and national traditions, raising issues that need to be discussed and eventually resolved if our vision, more or less shared, is to be developed into a viable theory.

## AFFIRMATION OF HAPPINESS

The shift from production-oriented to consumption-oriented society is not only a matter of theoretical emphasis but bears on key issues concerning the social and political order of affluent societies. Michel Maffesoli suggested in 1982, still hesitating, that 'we might be permitted to think that the technological innovation of the future will put itself at the service of Dionysian modulation, in particular at the service of the body' (1993, 11). We are about to enter an era of orgies, where the sense of community is no longer based on instrumental goals but on sensuality and sentiments, to a point of 'de-individualisation' (see also Maffesoli, 1995). Jean Baudrillard responded, saying that we are already beyond the era of the orgy. Orgies are impassioned·rituals of collective transgression but in today's world there are no limits to transgress. Everything is already transgressed, broken, and the community that results from such transgression is at most ephemeral and insignificant. The rather hopeless question we must ask is not whether we wish to participate but rather: 'What are we going to do after the orgy?' (Baudrillard, 1991).

Maffesoli and Baudrillard were in fact arguing not so much about consumption, culture and ways of life in their own right as about a new kind of community and communal social action that is no longer based on the instrumental social bonds of modern industrial society. Such a shift in focus does not imply, of course, that social criticism from now on could be 'value free'. On the contrary, a striking feature of the sociological postmodernity literature has been its openly evaluative tone. Norman Denzin, for example, is hardly issuing only a personal moral judgement when he writes: 'what started as colonisation of representations by the commodity form (the ideological commodification of objects) has now turned into a situation where the postmodern culture colonises the commodity' (Denzin, 1991, 61). It is this relocation of the nexus of power to the local, to the everyday practice, the most efficient means of which is laughter, that tears down Berlin Walls, forces governments out of office and elicits new issues such as environment, sexual freedom and equality, even anti-racism, in their agendas.

Both the dismal view of Baudrillard and the more optimistic tones of Maffesoli or Denzin testify to a new affirmation of happiness in affluent societies. The guilt for consuming rather than saving has lost its sway; the sentiment of sacrificing momentary pleasure for the sake of accumulation in the future has been dethroned by the spirit of 'hic et nunc'. We may place more or less value on this, or as Holmwood does in Chapter 4 in this volume, remind ourselves of the issues of poverty and inequality that remain pressing. Even so, it does seem to be a valid observation that social life and the principles of community have lost much of their *Gesellschaft* character. Instrumentality has fallen back to expressivity, social movement back to tribality.

The consequences are of considerable dimensions. First, the conception of time in a consumer society is different from the time conception in a society oriented to production. Throughout this century Western societies have been constructing themselves for a better future. Reason in modernity has been valued not only for its own sake, or for the sake of morality. It has been subordinated to the purpose of commanding nature, including the nature of humans (Adorno, Horkheimer). Enlightenment has been a project for a better world through Progress. Alain Touraine (1992, 79–108) has argued that both the political left and the political right, the great divide in modern industrial societies, have accepted this as their primordial cause; they have merely disagreed over the means, in accusing one another of obstructing the March to Progress.

Secondly, the coming of the new consumer society is related to a restructuration of space that has been called globalisation. The whole industrial process is operating on a global scale, and in consequence our material culture exceeds the boundaries of the nation states that have been the political units and frameworks of identity in modern industrial societies. Luxuries have always travelled far, and this is even more true now than in earlier epochs. The difference is one of scale. Now mass-produced goods have international markets. Cultural industries provide international luxury for great masses of the new middle class. Opera stars, orchestra conductors and even large ensembles seek audiences at great distances. Sports are no longer contests between nation states but between international teams and their sponsors. On the other hand, local communities attract masses of tourists from all parts of the world through museums and artistic or media events.

As the diversity of available objects and experiences has become almost unlimited there has been a shift in focus from achievement to inner experience in our life concepts. Gerhard Schulze speaks of the Society of Experience, *Erlebnisgesellschaft*, where we no longer ask how to get things but what kind of life we will have (Schulze, 1992, 33). In Schulze's view, this is not simply a matter of saturation at the lower levels of need hierarchies, as the post-materialists have argued since the birth of mass consumption society (Galbraith, 1962/1958; Inglehart, 1977). At all levels of needs, satisfaction simply is not enough. The way and manner in which needs are satisfied must be subsumed under the additional criterion of the Beautiful Life, and 'beauty does not come to the subject from the outside but will be imputed by the subject to objects and situations' (Schulze, 1992, 39).

The aesthetisation of life is part of the new affirmation of happiness in contemporary affluent societies, but there is a price to pay for it. Uncertainty and disappointments are an inevitable consequence of the possibility and necessity of choice. The less the aesthetic design of our lives depends on external factors such as needs, situations or traditions, the more uncertain we are bound to be about the value of our choices. The inner-directed personality becomes other-directed in a neurotic search of affirmation and reassurance, always vulnerable to disappointments.

Traditional criticisms of the mass consumption society seem now discredited, not because they are normative and should be reassessed in a non-normative light. The reason is that the yardstick by which they have judged mass consumption has become vague or invalidated. First, there is no way of arguing any more that the commodity form somehow simply denigrates the use value of products. It is true that planned obsolescence works in industrial design, most notably in the mutual requirements of developing hardware and software in data processing. Nevertheless, the technology of everyday life in advanced societies has reached a point where essential improvements are hard to envisage. Means of public and private transportation, food, housing and entertainment have improved in quality, comfort and even safety to a degree that is beyond question. It is the use to which they are put that causes problems.

A second criticism of mass consumption society has also lost its rationale although its moral importance has increased. In affluent Western societies poverty and inequality remain problems and they may be increasing in severity, a point stressed by Holmwood in Chapter 4. However, the old Marxist way of arguing about reproduction deficits is now much less convincing than openly moral appeals for justice, unrelated to production, progress and general welfare. Inequality is no longer a matter of practicality but a question of morality and values.

Thirdly, the Veblenesque criticisms of conspicuous waste are still relevant, but hardly in the original sense in which Veblen himself meant, namely that they obstruct natural technological progress. Now the question is about distributing the burden of environmental overloads, protecting the public health and directing public expenditure from conspicuous military waste to peaceful and environmentally sound consumption.

A fourth criticism has been that secondary satisfaction in socio–cultural games of distinction colonises the primary use value functions of consumption. This argument deserves continuing attention, but less as a moral defence of use values than as a question concerning the kinds of secondary uses to which they are put. Consumption style does build up identities, but the issue is to what extent these identities are any longer related to the traditional class system which is based on market positions and relations of production?

## THE BODY AND THE SOCIAL BOND

The scope of the change in perspective from production-centred society to the consumer society is evident in the recent sociological literature on the body, largely inspired by Foucault, whose influence is also felt in several of the chapters in this volume. The issue of the social constitution of the body is important in consumer society not only because everything we consume is taken in, enjoyed and processed by the body, whether through the tactile senses of touch, taste and smell, or through the distant senses of the eye and the ear. The body is important also because in its social and historical constitution the nature of the social bond is at issue.

Consumer society is individualistic by definition. Consumption reflects and embodies our relationships not only to objects but also to others as choice and pleasure through the exploitation of goods and services usually produced by others but also through our own judgements as free decision makers. This has brought the body into focus, for it is as embodied beings that we experience our separateness from others, whereas that which resides in the 'soul' represents the social order: culture, organisation, discipline.

Standard sociological theory has proceeded from the 'soul' in its attempts to understand how modern society stays together despite the division of labour, differentiation, market competition and universalistic individualism. The rationalistic conception of action as an issue of means and ends, mediated by different kinds of cultural factors such as value orientations and collective consciousness, has been taken as a given in sociological theory from Weber to Parsons and onwards. It is only recently that the perspective has become reversed, and writers have begun to look for other possibilities and other kinds of social bonds that might better describe the incorporation of individuals into society in our contemporary reality (Turner, 1984).

A similar bias in favour of the social order has been observed in Foucault's (1979) early conceptions of disciplining the body through technologies of power (Falk, 1994; Radner, Chapter 6 in this volume). The clinic and the prison were for Foucault models of disciplining the body by the outside order, and some followers have taken this in a quite literal sense, arguing that modern society is inherently repressive. A more reasonable way of reading these studies is that modern technologies of power were in fact new in that the discipline they exercise through the body aims at internalising the social order as anonymous norms guiding individual conduct. Nevertheless, in the early Foucauldian formulations the body remains the prisoner of the soul, not vice versa (see also Falk, 1994, 5–8). In the 'History of sexuality' (Foucault, 1988) the perspective changed from technologies of power to technologies of the self that are crucial in constructing the modern individuality. This change of perspective is vital to Hilary Radner's interpretation of the Jane Fonda workout programme and its history. Against a strong feminist tradition she argues that production of the public female body is not simply repression but a process of constructing the feminine self by taking 'your pleasure in your own discipline', to quote Fonda's own words. This shift in emphasis reflects in very concrete terms what B.S. Turner calls the liberation of the body from the prison of the soul so that it comes to be its mirror and a personal project. The techniques of body formation such as dieting are no longer subordinating desire in the interests of the salvation of the soul; instead they are focused on constructing the modern person's sense of self-identity. In this process of secularisation, the body becomes eroticised and public (Turner, 1984), corresponding to the images and expectations of the requirements of this selfhood (to a point where even feminist writers have accepted plastic surgery, as Radner also shows).

It may not be difficult to agree on the newly acquired role of the constructed body as the mirror of the soul, and normally it is interpreted as just another aspect of intensified individualism. For example Pasi Falk (1994, 25) argues that the multiplicity of body forming technologies speaks of the openness of the soul although the body itself becomes increasingly closed and disciplined. A contrast to this is Michel Maffesoli's thesis in Chapter 2 that the 'epidermic conscience' marks a point of saturation in the apparently linear progress of individualism such that the centrality of the body in fact represents an upsurge of new kind of orgiastic collectivism. This is not the place to take a stand in the issue, but it is justified to pay attention to the increased and changing role of the body in constituting social relationships in the new consumer society. It underlines the continuity between what Colin Campbell (1987) has called the romantic ethic of modernity and the contemporary hedonism and individual sovereignty that appear frequently in political debates as arguments against welfare state paternalism. Several chapters in this volume demonstrate this change of balance: Jensen and Kjærnes on Norwegian nutrition policy (Chapter 11), Kingma on Dutch deregulation of gaming (Chapter 9), Sulkunen on Finnish alcohol policy (Chapter 13) and Ilmonen and Stø in Nordic discourse on general consumer policy (Chapter 10).

## ORGANISING IDENTITIES

Another related issue concerns the socially constructed content of consumption itself. This has been a haunting problem for researchers of specific consumer behaviours such as the use of food, alcohol, tobacco, drugs or the media: what actually is 'it' that we consume in these substances and that arouses our desire for them (see Falk, Chapter 5 in this volume)? Ever since it became apparent that the naturalistic need-based theory of use values, subsumed under the aegis of commodity form, leads nowhere, new starting points have been examined not in the relationship between objects and their consumers but in the consuming subjects' relationships to the complex network of subject and object relations outside themselves.

A long tradition exists in sociology, from Gabriel Tarde and Thorstein Veblen to Pierre Bourdieu, in which the desire for objects has been situated in processes of social comparison. Commodities stand for desired social properties or positions, and this is more important than the needs and their satisfaction that the commodities represent. Veblen's concept of status emulation emphasised the competitive aspect of such comparison, Tarde's point of view giving more weight to processes of imitation and its converging effects. Both lines of argument have been taken in criticisms of the consumer society, but this may no longer be their most relevant employment.

For Veblen (1970), the leisure class represented something more than the innate human desire to be liberated from labour. Behind this notion lies a distinction between 'predators' and 'producers', those who create resources and those who merely consume them. Producers include not only the working class but also engineers and industrialists, and of course farmers. Banking capital, bureaucracy and especially the military are predators, and for them the social networks and symbols of not-work are an important resource. Bourdieu's (1979) thesis is close to Veblen's ideas about the symbolic and social functions of style but is fixed on the classical class division of industrial societies. Given the availability of choices and the relatively easy access to any life-style – at least in appearance, images and imagination – we may now ask to what extent the Veblen–Bourdieu line of thinking is valid any more. Is consumption or life-style really capable of reproducing class structures?

Many would say 'no'. Not only the ease of access to different styles but also the underlying class structure itself has become so indistinct as to make the old production-centred thinking about social structure almost useless. The new middle classes, by their very numbers, by their educational resources and by their consumption potential, are capable of imitating and even outdoing the old bourgeois way of life. The classical class structure of industrial societies has become invisible.

Even in contemporary affluent societies ways of life and associated communities are not completely arbitrary and disorganised, but the splintered structures of time (accumulation and progress) and space (nation state and local community), as well as the inner-directedness of contemporary culture, raise new theoretical and empirical problems in distinguishing historically relevant groupings. No presumed identity of interest, no presumed functions of style in reproducing existing class structures, will do as a basis for interpretation, at least as a general guideline. This is the reason why the Birmingham approach (Willis, Clarke, Hebdige) has proved to be problematic outside of its original context, despite the promising idea of homological correspondence between subjectively experienced cultural forms and objective (class) conditions.

Symbols are now more indispensable than ever for the legitimation of social organisation and its hierarchies. The problem is that they now are also more contestable than ever before. If going to an art exhibition, appreciating the works and expressing this appreciation, turn into symbolic constructions of the habitus or of the identity of the audience, they may in the end have nothing to do with the art itself. Aesthetic experience becomes a social convention, a display of cultural capital and a way of accumulating it. Art may just as well be an empty surface within a frame, or music can be total silence in the concert hall. What matters is the social framing, not what is framed. Arbitrariness of the sign becomes complete.

That is why the symbolisms of consumption and life-style wear out as they are used. If commodities no longer represent the needs that their use can satisfy, nor the social properties or positions of their users, consumption is reduced to mere imaginary simulation. In his analysis of modern advertising in Chapter 5 in this volume Pasi Falk comes close to this idea, developed originally by Jean Baudrillard. Commodities are presented in modern advertising as something 'simply good', for example Aspirin being no longer promoted as a pain killer that alleviates the lack of good feeling but as an object of

consumption that stands for the experience of good life as such (see also Falk, 1994, 143–5).
Again Maffesoli offers a radically different point of view. He speaks about the time of tribes (1995), implying that individuality has saturated to the point of falling back to a new kind of tribal community held together by bodily contact and consuming together. The word may be misleading: normally we think of tribes as communities which cannot be escaped; we do not speak of freely choosing them. But even modern tribes are communities for their own sake rather than instruments for higher purposes. They have their own myth and ritual and a sense of togetherness. Also the tribes of contemporary mass consumption society are held together by emotional cohesion rather than instrumental commonalities. They are voluntarily chosen, not based on functional similarity such as class, kin or neighbourhood. Even work-based tribes often function less as work collectivities than as social clubs. Membership in these tribal associations is segmental: it occupies not the whole individual but a role specific to each group. Roles can easily be changed from one tribal group to the next; there is no lasting and total commitment to just one.

Maffesoli has little to say on what kind of tribal communities we might expect to observe in contemporary society or how they could be structured. Gerhard Schulze (1992) has suggested a new kind of solution to the problem of relating subjectively experienced cultural practices to situations and to resources. He distinguishes three 'schemes of everyday aesthetics' or formations of consumption, as they might also be called. These are the 'high cultural', 'the triviality' and the 'tension' schemes. The first is characterised by preferences for the most legitimate culture (classical music, fine arts and so on), intellectual and media practices and a spiritual, contemplative and non-bodily attitude towards pleasure. The ideal is perfection, but unlike in earlier periods of high culture, the contemporary aspiration towards high standards is indifferent to the substance of the life philosophy represented by arts and literature. Any styles, any ideas from any historical period are respectable, irrespective of their way of seeing the world, as long as they are competently classified as High Culture.

The second, triviality scheme is characterised by aspiration to harmony, comfortable sociability (*Gemütlichkeit*) and physical pleasure. It does not conform to the 'taste for the necessary', as Bourdieu describes the aesthetics of the lower classes that are poor in cultural capital. This cultural scheme represents exactly an escape from the necessities of everyday life. It is a culture of the beautiful illusion (1992, 153). Thirdly, the scheme of tension is characterised by a high intensity of bodily experiences, irony towards the established order and the rituals of high culture, antipathy towards the stable patriarchal family and a self-centred individualism that Schulze calls narcissistic (1992, 157).

The schemes are not only sets of attitudes; they are social groupings and identities related to resources and situations, especially education and age. Schulze's analysis exemplifies the unavoidable complexity of descriptions of social structure on the basis of cultural preferences. The complexity is essentially related to the fact that the formations of consumption are not determined by the situation but subjectively chosen. Especially they are not by definition based on (1) work, occupation, income or possessions; (2) or on a hierarchical order of major social groupings; (3) or on conflict between a dominating culture and a counter-culture; (4) or on one-sided determination of the subject by the situation; or (5) on a spatial segregation of major social groupings (1992, 175). These are dimensions of empirical reality. For example the different schemes may or may not be engaged in an open cultural warfare one against another but their definitions and empirical manifestations are – at least in principle – independent of such observations.

The complexity and arbitrariness in the process of assigning meanings to consumption is exemplified by Denise Herd's Chapter 7 in this volume. In the culture of American black youth alcohol takes on the traditional symbolism of masculinity and power. But in rap music the promotion of alcoholic beverages in black communities is also seen as racial domination using

> black bodies as receptacles for consumption ... when markets for alcohol, tobacco, and drugs and other 'sin' products are rapidly shrinking in a drier, 'recovering' middle class white society.

Herd's analysis also usefully points out two limits of the arbitrariness of symbolism attached to consumption. First, the racial groupings and conflicts between them are reflected but not created in consumption. The stereotypes of the black man as a drunken brute and the black woman as sensual, exotic primitive are images in the interest of the white society to refuse equality to the racial minority. The attack of rap musicians against alcohol is part of a struggle over these images. Secondly, alcohol has become the site of this cultural struggle not completely by accident: the American black society has a long tradition of anti-alcohol movements and even today drinking is a less serious problem in it than in some other ethnic groups including the whites.

GOVERNANCE OF SATISFACTION

To say that the new consumer society marks a change in perspective is not meant to imply a neglect of processes related to production and distribution. It does, however, mean that we should be looking more closely at consumption not only as something in its own right but also because the logic of social processes is different. This relates especially to social conflicts. Not denying the continuing importance of conflicts related to work life or equality and security of the distribution of goods and services, the conflicts related to consumption have become central in affluent societies and they cannot be interpreted in the same way as classical conflicts in industrial societies.

Herd's is only one example of this. Refusal to consume is not necessarily imposed by the interest of the dominating social order but can also be a form of resistance. This, in fact, is nothing new. The history of temperance movements provides many similar examples, and some were in effect early steps in the formation of massive nationalistic and labour movements (Sulkunen, 1985). A new kind of conflict, and a new and unexpected outcome of that conflict, is exemplified by Chapter 8 by Justin O'Connor and Derek Wynne in this volume. It is a rivalry between the local spontaneous creation of cultural consumption in the city of Manchester, and centralised planning in the interests of economic reanimation of the area. When the submission of culture to capital is too apparent and follows too closely the global tastes of the business community, the creation of urban 'landscapes' out of local 'vernaculars' (these are Sarah Zukin's terms) may fail. This is only one example of the positive possibilities of deregulation that many sociologists see in the new consumer society.

A similar process of deregulation is going on in many morally sensitive areas of consumption, but for different and less spontaneous reasons. A basic contradiction in consumer society, comparable to that between labour and capital in the society of production, is that between the sovereignty of consumers and their need for protection against various ills related to consumption. The difference is that labour and capital are represented by different groups of people, but the dividing line of the conflict between sovereignty and protection cuts through all of us. Today it seems that in many countries consumer sovereignty is getting the upper hand in negotiations over the balance between individual responsibility and government direction. This is exemplified by the chapters in this volume on different aspects of consumer policy: gambling in the Netherlands (Kingma, Chapter 9), food (Jensen and Kjæjaernes, Chapter 11), alcohol (Sulkunen, Chapter 13) and general consumer policy (Ilmonen and Stø, Chapter 10) in Scandinavia.

There is one important point to note about such deregulation, however. It is made by Gary Wickham in Chapter 14 of the volume on the 'governance of consumption'. Even if 'deregulated' in the sense of being subject to less governmental restrictions, consumption is always directed in some ways. Deregulation in one way brings about new needs of direction in others. This is interestingly shown by Sytze Kingma in Chapter 9 on gambling, which points out that more liberal legislation on gambling has created a new problem of gambling addiction that again is an object of public intervention. A similar pattern is evident in alcohol control and nutrition policy. When the moral grounds for direct restrictions on drinking or eating fail, the discourse of their governance will be formulated in terms of addiction. Wickham's main point is that whatever the regime of governance is, it always involves resistance, and that attempts at directing consumption and equally the forces of resistance have a ritual and therefore cohesive aspect in them, whatever the explicit rationale of governance. Thus the tribes of which Michel Maffesoli speaks in the context of consumption may get counterparts in tribes that are opposed to consumption. This is already evident in the effervescence of social debates around alcohol, gambling and tobacco smoking but could be understood more generally as tribalistic conflict between different and contingently chosen life-styles.

Addiction and other health problems related to consumption are comparable to other risks such as the environmental problem. We have enormous quantities of information, both of the causes and the consequences of environmental problems, just as we have of healthy nutrition and healthy lifestyles. An essential part of this information is not of immediate experience but produced by experts and delivered to us by the media (Beck, 1992).

The new consumer society is therefore a culture of suspicion. Peter Simmons shows in Chapter 11 in this volume how the fraudulent use of eco-labels has turned into a new form of regulation and conflicts over it where the distinction between moral, technical and interest-bound discourse is almost impossible to make. But similar suspicion cuts even deeper into the divided hearts of sovereign consumers in need of protection and reassurance. As the situational determinants of life-style have become weak and the inner-directed drive to the Beautiful Life has become imposed on us by the necessity to choose, individual happiness and pleasure are elevated to the centre of our existential order. The quest for certainty about the value of choices, but also about their rationality in terms of risk avoidance, has nowhere to look. Mistrust places a new moral burden on individuals but also on social theory. If the unifying horizon of production and progress is replaced by a particularistic spirit of the here and now, there are no agreed criteria to assess the value of public policy in protecting health, environment or equality, often in the face of strong particular interests. Yet, as Schulze argues in Chapter 2 in this volume, such situational exigencies may again come to the focus of social life, this time attacking subject-centred thinking instead of being attacked by it.

## FRAGMENTATION

In sociological theory such indeterminacy has appeared as the fragmentation of society. An apparent radical incommensurability of ends is the problem of social order in a subject-centred culture, where the way of life, style, identity and even adherence to social groupings are chosen rather than situationally determined.

This has led some writers to the conclusion that sociological theory must also be fragmented and partial, dependent on a point of view. Many say this in order to avoid normative judgements on the way people choose to live. Others, like Michel Maffesoli, take an openly affirmative position on the free and uncontrolled uses of pleasure. John Holmwood takes a critical stand in Chapter 3 in this volume towards such postulations, arguing that those who accept them capitulate before the incommensurability of ends and may sacrifice the values of inclusive citizenship and equality, represented by the welfare state, to the benefit of the free reign of market forces. One epistemological reason for this laxity is that theoretical constructions of the postmodern society are often ideal types. Deviant observations can be pushed aside as unimportant exceptions instead of leading to critical examination and correction of the theoretical model itself.

There is a contradiction at hand when theorists celebrate heterogeneity, both of social reality and of theory, but nevertheless base ideal types on one dominating feature of contemporary social life and use them as comprehensive interpretative frames. Indeed, one might argue that there is much less heterogeneity between these ideal types than one is often led to believe. The lost idea of progress, the corruption of the values of Enlightenment, the primacy given to the body or to ritual and emotions instead of instrumental reason are common elements in many different attempts to construct tools for understanding the postmodern condition. An interesting point of convergence is brought out by Maffesoli's and Schulze's contributions to this volume (Chapters 1 and 2). Both understand social change in cyclical terms, and this may reflect the disappearing vision of linear evolution so dear to modernity.

Nevertheless many important issues remain open and the time has not yet come when all of them are resolved or even identified. Despite any convergencies, debate in social theory is in this sense heterogeneous and incommensurable. Especially striking is the influence of national traditions and the difficulties they create in locating common theoretical problems. In the long run a comprehensive theory may be developed of advanced society where consumption has taken priority over production. Such an understanding will require rigorous conceptual analysis but also visions and empirical case studies. This volume employs the two latter means to make sense of the consumer society that is being constructed before our very eyes.

**Note**

I wish to thank John Holmwood for his valuable help in writing this Introduction and Pasi Falk for his insightful comments.

**References**

Baudrillard, J., *The Disappearance of Art and Politics* (New York: St Martin's Press, 1991).
Beck, U., *Risk Society: Towards a new modernity* (London: Sage, 1992).
Bourdieu, P., *La distinction: Critique sociale du jugement* (Paris: Minuit, 1979). Trans as *Distinction*, London: Routledge & Kegan Paul, 1984).
Campbell, C., *The Romantic Ethic and the Spirit of Modern Consumerism* (New York and Oxford: Basil Blackwell, 1987).
Denzin, N., *Images of Postmodern Society. Society Theory and Contemporary Cinema* (London: Sage, 1991).
Falk, P., *The Consuming Body* (London: Sage, 1994).
Foucault, M., *Discipline and Punish: The birth of the prison* (Harmondsworth: Penguin Books, 1979; New York: Vintage Books, 1979).
Foucault, M., *The Care of the Self* (Harmondsworth: Penguin Books, 1988).
Galbraith, K., *The Affluent Society* (Harmondsworth: Pelican Books, 1962/1958).
Inglehart, R., *The Silent Revolution* (Princeton: Princeton University Press, 1977).
Maffesoli, M., *The Shadow of Dionysus – A contribution to the sociology of the orgy* (New York: SUNY Press, 1993) Originally published as: 'L'ombre de Dionysos: contribution à une sociologie de l'orgie'. Paris: Méridiens Klinckesieck, 1982. English translation by Cindy Linse and Mary Kristina Palmquist.
Maffesoli, M., *The Time of the Tribes: The decline of individualism in mass societies* Originally published as 'Le temps des tribus, Le déclin de l'individualisme

dans les sociétés de masse.' Paris: Méridiens Klinckesieck 1988. (London: Sage, 1995).

Schulze, G., *Die Erlebnisgesellschaft: Kultursoziologie der Gegenwart* (Frankfurt am Main and New York: Campus Verlag, 1992). (To appear in English as *The Experience Society* (London: Sage, 1995.)

Sulkunen, I., 'Temporance as a Civic Religion', *Contemporary Drug Problems* 12 (1985), 267–85.

Touraine, A., *Critique de la modernité* (Paris: Fayard, 1992).

Turner, B. S., *The Body and Society: Explorations in social theory* (Oxford: Basil Blackwell, 1984).

Veblen, Th., *The Theory of the Leisure Class* (London: Unwin Books, 1970).

# Part I
# The Vision

# 2 The Return of Dionysus
## Michel Maffesoli

### INTRODUCTION

It is not a new idea that any given era can be understood as
structured by a specific dominant logic. The 'anthropological structure' as understood by Gilbert Durand, Foucault's
epistème or Kuhn's paradigm are heuristic propositions of
great interest to the effect that the actions, feelings and
prejudices that rule social relations either in particular
institutions and spheres of life or in the civilisation as a
whole, are organised and ordered around a central value
principle. J. G. Merquior (1988, 41) makes a pertinent distinction between several notions of this kind, speaking of
'underground thought', 'mental infrastructure', or an 'historical a *priori*'.

Each of these expressions articulates, in different ways, the
fundamental and existential essence of an 'epochal point of
view'. Combining the static and the dynamic, this point of view
allows us to see a certain epoch as organised around a constant value principle, while also permitting us to interpret
changes and variations within it as modulations of such a
principle.

This is how I see the new consumer society which is constructing itself before our very eyes, not only in advanced
Western societies, but, increasingly and sometimes even more
frenziedly, in cultures that are imitating the occidental culture
while being dependent on it. The current efflorescence of
values glorifying consumption, pleasure, and satisfaction in
the ex-socialist countries is a good case in point.

The rise of the new consumer society is not simply a matter
of reordering priorities in everyday life. What we are observing is an unexpected and frivolous revaluation of everyday
life itself. It would not be appropriate to reduce the change
into a mere restructuring of the market from production-
oriented industries to the splendour and abundance of
consumer goods, services and entertainment. The epochal

change penetrates all spheres of life and ideology, and, to make sense of it, it should be seen as a new and emerging epochal regime of our culture as a whole. From empirical research, we can see the emergence of this new '*Zeitgeist*'. The great explanatory systems which have ruled modernity seem powerless to grasp the new logic of social existence. It is a logic that is centred on being together. It is a logic which no longer aims towards an end, or is directed towards a distant future. On the contrary, this logic is immersed in everyday life here and now, *hic et nunc*. Metaphorically speaking, it is a structure of the 'domestic' rather than the 'politic', and is directly related to what has been called the 'despondency of the political age' (Hocquenghem and Scherer, 1986; Maffesoli, 1992). This formulation indicates well the need for a new way of understanding life and living in society, nested in the vacuum left by the *absence of a plan*.

To explain this in a brief and necessarily partial way, I would say that the classical duality of the moral and the political that has characterised modernity as a specific epochal structure, is now being succeeded by a new duality of hedonism and aestheticism. This latter duality can be said to be the nexus of postmodern culture and existence. The modern duality of politics and morality was based on an ambition for perfection and unity. In a more or less conscious manner, it was a matter of eliminating all confusion and disorder, to reabsorb the anarchy of life to the framework of order, to replace the polytheism of values by the monotheism of utilitarianism. '*Uti et non frui*' was the golden rule. From this followed the imposition of a certain dialectical logic that sought to squeeze aside anything that did not fit its logic. In the modern perspective anything that did not correspond to the useful, to the projective, to the serious, was to be cast aside from the correct, logical political discourse. (Maffesoli, 1993b, 54).

In modernity the emphasis was placed on a progressive view of history, the creation of the future from the promises of the past. In contrast, the postmodern duality of hedonism and aestheticism is acted out in the spirit of destiny, or, the *amor fati* (fatal love) of the tragic. It is concerned with a multiform sliding of different aspects of our culture, which merge into a heterogeneity that can be illustrated by the importance of pluralism, fracture and relativism in many domains of life. All these things emerge from the primacy of everyday life in all its concreteness. The postmodern heterogeneity defies simplification. It defies predilection for unity and abstractness of the modern rational view. Here we rediscover the antinomy between the Apollonian and the Dionysian world view, formulated at the end of the last century by thinkers such as Nietzsche and Walter Pater. According to their views, there is a constant oscillation between the severe and calm unity of classical periods and the disordered efflorescence of periods that could be described by analogy as baroque. While the Apollonian periods are regulated and systematic, clarified by the light of understanding according to what Pater calls the 'Parmenidian abstraction's ideal', the Dionysian periods abandon themselves to 'the endless game of the unbridled imagination' (Pater, 1988, 154–9).

This scheme has become so familiar that there is no need to elaborate on it any further. It suffices to point out that in postmodernity a general process of extroversion can be observed in domains as diverse as architecture, clothing, relationships with the social or natural environment, and even in political life. This extroversion is a product of *somatophil* societies that exalt and value the body.

This re-epiphanisation of the body is by no means an individual or narcissistic fact, but rather a global phenomenon. It is a crystallisation of individuality within a completely collective ethos. The history of ideas illustrates how the density of one dominant logic such as the rational individualism of modernity gives way to its opposite when it exceeds the limit of saturation. No value principles, or figures, as I also have called them, are eternal. But it is well to keep in mind that nothing stops them from being reborn when their time returns, albeit in different forms. The *homo economicus* that succeeded the *homo politicus* of Ancient Greece has repeatedly appeared in multiple modulations in the history of mankind, and its specific reincarnation in modernity has been only one of these. On the basis of such cycles, it seems to me that today, in the new consumer society, we are observing the (re)birth of *homo aestheticus*. For me, this is just another way of saying postmodernity.

## HOMO AESTHETICUS

By 'aesthetic' I mean, according to the etymology of the word, the ability to feel emotions and sensations collectively. It is to 'vibrate' together in harmony. As Alfred Schutz (1984) has expressed it, aesthetic experiences are those in which we enter into 'syntony'. In contrast to modern individualism, collective sensations or 'vibrations' are the kind of nuclear experiences that give meaning and structure to the postmodern era. The linear evolution that modernity imagined to persist and lead to a total dissipation of the imaginary and the collective, is thereby broken.

In the new consumer society Prometheus is under suspicion.

The rationalism of modern societies has refused to see that no social life is possible without non-logical collective figures or representations that constitute the framework within which social life is possible. These can be the mythical representations of Antiquity, or the scientific representations of our time; the difference is of small importance. What is changing now is not the foundational figurative logic itself. Only its form is undergoing a process of transformation from the individualistic and utilitarian to the hedonistic and collective (Maffesoli, 1993a, 162).

We need only to observe the contemporary collective effervescence experienced in large musical concerts, sports events, festivals and collective consumption. This seemingly aimless and pointless excitement centred on the here and now is nothing else than a manifestation of a radical criticism of productivist mentality in the midst of everyday life. Work and progress are no longer the only legitimate categorical imperatives. Many economists, experts and philosophers agree today that these value principles have had their day, even in a simple chronological sense.

We need not be limited to examples that are obvious but which, to many, will appear trivial. Similar shifts are occurring in contemporary management doctrines that stress affective identification, group work and cooperation instead of mere instrumental efficacy. The whole of our contemporary social life with voluntary associations, charitable societies, hobbies, parents' associations, local clubs, environmental and moral lobbies, in fact anything we do, is structured by small interchangeable groups whose explicit goals and purposes are served by them much less than the 'affective participation' or, in Max Scheler's word 'Mitgefühl' itself (Maffesoli, 1993b, 15). Finally, it should be pointed out that the emerging aesthetic order of things has an epistemological dimension. It is a culture of the image, of the visual, in contrast to the rationalistic culture of the Concept. An image does not aim at exactitude or truth. It has what might be called an iconic function that has no validity in itself, its function is to 'present' something else, here and now. Pictures are there to be looked at now, together with others, and in that sense they are vehicles of tactile communication. Against contrary interpretations, we should remember that Narcissus is not drowning when he wants to be fused with his own image. When he falls into the well he is merged with the cosmos that the well stands for. Metaphorically speaking the same is true of the television screen. Mass Narcissism falls into its own image, but in doing so it merges with the social body. This means that televised messages have no prefixed meaning, the community of their meaning is created in the collective experience of the viewers. In a sense, Jean Baudrillard's (1990, 25) analysis is correct when he says that an overflow of communication is a symptom of a failure of communication. But this is incorrect as soon as we realise that there is a kind of communication that in all meanings of the word attempts to contact the other. Nonverbal communication to which 'meaning' is of secondary importance is predominant in today's culture that deserves the name 'imaginal', in contrast to the rationalism of modernity. It is a relativistic form of communication that supports relationships at the expense of concepts (Maffesoli, 1993a, 121).

It is a mistake, therefore, to lament the individualistic privatisation, egoism, or loss of the spirit of citizenship that are often said to be characteristic of our time. The contemporary ideals of community are not definable within the framework of the political project of modernity. They explode that project, attack it with mockery or simply take it with total indifference. This does not mean that another kind of solidarity could not be possible. On the contrary, what we are witnessing is a new organic solidarity, in the strongest sense of 'organic'. It is a solidarity that puts back together all the elements separated by modernity. It is a solidarity through actually lived experience rather than via concepts, it ties the whole personality to a familiar group, in which the members can invest their energies in proximate affairs or at least in activities that nourish the community itself (Maffesoli 1995, 53).

All this is familiar, and the frequent question one hears is why it should be so. My answer would be that the question is misplaced. Usually it only articulates a worry or a disappointed nostalgia for the fallen Promethean idol. The 'why' question asks for criticism of that which is to be explained, so as to say what went wrong. Or, vice versa, it may articulate a critical distress about modernity itself so as to affirm and exalt our emancipation from repression under the aegis of Progress.

Themes such as liberation, activism or the culture of production have all had their day. They will certainly return, just as their decadence and their renaissance have repeatedly occurred and reoccurred in the course of human history. For the time being, however, we need not necessarily take a moral stance. It is not our task to say what should be but to insist on what is. To quote van Gogh, 'we must unscrupulously believe that what is, is'. What is today is the plenitude of groupings and communal and communicative myths. That is enough (Maffesoli, 1993a, 111).

In my view, such alternations are sufficiently accounted for by the mechanism of saturation, which Pitirim Sorokin described so well. It is difficult to determine the point of saturation in the solution one is salting until that point is reached. By the same token, it may appear presumptuous or even insane to indicate, in a world which is apparently so dominated by the economy of goods and effects, the emergence of the values of sensuality and sociality. My hypothesis is that the sentiments that utilitarian individualism has relegated, like women, to the home, now tend to reassert their efficacy in the societal game through a process of saturation of the very same individualism (Maffesoli, 1993b, 14).

Other themes, other ways of seeing, other concepts that may be equally nebulous as the preceding ones when they were newly (re)born are nevertheless now attracting the attention of sociologists as powerfully as they are capturing the lives and conceptions of the heroic common men and women in their contemporary everyday lives.

Of course, any social analysis which starts off from such premises is destined to be a caricature, in the sense that it will describe and interpret by way of exaggeration, even absurdity, to make that which 'is' obvious and visible to the naked eye. Using an expression of Nietzsche, we should look for the depth of the new order on the surface of things, we should reach for an approach that will take seriously the appearance of things, to give them their true weight without forcing them into a finite form in which their meaning would be distorted.

## UNPRODUCTIVE EXPENDITURE AND THE EROTIC BODY

As though a revengeful return of the repressed, it is unproductive expenditure which now is taking the place of the activist progressism that structured life and culture in the modern era. Gilbert Durand (1979) showed a long time ago with great insight how Dionysus was lurking beneath the surface even at the height of the progressivist myth (and its cult of the machine) in the nineteenth century. Others, such as Colin Campbell (1987) or Daniel Bell (1976) have underscored that modernity itself had two heads, the ascetic and the romantic. Be that as it may, it is no paradox that the Dionysian spirit today has the upper hand, nor do I find any reason to construct critical theories in favour of one against the other. What we must try to do is understand that which is instead of arguing for what should be.

It is from this perspective that we should look at the recent emphasis on the body in the new consumer society. The human body, once the organ of production, has now given way to the erotic body. Is this a simple rebellion as in the classical scheme of liberation, such as those promulgated early on by such Freudo-moderns as Erich Fromm, or Charles Reich? Not necessarily. Rather, the resurgence of the erotic body testifies to a positive force, one that says 'yes' to life as such and in general and not only to sexuality as a means of liberation. It is a force that resides under many surfaces and surges up from time to time irresistibly, as if it were a ground swell of such depth and strength that nothing can stop it. It is indeed an ambitious project that accounts for what is most characteristic of the new consumer society: the upsurge of popular expenditure that exhibits the classical features of Durkheimian theories on ritual waste. What once was only a popular emulation of the avant-garde, of the artists, of solitary and proud geniuses, now diffuses as if by capillary action throughout the social body. The *jouissance* of the present, the '*carpe diem*', is becoming a massive and incontestable value.

The current concern for the body indicates something about the new forms of organic solidarity that is antithetical to the modern democratic ideal that rested on a conception of the individual as autonomous, master of the self and of history, entering in relationships with other autonomous individuals through contracts in order to make History and society. In contrast, it is a fusion, even confusion, that replaces distinctions and elaborates the postmodern social bond. Researches on the cult of the body – cultural tourism, dietetics, fashion, sports – show beyond doubt that the body is constructed, cultivated and embellished under the eyes of others and for others to see. Thus even that which might appear as a sign of perfected individualism is in fact part of our tribal, collective hedonism (Maffesoli, 1993a, 74).

It is in this sense that I understand what Octavio Paz (1976) calls 'an exaltation of organic values'. They are expressions of the senses, images, passions and feelings of a given moment. An ethic of the moment, until now in mezzo-voce, is rising to an unforeseen crescendo.

It would be both naive and a misrepresentation of the case if we were to understand this momentary ethic only from a chronological perspective as something that fashionably comes and goes. Instead, what we are observing is an archetype of sociability that gives structure to our world and our social existence. What is historical is not the archetype itself but its cyclical movement as it now enters the front stage after having played minor and nearly invisible roles in the shadows of backstage. The cyclical rise and fall of this archaic social form have now led to the return of Dionysus, as a phase of the war of the Gods that in the language of the Homeric ethic takes the form of the rise and fall of diverse and contradictory fortunes. There is no hell and no heaven for us to resist or to pursue, there is no single God, nor his necessary opposite. Instead we are confronted by a pantheon of divine beings that correspond to the plurality of our existence. Indeed, it is this very plurality of the divine that is the source of our uncertainty and the tragedy of our social existence. Coming to terms with destiny is tragic not because destiny is one but because it is a plurality.

The unproductivity of popular expenditure is comparable in its effects to the luddism that has been relegated to the shadow of Prometheus by current, but now fading, rationalism. The ritual and social functions of waste and destruction by the luddites have been comprehensively analysed in the classic writings of those such as Huizinga (1975, 26), Caillois (1958, 70) and Duvignaud (1973, 5), and we need not go into details here. All we need to keep in mind is the concept of 'residue' in the sense that Pareto uses this term: an irreducible core around which diverse 'derivations' are arranged. The symbolism of economic war in the financial market, pecuniary emulation (Veblen) and the political spectacle are examples of such wasteful and belligerent expenditure that I have elsewhere called 'the game of the world', which fashions in one form or another all social life. Therefore, far from being just a passing fad, the splendour of popular expenditure is a manifestation of a basic ritual of all human existence.

Luddism is only one occurrence of this ritual and demonstrates its persistence and power in the midst of a society that professes both individual utilitarianism and reason. Mystics, whose ideas have long been refused in concert with the general spirit of the modern era, were conscious of this power and they merit our renewed attention. Jacob Böhme, in whom I am particularly interested at the present, considers that the maintenance of contemporary existence is made possible only by the 'joyous game of eternal reproduction' through aimless pleasure and purposeless waste (Faivre, 1969,14). This trail of thought is worth pursuing, but it could perhaps be better formulated in terms of Fourier's 'hyperrationalism': there is a reason behind the unreasonable, and this reason relates to the primordial logic of community, love and attraction (Fourier, no date, 157). The recognition of such 'hyperrationality' of the social implies the re-integration of elements into social theory that until now have too often been put aside (Maffesoli, 1993b).

In fact recent sociology has taken steps in this direction. We no longer hesitate to recognise the primordial role of illusion, the imaginary, or of simulacrum, which evoke the randomness of human life and account for it in figurative forms of speech. Death is the ultimate randomness and death is also the situation in life that can be thought of in no other way because that is where the social existence of humans becomes concrete and irrefutably evident. Only in fantasy and imagination can this otherwise unspeakable fact be expressed with shining lucidity. The same goes for orgies, whatever their diverse forms. They are the expression of the erotic body, the body that enjoys together with other bodies and produces an exaltation of the experience of being together, unchained from the exigencies of productivism.

We should therefore not be at all surprised to confront such Dionysian luddism in the contemporary world of heedless pleasure and consumption. Nor should we think of it in terms of 'past' and 'future', to explain it away today as a moral failure or to lament its past repression as deviance from the free rein of true human nature. Its constancy and persistence appear as astonishing only because the primordial desire of waste and destructive expenditure appear as emptiness or hollowness in a world which, in modernity, turns everything into something positive and evaluates the outcome from the perspective of construction. It is in this sense that we must understand the Maussian concept of unproductivity.

THE ORGIASTIC RITUAL

Rituals, as we know, have religious roots and more precisely orgiastic ones. They are 'embodied fantasy', taking the expression 'embodied' with its full semantic force. It is indeed the body which confronts, caresses, collides, loves. Instead of getting lost in the notorious euphemisms of political or religious liturgies about 'soul', 'spirit', 'faith', 'ideology' and so on, we should recognise above all that ritual experience is lived through and in the body, whether violently or tenderly according to the case. Fantasies associated with rituals always refer to the body in one way or another, and they always imply waste, expenditure, even destruction, all that is useless. Their function is the same as in religion, although religion no longer exists unless the word is understood literally in its etymological sense (*religare* = to tie back, to re-bind). Rituals form a bond between those who without religion would remain isolated. From this comes the importance of those contemporary rituals that involve the body: drinking together, eating together, banquets, dances, music, sports and so on. These rituals provide a bond of aggregation, and they play an important part as expressions of the need for communion in everyday life.

Given the presumptuous existence of the industrious Prometheus in modern culture, the problem today is to recognise the presence of the noisy Dionysus as a necessary and increasingly rampant figure of sociability. The return of Dionysus to the front stage changes everything, from world view to aesthetics and the everyday life. The question from now on is no longer knowing how to master life but how to waste and enjoy it. 'The problem is no longer knowing how to make the true me flourish inside myself, but to bring in the harvest and to consume my life' (Max Stirner). This admirable perspective captures precisely everything that is involved in the opposition between the culture of production and the culture of expenditure, and it also insists on maintaining the irreducibility of this opposition.

What Stirner wrote about subjectivity can be extended to the social framework. Although the new consumer society appears as a gigantic ritual of expenditure by individuals, that extravagance is made possible by an underlying popular expenditure of the masses.

What Freud called the 'polymorphous perversion of the child' is close to this idea of expenditure. When the child is exploring all the erotic possibilities of its body, this activity has no finality or purpose. It is a game without a goal, but even games without goals do have rules, one of them being that they are games with the body. Neighbourhood sociability, evenings of drink and merriment, various carnivals, wine and beer festivals and many other forms of communal consumption remind us of the persistence of a certain village and peasant paganism that has refused to follow the Promethean path to rationalisation and to Weberian 'disenchantment of the world'.

The unproductivity of the child's play is only one manifestation of 'the joyous game of eternal reproduction' that Böhme

talks about. It is useful to contrast production and fecunda-
tion in order to understand that it is in the latter where what
I have called '*the will to live*' matters most. The will to live,
individual as it often appears as in the play of the child,
depends in the end on the unproductive persistence of
sociability.

## THE NEED FOR FUSION

Two centuries of autonomy, separation and frantic individualism have led us to believe that these are natural states of the
world, and that if there is any evolution left it is towards an
ever-accentuating perfection of these ideals. Therefore, we are
particularly struck today by observing the persistent and impe-
rious need to be '*en reliance*', to be bound together, which is
manifested in the unproductive expenditure and bodily game
of consuming together. It is in this sense that I speak of tribalism, which is a way of being that favours fusion, or perhaps
even emotional confusion (Maffesoli, 1995).

It is important to note that the contemporary tribal togetherness is a specific form of sociability, diametrically opposed to
the modern figure of being social. Its existence reminds me of
Edgar Morin's formulation, according to which we need to reconsider the complete set of solidarity rules (Morin 1983,
130). The thing which dominates all others is the desire, the
warm desire, to be together. This desire is no longer characterised by the rigid modes of organisation that are familiar to
us from the modern individualistic collectivism, but rather
refers to an ambience, to a state of mind that is best articulated through life-styles that gives priority to appearance and
form rather than goals and means to their achievement. It is
in a sense a collective consciousness, or rather a collective un-
consciousness that acts as a matrix of a multiplicity of experiences, situations, actions or of group affiliations. It is striking
to observe how contemporary mass rituals consolidate micro-
scopic groups that, on the one hand, are distinct but, on the
other hand, constitute an indistinct whole, that is to a certain
degree even confusing. This is what has led me to use the
metaphor of the orgy to underscore that contemporary group
attachments, even if often transient and momentary, may be

emotionally so strong that individual identities sink completely into their common feeling of togetherness.

Let us pursue a paradox: the tribal mass rituals of the new consumer society are at once local and emotional *and* nevertheless shared by large masses. They can be observed in diverse sporting events that are diffused by the media and gain importance far beyond those who participate directly in them. They are present in the frenzy of consumption and spending in large department stores, hypermarkets and commercial centres that of course sell commodities but which above all emit a symbolism. They generate a sense of participation in the life of a common species. It is apparent in the aimless wandering that takes place in the streets of big cities. Finally, we meet this desire of fusion in the rituals of evasion during summer holidays that offer the spectacle of crowded beaches, a spectacle that many observers deplore for its promiscuity and for the discomfort of that swarm. Again, we should remind ourselves that such rituals allow us to experience an euphemised communion, and as Gilles Dorfles has formulated it, 'to abandon any space between the self and others, to construct a single amalgamated social body' (Dorfles, 1984, 30).

Such a swarm is subtly differentiated, and tastes in dress or sexual preferences, sports, music and the very regions one likes to visit reveal a willingness to share a coastal territory with others, thus creating a communal ensemble with different and complementary functions. From such anecdotes we can retain a constant movement between the tribes and the masses that belongs to a fear of emptiness and loneliness. This '*horror vacui*' that is manifested for example in the non-stop music on beaches, in department stores and in many pedestrian streets creates an atmosphere that reminds us, perhaps not by coincidence, of the permanent noise and uncoordinated agitation in oriental and Mediterranean cities.

Be that as it may, this atmosphere can be found in all domains of contemporary societies, and to understand it better we only need to remind ourselves of its theatrical nature (Duvignaud, 1973). Theatre is a mirror of society, and one part of the 'hustle and bustle' of our cities comes from diverse street entertainments. Another part is a version of the 'barbaric theatre' and diversity of cults of possession that have African, Brazilian or Hindu origins. This is not the place for a detailed analysis of such phenomena (see Maffesoli, 1995); I only want to indicate that they all rest upon a tribal logic that is only possible in concatenations of individuals into networks, within masses.

All the aforementioned elements contradict the spirit of the serious, of individualism, of 'separation' (in the Hegelian sense of the term); a spirit which is characteristic of the modern bourgeois and productivistic way of life. Both productivism and the bourgeoisie have done their best to render aseptic any forms of social life that can be compared to dances of possession or that otherwise bear signs of popular effervescence. Perhaps we should see here a justified vengeance of the values of the South over those of the North, a kind of 'choreographic epidemic' (de Martino, 1966) that tends to contract to it a growing number of people. Dances of possession have the function of aggregation. Lamenting or rejoicing collectively have simultaneously aimed at healing the sick and at reintegrating them to the community. These cults, characteristic of the Mediterranean area (maenadism, tarantism, various bacchanalias), of India (tarantism) and of African or Latino–American regions (condomblé, shango) are of particular interest for understanding group therapy, the networks of alternative medicines or mutual help groups now in vogue. They are all manifestations of what Schutz called 'making music together'. The rise of sectarianism and other similar phenomena are manifestations of contemporary modulations of the choreographic epidemic.

These examples, and many others that could be given, are indeed metaphors of what I have called the '*Bacchus fédérateur*', the connecting god (Maffesoli, 1993b). Among the diverse vehicles of such federation, alcohol plays an important role in sustaining communion and integrating in a homeopathic and ritualistic way the 'cursed part' (Bataille, 1949) within social structure. In this sense it is not possible to say which existing life-styles will prove to be prophetic. All we know is that their very mix, in all its heterogeneity, will. If it is not yet possible to say in a positive way what kind of new culture is now emerging, we can nevertheless say that it will be structurally multi-faceted and contradictory. It will rest on the pleasure and desire of sharing emotions and affections with others, in one word: it will be Dionysian.

# POSTMODERN 'ENVELOPE-MENTALISM' AND THE CONSUMER SOCIETY

There is a dialectic of depth and surface that essentially determines the style of life at any given moment. The pleasure of the body, the stress placed on the superficial, is that which best characterises the postmodern era. This is how we might formulate the 'aesthetic ethics' of our time: it is a morality determined by a body that with all its powers engages itself with pleasure. This has two important consequences, first an epidermic self-awareness and second, the fact that the body is a 'communicating machine'. For these reasons, the anthropological construction that we call the 'body' sometimes becomes both the cause and the effect of an intensified social activity.

The concern with the appearance of the body that is manifested in advertising, in the consumption of drugs, alcohol, food and fashion, and which is manifested *par excellence* in body-building sports, is much more than a superficial or inconsequential phenomenon. It is part of a great symbolic game, a certain way of touching others, being in relationships with them, in other words of constructing society.

A reflection on the diversity of modulations in which the body is socially valued makes available an important theoretical lesson too often neglected in classical sociology. The individual body is the foundation of the social body. It constitutes its specific economy in the simplest sense of the term. The figure, the form, the image of the body have often been misrepresented as static, while in reality they are mobile and in constant cultural transition. Marcel Mauss wrote of the technique of the body, by which he meant the correlation between society and the manner of making use of the body. More recently Michel Foucault refers to the same fact in his last books (1984a, 1984b) when he writes about the care of the self (*souci de soi*) and the uses of pleasure (*usage des plaisirs*). In each case, the stress is on the idea that culture, which is the foundational matrix of social life, cannot be understood without understanding the body. Both Mauss and Foucault aim to show that the social body cannot exist in abstraction from the individual body, which is the basis for constructing social reality.

This point invites us to reconsider the frivolity of the new consumer society in its fascination with fashion, design, gustative pleasures, eating and drinking, anything that expresses the cult of the body that constitutes the atmosphere of this society. The care for the body is both cause and effect of all social dynamics. It is also the privileged manifestation of what I have above called the aesthetic experience: feeling emotions together, sharing the same ambience, to participate in practising the same values or to get immersed in a general and overwhelming theatricality. This banality is worth repeating to remind us that the 'psycho–physiological unit' that we often think of as individuality does involve the body, a fact too often forgotten in modernist sociology. The body is an envelope enveloped in the external world. Many philosophical, psychological and sociological analyses recently have correctly drawn attention to the epistemological consequences of this fact. A body is not capable of constituting identity unless it is situated in the social world. Situationalism or, to create a word, 'envelope-mentalism' is a correlative to the numerous bodily practices that are an integral part of the new consumer society today, including apparently contradictory phenomena such as drinking festivals as well as care of the body, dietetics, cosmetics and theatricality.

In particular, the cult of the body helps us to see that such games of appearance are part of a great symbolic system that is not insignificant from the point of view of our social existence. The increasingly predominant culture of communication is indeed the current modulation of such a symbolic system. We are living in a period which is like some others that have been thought of as naive or primitive, in which the individual or the social body has been intensively charged with 'envelope-mentalism' or communicational symbolism. Our own bodily rituals represent an anthropological constant, a means of situating the self in a web of relationships with others. The body is cause and effect of communication, of symbolic order: in brief, of society.

### References

Bataille, G., *La part maudite* (Paris: Minuit, 1949, trans. 'The Accursed Share', New York: Zone Books, 1988).

Baudrillard, J., *La transparence du mal* (Paris: Gallimard, 1990).

Bell, D., *The Cultural Contradictions of Capitalism* (New York: Basic Books, 1976).

Caillois, R., *Les jeux et les hommes* (Paris: Gallimard, 1958).

Campbell, C., *The Romantic Ethic and the Spirit of Modern Consumerism* (London: Basil Blackwell, 1987).

Dorfles, G., *L'intervalle perdu* (Paris, 1984).

Durand, G., *Figures mythiques et visages de l' oeuvre* (Paris: Editions Berg, 1979).

Duvignaud, J., *Les ombres collectives. Sociologie du théâtre* (Paris: PUF, 1973).

Faivre, A., *Eckartshausen et la théosophic chrétienne* (Paris: Klincksieck, 1969).

Foucault, M. *Histoire de la sexualite 2: L'usage des plaisirs* (Paris: Gallimard, 1984a).

Foucault, M., *Histoire de la sexualité 3: Le souci de soi* (Paris: Gallimard, 1984b).

Fourier, Ch., *Oeuvres complètes* (Paris: Anthropos, no date).

Hocquenghem, G. and Scherer, R., *L'âme atomique. Pour une esthétique nucléaire* (Paris, 1986).

Huizinga, J. *L'automne du Moyen Age* (Paris: Payot, 1975).

Maffesoli, M., *The Shadow of Dionysus – A coutribution to the Sociology of the orgy* (New York: SUNY Press, 1993b).

Maffesoli, M., *La transfiguration du politique* (Paris: Grasset, 1992).

Maffesoli, M., *La contemplation du monde: Figures du style communautaire* (Paris: Grasset, 1993a).

Maffesoli, M., *The Time of the Tribes: The decline of individualism in mass societies* (London: Sage, 1995).

Martino, E. de, *La Terre des Remords* (Paris: Gallimard, 1966).

Merquior, J. G., *Foucault ou le nihilisme de la Chaire* (Paris: Presses Universitaires de la France, 1988).

Morin, E., *L'esprit du temps* (Paris: Livre de Poche, 1983).

Pater, W., *Essai sur l'art et la Renaissance* (Paris: Grasset, 1988).

Paz, O., *Point de convergenge* (Paris: Gallimard, 1976).

Schutz, A., 'Making music together', *Sociétés*, vol. 1, no. 1 (Paris: Massors, 1934).

# 3 From Situations to Subjects: Moral Discourse in Transition

Gerhard Schulze

## INTRODUCTION

Forty years ago, making a case for a public morality would have been strongly encouraged. Twenty years later you would have run the risk of being attacked as a boring puritan idiot for expressing it. Today, moral appeals are often no longer understood. The rhetoric of everyday verbal intercourse has undergone a significant loss of normative concepts. Notions like 'sin', 'guilt', 'good', 'evil', 'decency', 'selfishness' and so on are dropping out of collective memory. They provoke helplessness rather than consent or aggression. 'What do you mean?', is a common response.

At first glance, it seems that reflections on moral discourse have to be limited to the observation that there is nothing left to be observed. But it would be sociologically naive to interpret the disappearance of moral notions as the end of the history of morality. On the contrary, the history of moral discourse remains very dynamic and, while we are still trying to comprehend the past period, we have already entered a new one.

The following chapter deals with the change in the moral discourse concerning consumption. Exactly where this change will lead is one of the key questions at the end of this century.

Moral discourse is embedded in general universes of thinking. I will analyse morality within two such universes of thinking which I call 'situation-centred' and 'subject-centred'. After comparing both frames of reference I will distinguish three subsequent stages of moral conflict. My concluding remarks concern the role of elites in the transformation of moral discourse.

38

## MORAL DISCOURSE: THE DIALECTICS OF TAKING AND RENOUNCING

Moral discourse crystallises around two topics: taking and renouncing. On an elementary level of thinking all of us are convinced that taking is better than renouncing. Therefore, moral discourse traditionally is centred on renouncing; the great bulk of moral effort since antiquity has been prohibitive. In European history, the classical manifestation of moral discourse has been the sermon. The lasting meaning of the word 'sermon', even more durable than its association with 'church', is the caricature of a moraliser trying to spoil other people's fun.

People need a lot of argument to be convinced that it is good to renounce while, on the other hand, it is taken for granted that it is good to take. Appeals to take are reinforced in an advanced culture of consumption, in which the individual has to digest many more goods and services than are needed for survival. Since the nineteenth century we can observe such a change of the mix within the moral discourse on consumption, the positive and inviting elements becoming increasingly explicit and frequent. The history of advertisement can be interpreted as the transformation of the moral discourse on consumption, with the preacher being gradually drowned out by the salesman who suggests that it would be a great fault not to take.

The weakening of the voice that preaches renunciation may easily be mistaken as the disappearance of morality itself, but perhaps in no former period have the morals of taking been so omnipresent as they are today. We are permanently admonished to take; renouncement seems to have become obsolete. Take, for instance, the message of an advertisement for Martini in the Italian magazine *Panorama* (1993), showing a bottle and a smiling woman: *Potete benissimo vivere senza di lui, o di lei, ma che noia!* (You surely can live without him or her [the Martini], but how boring!)

Because of the dialectical relationship between taking and renouncing, the morals of taking might however contain the germ of a renaissance of the morals of renouncing. In the same magazine, another advertisement shows a woman stretched out on a wooden bench looking up to the dark sky where one can read the words *Sedile scommodo – osservatorio per le stelle* (uncomfortable seat – observatory for the stars). The message is: You need nothing to be happy – a rather paradoxical redefinition of the situation in a context of consumption.

Beyond this aesthetisation of asceticism (well known in the history of civilisation) quite another moral pattern of renouncing has arisen: the motive of damage avoidance which is basic to various green movements throughout the world. But can this pattern ever become popular?

## UNLIMITED CONTINGENCY OF CHOICE

There is a world wide trend towards a transformation of living conditions. Nearly all societies follow the agenda of attempting to increase options in everyday life. One of the codes by which this agenda is represented in public opinion is the concept of wealth. What exactly does wealth mean? At first, one thinks of wealth in terms of money, but money in itself is worthless. Its value exists only in relation to the products that it can purchase. I emphasise this expression, 'can', because it indicates an understanding of wealth based on behavioural logic. Wealth as the availability of possibilities – this is what determines human behaviour in the end. Increasing wealth in this sense means increasing possibilities; a new unlimited contingency of choice.

The paradigmatic place where the new contingency of choice became visible for the first time was the department store, the institutional locus of the late nineteenth century consumer society.

This new institution helped change the nature of aesthetics by which goods were marketed, introducing powerfully persuasive techniques in film and decor that are still being refined. The department store also changed the very nature of the place in which people consumed, what they consumed, the information they needed to consume, and the styles of life to which this new consumption was devoted (McCracken, 1988, 29).

The last few decades have brought an acceleration of the new contingency of choice or, as it were, an expansion of the department store over vast territories of the social world.

The situation with which one's senses are confronted during a trip through the supermarket plainly illustrates everyday life in rich societies. The visitor, with his or her minute psychological and physical digestive capacity, is faced with thousands of consumption possibilities. Another relatively new phenomenon is that people take for granted the fact that they can drive anywhere at anytime.

Other modes of unlimited choice are not even related to the economic concept of wealth. For instance single pregnant women have to make a choice: they can of course marry the father but they can also simply move in with him, or not move in with him, or even just leave him. Who would have thought in the early 1960s that today we would have a sexual contact market for every possible alternative, from heterosexual to homosexual, lesbian, bisexual, group sex, sado-masochism, rubber, leather, and so on? It all reads like a menu, and that is exactly the intention.

The examples above illustrate that the new contingency of choice is more than just a phenomenon associated with prosperity. Contingency means an increase in possibilities. The increase in consumption possibilities is only one of many aspects of this phenomenon. This is not simply a phenomenon caused by prosperity; more generally it is a phenomenon of modernisation which will not be driven away by unemployment, recession, and stagnation of real income.

## THE NEW PARADIGM OF EVERYDAY THINKING

To the same extent that societies advance upon this path of transformation, traditional systems of orientation developed for a situation of scarcity become inadequate. How should we deal with the world when it becomes difficult to identify our goals? This formulation is, of course, exaggerated. Yet one can not overlook the fact that the obvious challenges of getting things with which one is faced in everyday life have sharply decreased in affluent society. One explanation for the intensified advertising competition at the turn of the century was that demand was insufficient to absorb the supply (Fraser, 1981, 146).

But the problem of answering the question 'What do I want' during this period was only a foretaste of the uncertainty of consumers at the end of the century. An orientation vacuum has arisen. Under these circumstances a type of Copernican turning point is implied. Goals will no longer be defined in terms of situations, but rather in terms of oneself.

The paradigmatic personality type in the new consumer society is the 'selector'. The requirements of unlimited choice in everyday life transform us into catalogue page turners, composers of menus, possibility managers. What type of psychodynamism occurs in the phase of this new freedom to choose? The basis for understanding this issue is the difference between influencing and selecting. I will make use of both concepts in order to indicate the relationship between subject and situation. When the limits of objective conditions become very constraining, one attempts to influence the situation. The expansion of possibilities leads to a decline in this type of behaviour, and at some point selection replaces attempts at influence. The difference between the two concepts can be illustrated by using the example of eating. The attempt to influence the environment in this realm encompasses not only cooking habits, but also farming, hunting, and stockpiling. Selection, on the other hand, consists of reaching into the freezer to grab a precooked meal, or choosing a number on a menu.

> For example in English diet the outstanding and apparently irreversible trend is the growth in demand for manufactured 'convenience foods'. (Burnett, 1979, 344)

Influencing refers to accepting a situation and attempting to change it to one's own benefit. The fundamental question used to plan actions is: 'What can I do, if anything?' The positive experience for those who attempt to exert influence is the triumph over circumstances. The negative experience is the feeling of weakness or powerlessness. One can either do nothing, or attempt to do something, and fail.

Selecting, on the other hand, implies quite another relationship between subject and situation. The chief question now is: 'What do I want?' The first question ('What can I do?') describes a problem of survival. The second question ('What do I want?') takes survival for granted. Survival stress has been replaced by the stress of getting through life.

Influencing implies labour on the situation, while selecting implies situation management: taking on and disposing of life circumstances. Situation management proceeds much more quickly and comfortably than situation labour: turn it on, turn it off: drive somewhere, drive back; start something, stop doing it; move in together, separate.

In a situation of many options the actor is forced to know what he or she wants. The normalisation of a life of choosing has induced a revolution in thinking. In conditions of scarcity, thinking is situation-centred; in a situation of many alternatives it is subject-centred. Often this development is misunderstood as a shift towards extreme selfishness, but it would be ridiculous to portray past times as being a paradise of altruism. Selfishness and altruism are persistent phenomena within a changing frame of reference.

As Forty points out in his study on the history of design, subject-centrism is not only a by-product of the increase of supply, it also has been systematically supported by the symbolic expansion of the space of alternatives.

> A masculine-looking pocket knife might underline the purchaser's view of himself as manly, but as long as it was the only men's knife available, it would do nothing to make him feel different from other men. What would do this would be the opportunity to choose from a range of knives or to have a particular design which he alone among his acquaintances might possess. (Forty, 1986, p. 87)

Today, extreme symbolic and practical variety has become a common feature of all types of commodities. Now, self-reflection as a consequence of choosing between many alternatives is permanent and ubiquitous in consumer society.

The revolution of thinking can be characterised as a diametrical turn of perspective: from outside to inside. Indeed, the term 'revolution' which Kuhn uses to describe the displacement of a scientific paradigm by a new one now has to be extended to paradigms of common sense.

Within this new frame of reference, the whole society is subject to a profound metamorphosis, as I have analysed with respect to the case of Germany in the last few decades (Schulze, 1995). In the subject-centred society nothing remains as it was: symbols and aesthetic patterns, mechanisms of group affiliation, social milieus, basic semantics of social perception, market relations and, of course, moral discourse.

## TAKING AND RENOUNCING WITHIN THE SITUATION-CENTRED UNIVERSE

Sociologically, the most important feature of moral discourse within the situation-centred universe is the objective anchorage of the notions of good and evil. Thus moral reasoning about both taking and renouncing has a concrete meaning which ensures interpersonal communicability of moral meaning. The idea of the good life is patterned as 'life in good conditions'.

The Great Exhibition of 1851 in London was an overwhelming symbolisation of the heroic battle for better conditions. Samuel Smiles's book *Lives of Engineers*, written a decade later, is an example of the enthusiastic appreciation of progress as defined in terms of situation improvement.

England was nothing ... until she had become commercial ... until about the middle of the last century, when a number of ingenious and inventive men, without apparent relation to each other, arose in various parts of the kingdom and succeeded in giving an immense impulse to all the branches of national industry, the result of which has been a harvest of wealth and prosperity. (See Wiener, 1985, 29; 80–1)

The great industrial expositions which attracted worldwide attention signalled the inauguration of consumer society.

The arrival of the twentieth century was celebrated in Paris by a universal exposition spread over 550 acres and visited by 50 million people from around the world. The 1900 exposition was the climax of a series of similar events that in the popular phrase of the time, were arranged to teach a lesson of things. 'Things' meant, for the most part, the recent products of scientific knowledge and technical innovation that were revolutionising daily life; the 'lesson' was the social benefit of this unprecedented material and intellectual progress. (Williams, 1982, 58)

The spiritual climate during the era of Germany's 'economic miracle' offers a perfect example of this mentality. During this period happiness was defined through terminologies referring to situations. People's desires were externally oriented, based on external conditions – money, an apartment, furniture, automobiles, household appliances, holidays, prestige. The opposite of happiness was the objectively identifiable lack of desirable goods, the desirability of which was self-evident; the more one had of these goods, the better one was doing. Whereas today the question 'how are you doing' is usually interpreted as an inquiry concerning one's inner feelings, it was at that time mainly interpreted as a question about one's objective living conditions.

What is the reason for taking within this frame of reference? It is the improvement of the situation of the actor. Everybody can understand the justification of taking because everybody knows, at a rough common sense level, the distinction between better and worse living conditions.

The same holds true for the moral justification of renunciation – it refers to objective facts. Why should consumers renounce? Let us cast a view on three important patterns of renunciation: saving, transfer of resources, and abstinence. The meaning of saving is to guarantee good conditions in the future; the meaning of transfer is the improvement of the situation of the needy other; the meaning of abstinence is to maintain good psychophysical and social conditions. For instance, the concern about reading addiction in the eighteenth century was motivated by the fear that women reading too much would be driven into a sort of moral illness which was seen as a quasi-measurable fact like influenza. In all three examples – saving, transfer and abstinence – the meaning of renunciation is to avoid or to reduce problems that are believed to be visible, measurable, experienceable facts.

There are also anti-materialistic patterns of renunciation, above all the moral justification of the simple life in the Christian tradition.

Early New England Puritanism was not opposed to prosperity itself but to the selfishness and avarice that seemed to accompany it. Superfluous wealth almost inevitably diluted one's piety ... Quaker social thought ... did go beyond Puritanism in insisting that the widening gap between the wealthy and the indigent should be narrowed. Leading a plain and benevolent life, at whatever level, would benefit the community as a whole and would ensure that one's heart was wedded to the eternal rather than the temporal world. (Shi, 1985, 12; 29)

At first glance it may seem a strange point of view, but I think there is an important common feature between materialistic and spiritual modes of renunciation – the focus of action is imagined outside the subject, either in the situation or in the Kingdom of the Lord. And in both cases good and evil manifest themselves in the same objective manner. Good and evil become visible as things which people have, or desire but do not get, or could get but do not renounce. How does moral discourse change when extrinsic thinking becomes peripheral and the intrinsic pattern conquers consciousness?

## TAKING WITHIN THE SUBJECT-CENTRED UNIVERSE: RATIONALITY OF EXPERIENCE

The turn towards the subject-centred universe of thinking does not imply the loss of morality itself, but only the loss of objective references for goals and problems. This loss was prepared for by an increasing vagueness of the objective characteristics of things in the perception of consumers under the influence of advertisement.

The usefulness and value of most things depend, not so much on their own nature as upon the number of people who can be persuaded to desire and use them. (*An Advertiser's Guide to Publicity*, 1887; see Fraser, 1981, 134)

Slowly the focus of interest has moved from things to the person. Now the good life is defined in terms of experiences.

Life is intended to be 'interesting', 'fascinating', 'exciting', 'pleasant', and the like.

Because of the loss of objective references, moral discourse has changed dramatically. Little is left to discuss; so moral notions have nearly disappeared from ordinary language. Moral discourse is restricted to the fervent confession that everybody can do what they want, or even has to do what they want. The last moral position discussed with the claim to be binding is that nobody should be bound. Thus, the general structure of moral arguments is pure self-reference: legitimation by subjectivity.

The moral nature of that discourse is revealed by the reactions of disapproval and aggressiveness when other modes of legitimacy are propagated, such as duty, tradition, convention, religious commandments. After the Second World War, American

> economists expounded the basic marketing strategy of the 1920s: the public must be taught to consume more and expect more. And more people, both at home and abroad, must be brought into the marketplace. Still, many adults who had undergone the hardships of the Depression and the rationing required for the war effort had to be weaned from a decade and a half of imposed frugality in order to nourish the consumer culture. A motivational researcher told a business group that the fundamental challenge facing the modern capitalist economy was to demonstrate to the consumer that the hedonistic approach to life is a moral, not an immoral one. (Shi, 1985, 249)

Happiness has become a rather complicated construction: it is coded as 'feeling'. What do people who want to experience certain feelings strive for exactly? They are in search of psychophysical processes, and more, they are in search of certain self-reflections on their psychophysical processes. They want to observe themselves as involved in processes they believe to be pleasant. Here the central goal of the consumer is not having (as in the situation-centred mode) but being, as Erich Fromm (1976) puts it. In subject-centred thinking, having is not an end in itself but a means – it is not enough to have desired objects; the consumer also wants to believe that she is enjoying them.

The new morality of taking manifests itself in a pattern of reasoning I call 'rationality of experience' – that is, the attempt to optimise 'outside' means in relation to 'inner' ends. Generally, rationality means pursuing goals by using the most optimal means, and continually working to improve the means–ends relationship. The specific feature of rationality of experience consists in defining goals in terms of the subject itself. External circumstances are arranged towards the end of achieving the best possible internal effect. We choose, taste, exchange, throw away, affiliate, leave each other, travel here and there, eat this, drink that – always trying to improve the relation between situational input and subjective output.

The rationality of experience is the systematisation of behaviour under the control of internal orientation. The criteria of utility, quality, and wealth are projected internally. Acting within a framework of a technical, instrumental relation to themselves, people attempt to manipulate their internal existence through the use of situation management.

The particularity of the rationality of experience can best be seen by examining failure. If my thinking is externally-oriented, I will be disappointed if I am unable to obtain a desired good, or if it doesn't perform as guaranteed. On the other hand, if my thinking is experience-oriented, the above model will not be sufficient to explain my reaction. It is possible that I will be bitterly disappointed even if my desired object functions perfectly but nevertheless the product does not produce the desired effect inside of me.

## UNCERTAINTY AND DISAPPOINTMENT: THE PARADOX OF TAKING

What does one actually want when one does not wish merely to have something, but rather wishes to be something? At this point the person has become the goal of his or her own behaviour and activity. It seems that we have not fully understood what we are doing in such situations, and that our society has not only been shaped by subject-centred rationality, but also by a related epistemological self-misunderstanding.

Wanting to be something represents a project of self-reflection. The naive thought that one can search for and find oneself, as if this 'self' were a given, camouflages the fact of reflective self-construction at the moment of 'discovery'. Nothing is a given, and everything remains open. One is faced with incalculable possibilities of self-discovery.

Having is concerned with things, and things are concrete, and can be described. Being is concerned with experiences, and experiences can basically not be described. (Fromm, 1976)

If this is true, then our inner life will not be a basis for stable orientation. It is not so easy to induce desired psychophysical processes by mere manipulation of the situation because there are two problems, one before and one after the act of choosing. First, actors often do not know what feelings and experiences they want, and second, even if they do, they often fail to achieve the feeling they wanted. Intrinsic rationality inevitably is accompanied by uncertainty and disappointment – as a consequence of self-reflection.

People often try to specify what they want before the act of choosing: they try to 'find' their self. The central problem of the subject-centred orientation is, however, that the self does not exist independently of the process of seeking it. We have to construct it by self-reflection and there is no fixed design at all. So intrinsic rationality creates a new type of uncertainty – not knowing the ends instead of the traditional uncertainty of not knowing the means.

After the act of choosing, people try to construct happiness through reflection on their psychophysical processes – they want to believe that these processes are pleasant. But this reflection often fails: we are incalculable. Perhaps the person who has made great efforts to feel good is now in low spirits, or she has changed her mind, or she distrusts her own reflection that she is feeling good, destroying her reflection by metareflection. Even the most deliberate 'intrinsic rationaliser' cannot avoid the risk of disappointment which can occur as a result of subjectively induced incalculability.

Compared with the situation-centred pattern of happiness the new idea of the good life as a psychophysical process is a very unreliable promise. The happiness of having is accomplished if people get what they desire – objects, persons, situations. The happiness of being is not at all a matter of course even if people work as hard as they do to arrange situations with the intention of reacting in a manner they regard as being pleasant.

Paradoxically, the unattainability, or at least instability of the desired type of happiness does not weaken but rather strengthens the morals of taking. One of the reasons for this astonishing phenomenon is the incorrect but intuitively plausible theory of the constructed nature of inner states by outside arrangements. If everything can be achieved by technical control over circumstances, why not desired modes of being too? Every problem (uncertainty and disappointment) will be interpreted as a challenge to make it better; so the frame of reference producing failure is stabilised instead of being destroyed. A second condition is the idea of happiness as a psychophysical process. The absence of happiness is defined as an uncomfortable state of body and mind. If the notion of happiness is rooted psychophysically, we are addicts; after a period of learning, the pursuit of happiness becomes automatic, inevitable and self-preserving even in the case of increasing unhappiness. Thirdly, the mechanism of taking can sometimes be interrupted by the decision to renounce, but within the intrinsic mode of rationality, renouncing something almost inevitably leads to taking something else.

## RENUNCIATION WITHIN THE SUBJECT-CENTRED UNIVERSE

In the scheme of intrinsic rationality renunciation takes on the structure of the following argument: 'In order to elicit good psychophysical processes, I will not take this object.' But this seems contradictory. If we want to elicit subjective processes we have to change something. On the other hand, if we renounce, nothing changes. Normally, we cannot stimulate distinct inner episodes by doing nothing.

There is one important exception: renouncing things we already have or are accustomed to. In this case renunciation means positive action, replacement. This is consistent with the intrinsic scheme of doing something in order to feel good. However, this type of renunciation presupposes prior accumulation. It is the renunciation of the surfeited. The most evident example, of course, is the trend in dietary patterns that has led to deliberate avoidance of certain foods for cosmetic and physiological reasons. (Burnett, 1979, 348) But in most instances, there is no clear signal of 'too much', as in the case of eating. The desire for new clothes, cars, shoes, sightseeing, information, sexual relationships and so on is not balanced by a psychophysically rooted feeling of repulsion.

Within the subject-centred universe of thinking, renouncement expresses desire rather than rejection. This mode of thinking can be traced back to the beginning of the century.

> The aesthetic simplicity embodied in the American Arts and Crafts movement was frequently a salve for overindulged and overworked members of the urban middle and upper classes. ... The return to nature advocated by most Arts and Crafts spokesmen was not that of a Thoreau or Tolstoy but that of an Emerson, Downing, or Norton – a comfortable home and vegetable garden in the country, within commuting distance of the city, and blessed with the amenities of civilized living. (Shi, 1985, 193–4)

In rich societies, a type of hedonistic renunciation has become as normal as excessive consumption. The contemporary pattern of dieting, for example, fits exactly the general formula of 'doing nothing in order to feel good'. Actually, however, this 'doing nothing' is celebrated with certain rituals such as following diet rules, making the diet explicit in everyday talks, attending diet seminars, staying in a diet institution for a week or two, paying for not consuming. Through various rituals 'doing nothing' is transformed into 'doing something'; thus it takes on the character of the situation management necessary to put rationality of experience into action. The project of reflection of oneself as feeling good requires concrete triggers and constant reflection: 'Now event X has taken place, so let me see if my feelings correspond to my prior intentions, which motivated me to produce it in the first place.'

In this way renunciation can be reconciled with the logic of action in experience society. It is typical for Buddhism and meditation fashion, for not travelling during holidays, for not watching television, for not going shopping and so on. Always 'doing nothing' is made explicit by rituals transforming non-action into action: 'You know we'll simply stay at home next holidays. It must be marvellous to do literally nothing.'

In the experience society renunciation is not really the opposite of taking, but only one of thousands of alternatives aiming at the manipulation of one's own psychophysical state. The distance between taking and renouncing is as small as the distance between several television programmes that can easily be changed by remote control. So people switch between taking and renouncing according to what they believe to be more pleasant at a given time.

## THREE STAGES OF MORAL CONFLICT

In our culture of consumption there is an infinite, insatiable demand which has been answered by an explosion of supply. While this is occurring we can catch sight of the limits. If nothing changes the limits will be imposed by catastrophes, violence, and social breakdown. It seems that we are on the threshold of a new moral discourse – new in two respects: it will refer to problem specific for the twenty-first century, and it will have a new semantic structure.

What are the problems? In order to be brief, I will mention only three topics, each directly related to consumption: the environmental problem, the problem of international inequality, and the problem of various types of addiction. There is a common feature: all these problems are defined again in terms of objective facts. This, perhaps, is the beginning of a new stage of moral discourse. We can grasp its semantic structure more clearly if we distinguish it from two preceding stages:

At the *first* stage, in the universe of situation-centred thinking, moral conflicts were focused on problems of scarcity – antagonistic interests, justice of distribution, demands for charity, and the confinement of emotion by 'reason' in the life course.

The most prominent form of this traditional type of moral discourse is class conflict. In view of the cultural gap between the bourgeois and the proletarian way of life it may seem surprising to state that the moral discourse of class conflict is culturally homogeneous. Class conflict crystallises around common, objective reference points – money, ownership, living conditions, rights and obligations. Moral terms like 'exploitation' and 'subversion' refer to a world of desired goods which is essentially the same for both parties. Thus, the notion of 'antagonism' should not take our mind off the fact that both parties are very close to each other in terms of the definition of the situation. As Mukerji states with respect to early patterns of capitalist development in Europe:

> hedonism and asceticism seem on the surface contradictory, but they share one feature: an interest in material accumulation. The pure ascetic rationalist of Weberian theory accumulates capital goods, while the hedonist consumer revels in amassing consumer goods. The two types can be envisioned as extremes on a continuum of materialist tendencies, using opposite systems of values to organize and make sense of material accumulation. (Mukerji, 1983, p. 4)

Philosophically, the moral discourse of class conflict is simple. The history of moral discourse on consumption is a history of increasing philosophical complexity.

The *second* stage of moral conflict evolved in the 1960s and 1970s. People in almost all the rich societies experienced a conflict between two universes of thinking. The traditional situation-centred pattern was aggressively attacked by the subject-centred pattern. The new heroes proclaimed the abolition of moral restrictions, but actually they installed the new moral mode of intrinsic rationality, the clearest symbolisation of which was the new glorification of dropping out.

Some decades later, we can hardly understand the furious moral irritation with which 'normal people' reacted to the pattern of dropping out. In the traditional Wild West plot, violence evolves within the moral scheme of scarcity conflicts. In contrast, the act of violence at the end of the film *Easy Rider*, when 'normal people' kill the motorbike freaks, does not fit in to the Wild West routine at all. The victims do not violate the interests of their murderers. On the contrary they symbolise fundamental lack of interest with regard to the very logic of situation-centred action. They have dropped out of the traditional frame of reference. Thus, moral conflict evolves between different frames.

Under these circumstances, moral aggression is felt to be a fundamental existential threat that cannot be settled by giving things, but only by giving oneself. The solution of the conflict requires a personal conversion rather than an ordinary compromise, which is typical for the first stage of moral conflict. Since the late 1960s, the time of Easy Rider, this conversion has taken place collectively. The martyr death of the protagonists of the new subject-centred philosophy does not look at all like a symbol of resignation, but rather like a pathetic narcissistic apotheosis, revealing the fact that the 'killed' principle actually was the aggressor.

> Perhaps the sharpest penetration of the cultural politics of the hippies was their immanent critique of the protestant ethic, and of its accelerating internal contradiction in late capitalism ... More and more capitalism needs obvious, luxurious and unnecessary forms of consumption: it needs hedonism to maintain the driving-force of its asceticism. The protestant ethic needs its opposite in order to continue its own irrational progress. The hippies did not make this contradiction but they dramatised, exploited it – ground it out – in the minutiae of their life-style. They were the caricatured nightmarish incarnation of the bourgeoisie's own developing contradictory other nature. They did not earn, yet sublimely expected to survive. They watched and experienced nature as if there were no work to be done on it. They did not produce, yet they consumed without guilt. (Willis, 1978, 173)

At the present time, moral conflict is reaching a *third* stage: the reversal of the second stage. We can observe a renewal of the confrontation between subject-centred and situation-centred thinking, but this time the latter mode of thinking is the aggressor. This aggression has accompanied modern consumerism almost from the beginning, but it has become popular only in the last few decades. As Williams points out, the neo-ascetics at the turn of the century (for example George d'Avenel), believed that proliferation of needs would always outrun the proliferation of resources. They were sceptical of the nineteenth century belief in progress, fearing that material resources can never expand fast enough to keep up with the expanding consequences of unlimited human desire (Williams, 1982, 265).

So far, this new moral conflict has not yet fully evolved. What we see is not a moral discourse but a schizophrenic simultaneity of different universes of thinking without communication, and often within the same person.

On the one hand everyday thinking is encompassed in the subject-centred mode which allows only for an intrinsic motivation of renunciation: 'Don't take in order to feel good.' On the other hand we cannot ignore increasing situational problems – environmental crisis, aggravation of global economic imbalance, addiction. So we call for renunciation. But the necessary type of renunciation would be situation-centred which would require quite another behaviour than hedonistic, subject-centred renunciation. Basically the new claim for renunciation cannot be understood within the dominant subject-centred universe of thinking. It sounds reasonable but people do not put it into action. They are still living in a discursive state, the real conflict has not yet become obvious. It is a latent antagonism of different frames of reference.

Will this third stage of moral conflict ever become explicit in everyday thinking? Its elaboration requires philosophical distance – the competence to see one's own universe of thinking from a metaperspective. This expectation is not at all totally utopian. In the second stage of moral conflict the semantic structure was similar; indeed in that period there was an incomparable increase in everyday philosophising and theorising about the good life. Reflection about the ultimate existential goals became popular.

There is one important difference between the second and the third stage of moral conflict. Situation-centred thinking is now attacking instead of being attacked. One could be sceptical as to whether or not this will become a real new movement, because it is much easier to slip from the situation-centred universe into the subject-centred world than to go back the other way. Perhaps subject-centrism is like a 'black hole' in astronomy – a society once caught in its field of gravitation has passed a point of no return.

As Williams points out, the dialogue between hedonistic narcissism and austerity tends to turn the latter to Victorian moralising and only worsens the prevailing despair and anxiety. Its message is seen to be that people have to give up pleasures in retribution for past sins of overindulgence (Williams, 1982, 395).

Williams advocates the substitution of the negative morality of forbidding by a positive one that constructs new possibilities for social solidarity and collective action. The private car is one clear example. For individuals it may indeed be the only dependable means of transportation, given the circumstances. However, if the society as a whole decides to cut back on this form of consumption as inaffordable luxury, other alternatives become possible in a positive way that may lead to reinforcing new kinds of social bonds (Williams, 1982, 378).


## THE NEGLECTED JOB OF THE ELITES

In any case we cannot expect the arrival of a new era of moral discourse to be generated by mass movements or by political pressures exerted by voters. There has been a lot of words and much agonising about problems but no revolution in thinking. Many consumers are in a state of moral schizophrenia. They continue to mobilise anything in the hope of feeling good, and they feel bad in doing so.

This is a necessary but not a sufficient condition for a real change. If the new stage of moral discourse should become reality it must be accompanied by action that makes thinking visible. In the 1960s and 1970s this action was successfully demonstrated by individuals who manifested subject-centrism against the claim of institutions. Now the institutions have to come back into the arena of moral discourse and have to participate much more actively in the construction of a collective framework for solidarity in consumption. Clearly, the new consumer society has to be organised, because its morality has to be based upon the relationship between the individual and the community. A sense of common purpose must be brought back into individual moral thinking by collective action.

It is true that 'attempts to impose simple living have been notoriously ephemeral in their effects' (Shi, 1985, 280).

However, what should be concluded from this in the present situation? Should the change of consumption patterns be left to personal choice only, as Shi (1985, 280) proposes? I think that we have to draw the opposite conclusion – what is needed is an unparalleled intensification of institutional efforts.

This is the hour of political, economic and scientific elites, above all, because there is a necessity for nationwide and global coordination. The conference of Rio may be regarded as a symbol for the neglected job of the elites. Instead of governing, they behave as if they were being governed. They complain about restrictions which they claim are imposed by public opinion, lobbyists and objective conditions.

The next change of the frame of reference of moral discourse must, however, be imposed on social reality even in the face of initial resistance. The willingness of people to take another point of view in their personal philosophy of life already exists, although in an unstable, vague mode not very relevant for action. It will grow according to the extent that it is explicitly demanded.

## References

Burnett, J., *Plenty and Want* (London: Scholar Press, 1979).

Forty, A., *Objects of Desire* (London: Pantheon, 1986).

Fraser, W. H., *The Coming of the Mass Market 1850–1914* (London: Macmillan, 1981).

Fromm, E., *To Have or To Be?* (New York: Harper & Row, 1976).

McCracken, G., *Culture and Consumption* (Bloomington: Indiana University Press, 1988).

Murkerji, C., *From Graven Images* (New York: Columbia University Press, 1983).

Schulze, G., *The Experience Society* (London: Sage, 1995).

Shi, D. E., *The Simple Life* (New York: Oxford University Press, 1985).

Wiener, M. J., *English Culture and the Decline of the Industrial Spirit 1850–1980* (Cambridge: Cambridge University Press, 1981).

Williams, R. A., *Dream Worlds: Mass consumption in late nineteenth-century France* (Berkeley: University of California Press, 1982).

Willis, P. E., *Profane Culture* (London: Routledge & Kegan Paul, 1978).

# 4 Citizenship and Inequality in Postmodern Social Theory

John Holmwood

## INTRODUCTION

For a long time, the theory of industrial society has dominated sociological accounts of modernity. Our societies were argued to be defined by the large-scale production of commodities, produced and distributed according to a market logic of 'scarcity'. This logic became enshrined in the discipline of economics in the definition of its object as the study of the 'allocation of scarce means among alternate ends'. However, modern societies were also argued to confront a 'social' problem which was continuous with their 'economic' problem. This derived from the fact that large-scale production depended upon an industrial proletariat whose interests potentially went beyond the social structures of market capitalism. For many, the growth of the welfare state was to be understood as a strategy of class containment and incorporation. Social integration could be secured – though, perhaps, not indefinitely – it was argued, by the reproduction functions of social welfare services and the redistributive efforts of the welfare state. At the same time, any economic crisis tendencies of market capitalism could be reduced by Keynesian techniques of economic management.

Increasingly, however, this view of modern society is being challenged by theories of 'post-industrialism', 'postmodernity' or 'consumer society' as marking a radically new phase of social development. Writers identify a new 'logic of consumption' which is now relatively autonomous from production. Needs have become 'saturated' and exist beyond a traditional logic of 'scarcity' (see Schulze, Chapter 3 in this volume). At the same time, the social structures of post-industrial society have changed to displace the class interests whose accommodation was once held to underpin the welfare state (Lash and Urry, 1987). However, as the terms used to characterise this new period indicate, there is greater clarity about what the new phase is not – not 'traditional modernity', not 'industrialism' – than about what it is. Postmodernity, it seems, is the negation of our past certainties. Block expresses the situation well, writing that

> for generations, [our society] was understood as an industrial society, but that definition of reality is no longer compelling. Yet no convincing alternative has emerged in its absence. (1990, 1)

For some writers, what is required now is a sociology of postmodernity (see Bauman, 1988; Featherstone, 1988). For others, sociology itself must be transformed in order to account for the transformation in society (Smart, 1990). On this view, what we require is not merely a theory of postmodern society, but a postmodern sociology. But what sort of sociology is that? And what are its implications for the issues of inequality and citizenship that were so central to the sociological discourse of modernity? Indeed, some theorists of postmodernity argue that sociology is the discourse of modernity and with postmodernity comes both the displacement of sociology and the welfare state in which its professional ambitions (and job opportunities) were embodied (see Lemert, 1992a, 132; Crook *et al.*, 1992, 237).

In this chapter, my arguments will be directed against recent trends in sociological meta-theory. Most theorists (whether committed to a 'sociology of postmodernity' or to a 'postmodern sociology') attempt to theorise discontinuity, arguing, either that modern societies have entered a new phase organised by radically distinct new principles or, more usually, that although previous processes of industrial capitalism continue their effects have been rendered uncertain, transformed in their operation by the co-presence of radically new, additional principles. However, whatever is held to be novel about current processes will depend upon the adequacy of the representation of the past processes from which they are differentiated.

I shall argue that a major requirement is to theorise continuity rather than discontinuity. The sense that the present is a new phase of social development is, in part, a consequence of a misrepresentation of the trends of development in the previous phase. An adequate theory of the present would, of necessity, also reconstruct our understandings of the past. This aim of reconstruction in sociological theory has to be set against an increasingly dominant theoretical sensibility that accepts theoretical disorder as an inevitable and realistic existential condition of sociology. The issues are related. The acceptance of discontinuity between phases of social development is accompanied by a representation of the present phase as 'fragmented' – subject to the operation of multiple and contradictory determinations – and, in turn, that it requires a 'fragmented' theory to represent it (see, for example, Lash and Urry, 1987). Ultimately, I shall argue that the claims of postmodernism do not represent an answer to our current problems, but a capitulation in the face of them. As a first step, I want to trace developments in sociological theory over the last decade or so and their connection to contemporary issues of citizenship.


## FRAGMENTED REALITY OR FRAGMENTED THEORY?

From a sociological perspective, our times do, indeed, appear puzzling. Where change was expected, it failed to occur. Where change was considered unlikely, radical changes have taken place. These events appear to have resuscitated approaches that had only recently seemed well past their time. So, in the liberal democracies of Western societies, a period of political stability and social conformity up to the 1950s and early 1960s had led theorists to proclaim an 'end of ideology'. The defining ideological conflicts of early capitalism – essentially, those between a bourgeois ideology of 'radical individualism' and a socialist ideology of 'collectivism' – had, it was argued, lost their relevance in the 'mixed' and affluent economies and pluralistic political systems of modern industrial societies. As Bell put it,

> in the Western world ... there is a rough consensus among intellectuals on political issues: the acceptance of a Welfare state; the desirability of decentralised power; a system of

mixed economy and of political pluralism. In that sense ...
the ideological age has ended. (1960, 402–3)

As the decade came to a close, the 'end' of ideology gave
way to division and conflict. A 'new left' came into the
ascendant, accompanied by new forms of social and political
militancy, which seemed to indicate potentialities for fundamental change in Western capitalism. In Eastern Europe,
however, any resistance to their political regimes – in
Hungary in 1956 and in Czechoslovakia in 1968, for example
– was quickly crushed and most commentators gloomily
emphasised the capacity of sclerotic and bureaucratic
regimes to reproduce themselves almost indefinitely against
sporadic manifestations of popular will (or what, for the most
part, was a resigned acceptance on the part of their popu-
lace). By the end of the 1980s, however, the situation had reversed. Communist regimes in Eastern Europe had collapsed,
while government in Western capitalism was increasingly
dominated by 'new right', neo-liberal political ideologies.
The 'market' has come to the fore and welfare services are increasingly under attack. Postmodern theorists, once more,
proclaim an 'end of ideology', or 'end of grand narrative',
but, this time, it is the 'disorderly' rather than 'orderly' character of a mature industrial, or post-industrial society which is
held to have brought it about. At the same time, the welfare
state is assigned to an earlier phase of industrial society, now
superseded.

Given the recent dramatic transformations in our socio—
political landscape, it is perhaps not surprising that there is
uncertainty among social theorists. However, the bitter and in-
conclusive theoretical arguments of the last two decades have
also left their mark. The dramatic shifts in the post-war social
and political agendas of modern societies were accompanied
by equivalent shifts in social theory. In 1974, the first number
of the journal *Theory and Society* was issued under Alvin
Gouldner's editorship. According to the editorial statement,
the old paradigms were 'losing their ability to convince, let
alone enthuse' and new paradigms – 'critical theory, eth-
nomethodology, neo-Marxisms, linguistically sensitive sociology, structuralism, and neo-Weberanism' – were replacing
them (Gouldner, 1974, i).

The transformation of the sociological conscience collective from optimism in the face of a new theoretical (and social) order, to despair and fatigue has been rapid. Two decades later, the new paradigms seems to have fared no better than their predecessors. Alexander (1988), for example, writes of their increasingly 'enervated' and 'debilitated' character. The vital and creative phase of the 'new' paradigms has come to an early end; they, too, have lost their ability to convince or enthuse.

For postmodern theorists (for example, Baudrillard, 1983; Lyotard, 1984), the evident fragmentation of social theory into a series of mutually inconsistent, partial accounts is something to be acceded to as the irremediable condition of social inquiry. According to Lyotard, social theory now should give up any quest for generality and coherence, for the 'grand narrative' which will explain modern society. Social theorists, he suggests, betray a 'nostalgia of the whole and the one' (1984, 81) in seeking to reduce the manifold, contradictory particularities of social experience into a singular narrative. On this view, the 'social totality' cannot be grasped as a whole, but is made up of partial and mutually exclusive points of view. Social theory, therefore, should be concerned with the identification and elucidation of concrete, specific and located differences, denying the possibility of their inclusion within a coherent, and integrated scheme. 'A war on totality', is proposed and social theorists should be 'witnesses to the unpresentable ... activate the differences and save the honour of the name' (1984, 82). The condition of postmodern theoretical activity, it seems, is the diversity and context-specific nature of experiences, to be expressed in social theories which accept, and, indeed, embrace, contradiction. Thus, Baudrillard (1983, 4), argues that the 'chaotic constellation' of modern 'social reality' has now become 'unrepresentable', such that there is no such thing as 'the social' and no such thing as the 'individual' either.

On these views, social theory cannot ground its critical undertakings in social reality but, rather, as Lyotard puts it, it must, 'invent allusions to the conceivable which cannot be presented' (1984, 81). Undoubtedly, the wider political and social radicalism of the 1960s contributed to the demise of the old orthodoxies, just as it is the general collapse of this radicalism which has helped to undermine confidence in the theoretical alternatives. Postmodern theorists write not only in the shadow of the failure of general theoretical undertakings in sociology, but also of the failure of the social movements – especially, those of 'class' – which a previous generation of 'new left' social theorists had identified as the harbingers of social change. At least as important as the rejection of 'grand social theory' by postmodern theorists, is their rejection of the embodiment of 'universalistic' claims in social movements. After all, the 'proletariat' failed to live up to the claims made on its behalf. In place of 'grand social movements', post-modern theorists offer particularistic, temporary resistances to any inclusive embrace that would seek to reduce differences. The denial of 'difference' – whether explicit, or implicit – is seen as oppressive.

We might interpret this in the light of Habermas' (1981) critique of postmodernism as 'neo-conservative'. However, that would be to insulate the approach that he is defending from a similar sort of criticism. For example, Habermas (1976) is apparently open to the possibility that late capital-ism might entail the 'end of the individual'; that is, that there might no longer be mechanisms of socialisation which will produce the personality structure of an individual capable of self-reflection and social criticism. Baudrillard, with his thesis of the death of the 'social' and the 'individual', can be under-stood as simply affirming Habermas' worst fears. Habermas posits the 'end of the individual' in response to the failure of modern 'individuals' to act in ways embraced as 'rational' by social theorists. Baudrillard, for his part, mockingly accepts the situation of the 'end of the individual' as an indication of subversive activity, where what is subverted is the 'rationality' of social theory.[1] Their arguments are united by a common perception of the failure of social theory in the lives of those to whom it is addressed.

Postmodern positions, then, are not so easily distinguished from those arguments which, ostensibly, are ranged against them. In the next section of the chapter I shall trace this con-vergence, practically, in arguments over the welfare state. I shall not only show how postmodern claims arise on the back of the dashed hopes of radical, or new left, arguments, but also how these arguments have reinforced the 'neo-liberal' attack on the welfare state.

'NEW LEFT', 'NEW RIGHT' AND THE WELFARE STATE

Where the first generation of post-industrial theorists had argued that the welfare state was integral to post-industrial society, current theorists view the welfare state as the product and precondition of the production system of industrial society and are sceptical of its role in the 'new consumer society'. In current debates, the welfare state is assigned to a form of 'collectivism' which post-industrial social structures can no longer sustain, but this analysis must beg the question: what, then, explains the recrudescence of the ideology of market individualism?

Paradoxically, current interpretations of the welfare state derive much of their substance from arguments which were initially developed in criticism of theories of post-industrial society and the end of ideology. Thus, 'new left', especially neo-Marxist, writers criticised welfare arrangements as mechanisms of social control which failed to address the real, underlying issues of inequality and exploitation. The dominant view was that the welfare state was a form of 'administered capitalism' (Habermas, 1976), or that it represented 'class struggle from above' (Ginsburg, 1979; Gough, 1979). From this perspective, the welfare state was argued to be part of corporatist arrangements for the discipline of organised labour to secure the management of the economy in the interests of large-scale capital. As Ginsburg, put it, 'from the capitalist point of view state welfare has contributed to the continual struggle to accumulate capital by materially assisting in bringing labour and capital together profitably and containing the inevitable resistance and revolutionary potential of the working class' (1979, 2). In this way, 'reforms' are assigned to capitalism and become characterised by the 'exploitative' relation that is held to define it. 'True' amelioration of social conditions is represented as a future hope undermined by current realities. Often, the motivation for reform will have come from struggles from 'below', only to be incorporated from 'above'. Thus, as Gough put it,

> labour indirectly aids the long-term accumulation of capital and strengthens capitalist social relations by struggling for its own interests within the state. One could apply this approach to much social policy in this century. (1979, 55)

The consequence of doing so is severe. All victories turn to ashes.

Having challenged the extent to which political action within capitalism could produce an authentic amelioration of social problems, the 'new left' critics of the welfare state were unprepared for a political mobilisation by those who embraced capitalism, but shared their views on welfare arrangements. Where once they explained the growth of the welfare state by how it operated to maintain capitalism, 'new left' writers came to face the problem of explaining why the proponents of capitalism were prepared to jettison it and why, now, it should be defended (or what should replace it). If reforms are not to be understood as organised under socialist principles, the question is begged of what, precisely, are the principles under which they are organised? Some erstwhile critics of the welfare state (see, for example, Held and Hall, 1989) have sought the answer in ideas of social justice expressed in the concept of 'social citizenship' (see Marshall, 1950; Esping-Andersen, 1990). Yet, the positive substance of reforms is precisely what was denied during the period when the 'new left' dominated the intellectual agenda. Any revision of this view is undermined by the weight of previous denials.

Irony is one of the figures of postmodern theory (see Rorty, 1989; Lemert, 1992b). One irony in our current situation which repays consideration is the way in which 'new left' criticisms of 'welfare capitalism' mirror those of the 'new right'. Barry, for example, a neo-liberal political theorist, captures the convergence, writing that,

> some socialists, and all consistent Marxists, have to regard the typical welfare institutions as in a very real sense harmful because they are structured on a pre-existing capitalist order. Their thriving would be inimical to the future aim of abolishing the capitalist order ... Indeed, in theoretical Marxism, since the state is defined in essentialist terms as a coercive force to protect class interests, any welfare role that social theorists might attribute to it must be illusory. Almost all overt socialists saw welfare as a form of social control, as indeed it was. (1990, 41)

This convergence among 'new left' and 'new right' critics extends beyond the negative evaluation of state welfare arrangements as bureaucratic mechanisms of social control. It includes negative evaluations of any re-distributive measures associated with the welfare state (see Holmwood, 1991), as well as the representation of professional organisation (including the new professions of the providers of public welfare services) as self-interested monopoly (see Holmwood and Siltanen, 1995).

It is in this context that ideas of 'postmodernity' have become central to the justification of previous misjudgements. Thus, for some, the idea that capitalism has moved from a phase of 'organised capitalism' to a new, postmodern phase of 'disorganised capitalism' (Offe, 1985; Lash and Urry, 1987) becomes the means of explaining both an earlier expansion of state welfare arrangements and their current crisis. According to Lash and Urry, for example, the social institutions which were a product of 'class struggle from above' have been undermined by new social forces, those of, 'internationalising processes from above' (1987, 300). According to them,

the world of 'disorganised capitalism' is one in which the 'fixed, fast-frozen relations' of organised capitalist relations have been swept away. Societies are being transformed from above, from below, and from within. All that is solid about organised capitalism, class, industry, cities, collectivity, nation-state, even the word, melts into air. (1987, 313)

This new sensibility has not, however, produced any strong sense of a coherent alternative. Although Lash and Urry argue that postmodern ideology has its 'radical democratic side' (1987, 299) of pluralism and difference, it is its 'bourgeois side', associated with the 'new right', which appears dominant. Ultimately, I suggest, its supposed 'radical democratic side' is indistinguishable from its 'bourgeois side'. For example, the 'new right' avowal of markets takes its force from a claimed plurality and incommensurability of 'ends' (see Barry, 1990). On this basis, conceptions of social citizenship which imply a 'community of ends' are denied. Gray, for example, writes that,

conceptions of merit are not shared as a common moral inheritance, neutrally available to the inner-city population
of Birmingham and the secularised middle classes of
Hampstead, but reflect radically different cultural traditions
and styles of life ... needs can be given no plausible cross-
cultural content, but instead are seen to vary across different moral traditions. (1983, 44)

Any values of common citizenship, it seems, would involve an
imposition of the values of one group upon another and, in
these circumstances, the market is recommended as a
framework which allows different values to flourish.

Many postmodern theorists may wish to distance themselves from this implication, but their own versions of 'contradictory particularism' and celebrations of 'difference' are
difficult to distinguish from standard liberal conceptions,
whatever they may say about it. Turner, for example, writes
that,

if we wanted a slogan that might express the ambitions of
both a radical version of modernist liberalism and postmodern politics, it might be 'Here's to heterogeneity'.
Consequently, if we can understand postmodernism as gen-
uinely after- rather than anti-modern, it clears the ground
for new political and social strategies which embrace difference, pluralism and the incommensurability of cultures and
values. (1990, 12)

What makes this so difficult to accept is that it is, in effect, a
celebration of the impossibility of inclusive social citizenship.
Turner and Gray each accept that heterogeneous groups, sep-
arately and self-referentially, constitute a 'community of ends',
but deny processes across groups that could be the basis of
mutual recognition. However, in Gray's example, one group is
privileged compared with the other which is characterised by
low incomes, unemployment and other disadvantages.
Moreover, the two groups are not formed simply by self-
definition, but by processes of a system in which they each
participate. It is not clear why the disadvantaged should
regard it as a particular merit of the market system that it
secures the reproduction of their life-style!

Turner may look beyond the present to a hopeful future of 'heterogeneity' but, in the meantime, the situation is bleak. Whatever the hopes of its proponents, it cannot have escaped attention that the rise of postmodern theorising is accompanied by social conditions in which inequalities and poverty have increased and concentrated in some of the very groups whose 'difference' is being celebrated. At best, postmodernism appears to be a diversion. As Taylor-Gooby puts it,

> an interest in postmodernism may cloak developments of considerable importance. Trends towards increased inequality in living standards, the privatisation of state welfare services and the stricter regulation of the lives of some of the poorest groups may fail to attract the appropriate attention if the key themes of policy are seen as difference, diversity and choice. (1994, 403)

In the next section of the chapter, I shall suggest that the connections go deeper. Where theorists have come to deny 'inclusion' as a criterion of theoretical adequacy, it is hardly surprising that they cannot sustain a conception of an inclusive social citizenship.[2]

## CONTRADICTION AND INCLUSIVE THEORY

The ease with which 'new left' criticisms could be translated into 'new right' theories suggests a convergence deeper than a mere common hostility to a post-war 'welfare-state establishment'. One can identify a deeper conservatism in sociological theory than that which Habermas attributes to a postmodernism. This is a conservatism of method and a 'passivity' in the face of problems.

It is unlikely, I suggest – Baudrillard and other postmodern theorists, notwithstanding – that 'reality' has changed so as to make sociology impossible rather than simply in need of renewal. If current social developments cannot be grasped in the categories of current social theories, it is more likely that the problem lies with those theories than that 'reality' itself has become intrinsically upgraspable. It is hard to resist the conclusion that the perception of the 'chaotic constellation' of modern social reality derives from the 'chaotic' nature of modern social theories. If this is so, the challenge for social theory is to re-construct its explanatory categories, not to deconstruct the explanatory undertaking.

In detailing their conception of social theory, postmodern theorists have often drawn upon the philosophy of science, where 'post-positivist' philosophers of science (see, for example, Kuhn, 1962, Lakatos, 1970; Papineau, 1979; Hesse, 1980; Newton-Smith, 1981) have radically challenged the conception of natural science that has formed the backdrop to discussions of methodological issues in social science since the last century. Positivism is not simply an inappropriate approach to social science, it is deficient as an account of natural science. The implications of these 'post-positivist' arguments for the social sciences, however, are not straightforward. Certainly, post-positivist philosophies of science are anti-foundationalist, arguing that there are no pre-given methodological criteria, or other categories, from which scientific practices are derived. There is no 'grand narrative' of science, merely specific narratives associated with specific, historically located practices of science and, as those practices change so, too, do their self-conscious statements of 'method'. This view must, indeed, call into question all programmatic statements of science, including social science (see Bohman, 1991; Turner, 1992; Holmwood and Stewart, 1991, 1994), and seems to reinforce postmodern conceptions. However, unlike postmodernism in the social sciences, the post-positivist opposition to foundational accounts of natural science does not call into question its explanatory undertakings. Indeed, anti-foundationalism in the philosophy of the natural sciences is usually argued to be necessary in order to account for the explanatory success of science, while in sociology the anti-foundationalism of postmodern approaches is attached to a view of the necessary failure of social science.

In the natural sciences, any anomaly, or counter-instance, is regarded as a problem that calls into question scientific constructs. The explanatory drive in science, then, is firmly tied to problem-solving as the creative activity of science. 'Post-positivist' philosophies of science have not, in any fundamental way, altered the conception of science as a 'problem-solving' activity. Although they have given greater emphasis to 'conservatism' and 'tradition' within science, 'anomalies' and apparently 'disconfirming instances' remain as problems that research programmes must address. All forms of science advance as they solve located problems and, in that advance, ideas of their nature and appropriate methodologies change. The substance of the changes (and this is what undermines positivist accounts of science) is not an accumulative approach to unfolding reality, but the radical redefinition of theoretical objects and their relations, and standards of adequacy (see Holmwood and Stewart, 1991, 1994). However, where problems lie and how they should be addressed produces no one obviously correct strategy. All that can be said is that the 'correct' strategy is the one which, after the event, proves to be successful. It is in this sense that post-positivist theories of science eschew prescriptive, foundational methodologies. As 'ideologies' of science, however, they continue to emphasise 'problem-solving' as the creative practice of science and mutual coherence of theoretical statements and their empirical instances as a condition of adequacy.

'Post-positivist' theories of science, then, do call into question standard accounts of the social sciences, but not in the way that some postmodern theorists suggest. While there is no 'fixed point' to explanation, the conclusion is not simply that there are different points of view. Standards of evaluation shift in the process of the development of explanations which transform theoretical objects and relations, but scientific judgements are 'indeterminate' only in the sense that there is no one, pre-given best way forward. This does not imply that judgements of superior adequacy cannot be made. Superior adequacy must be an issue of the greater inclusiveness of one theoretical scheme over another. This does not mean that a conception of 'totality' is necessary in order to move in the direction of adequacy and coherence by the solution of specific problems. Inquiries in the social sciences may be regarded as 'particularistic', in the sense of beginning from particular, located problems. However, the dynamic of inquiry is that of inference and extension to other 'particulars' and the general requirement of such inquiries, in social science as in natural science, is consistency among statements of objects and their relations. Lack of consistency constitutes a problem to be solved. The solution of problems is a creative task which involves the transformation of theoretical objects and relations, including the observations associated with any problems.

In contrast, the claim of postmodernism is that theories must be contradictory because social existence is contradictory. Simply, this argument accepts that theories which, in their own terms are inadequate, are, in that inadequacy, descriptively adequate as statements of social experience. It is this which explains why postmodernism, in confronting the problems of 'modernist' theory, does not move to the need for a greater adequacy, but accepts the contradictory particularity which is the form of any problem. For example, as we have seen, Lash and Urry (1987) represent the postmodern phase of advanced societies as a state of 'disorganised capitalism'. But the only indication of 'disorganisation' is the deviation of current circumstances from the 'order' expected on the basis of theories of 'organised capitalism'. 'Observations' of 'fragmentation' are not independent of theory – 'real' – merely because they cannot be accounted for by an existing theory. A reconstruction of that theory would produce a new order (including new statements of observations).

The postmodern position is to affirm the validity both of the pre-existing theories and of the practical deviations from them. In this way, current circumstances come to be described as defined by a 'dialectic' of orderly processes and their negation. Crook *et al.* (1992), for example, argue that the social differentiation characteristic of modernity has, in postmodernity, produced its own reversal in social de-differentiation. Thus, they offer three theses on postmodernisation, where:

> first, its dynamic principles [differentiation, rationalisation and commodification] are the same as those of modernisation. Second, postmodernisation is not simply an accentuation of modernisation. The tension between these two theses generates the third: 'hyper'-differentiation, rationalisation or commodification produces outcomes which look very much like 'de'-differentiation, rationalisation or commodification. (1992, 47)

Similar conceptual 'displacements' have come to characterise recent discussions in the area of social inequality. Thus, an emphasis upon the centrality of 'production' relations has given way to an argument for the relative autonomy of 'consumption', the centrality of 'structure' has given way to an emphasis upon the importance of 'culture', 'class' has given way to 'status', and so on. As Turner puts it, 'economic class is declining in importance as the primary or leading division in sociopolitical life' (1988, 44), and Featherstone suggests that it is

> important to focus on the question of the growing prominence of the culture of consumption and not merely regard consumption as derived unproblematically from production. (1991, 13)

Eder (1993), for his part, seeks to 're-couple' class and collective action by asserting their [relative] 'independence'. At the same time, the original categories are maintained as necessary to a full explanation, without, it is intoned, committing the 'reductionism' of earlier arguments.

The characteristic of each of these dualisms is that one side lays claim to an 'order' that is unrealised, while the other side consists in the immediate apprehension of circumstances at odds with that 'order'. Each dualism retains the original explanatory structure as 'necessary' in any 'adequate' explanation, but not in terms of its own internal claims to adequacy. Such dualisms are the form of failed explanatory undertakings. The criteria organised under the dualism prescribe in contradiction to each other, and these contradictory 'possibilities' enter formal statements of the nature of social reality. In this way, the 'chaotic nature of social reality' takes on the character of a given of sociological analysis, rather than as an artifact of theoretical confusion.

Why is it that social scientists seem to be unwilling to engage in the activity necessary to the reconstruction of their theoretical problems to create new orderly theoretical conceptions, but regard the unreconstructed form of their problems as definitive and beyond transformation? Elsewhere (Holmwood and Stewart, 1991), a fallacy specific to the social sciences has been identified by which social theorists avoid what natural scientists accept – the need to reconstruct failed explanations. The fallacy is evident in claims of 'ideal typical' status for theoretical constructions in the social sciences, where it is held that theories are not called into question by the deviation of circumstances from the processes internal to theoretical statements.[3] On the contrary, theories are held to be valid as one-sided ideal types at the same time as the observations of behaviours at odds with them are accepted as descriptively adequate.

Ultimately, the claim for the 'reality' of 'deviant behaviours' alongside the validity of the schemes from which behaviours deviate is a form of sociological 'empiricism'. Notwithstanding any claim for novel epistemological insight, then, post-modernism (together with other, more standard sociological approaches, for that matter) is empiricist in its acceptance of the 'reality' of the 'observations' which deviate from the 'order' of pre-existing theoretical claims and its belief that those 'observations' have integrity as the expression of 'differences'. This is a position which could not be sustained in the light of post-positivist theories of science and, therefore, is usually justified by features peculiar to the objects of social inquiry. Where the objects of the natural sciences merely reflect routine processes, it is argued, human beings intervene in the world and thereby can produce novel and discontinuous effects. In contrast to natural scientists, social scientists, apparently, may regard any apparent explanatory problem as reflecting the peculiar nature of their objects, that is, as deriving from their status as human subjects capable of freedom and choice. Any decision by actors to behave differently need not, it is believed, bear upon the theoretical adequacy of the construct previously held to obtain. It could have been 'true' if it had been 'chosen'. On this basis, it is held that theoretical constructs can be valid despite their lack of application to the specific behaviours to which they are addressed and that there need be no requirement in the social sciences of a reconstruction of theoretical objects and relations.

The postmodern perception of the irreducible contingency of social life created by the unpredictability of human creativity and choice is bound up with the social scientific fallacy. By identifying human freedom with contingency outside social scientific determination, any improvement in social scientific explanation, which must reduce contingency would, by that token, reduce human freedom. Given this, it is not surprising that postmodern theorists arguing for theoretical

fragmentation should represent the aim of explanatory coherence and adequacy as 'totalitarian' and 'oppressive'. The
problem lies with the particular conception of human
freedom, rather than with any explanatory undertaking in
social science. It is a paradox that, in the name of human creativity, social scientists are being denied their creativity. In any
case, the only 'freedom' that actors are being given is 'uncertainty', at the same time as we are offered the possibility that
the worse social scientific explanations are, the more behaviours will deviate from them and, therefore, the 'freer' actors
will (appear to) be![4]

CONCLUSION

In this chapter, I have tried to show the connection between
trends in sociological theorising and the shift in the political
agendas of most Western societies. Whatever the differences in
basic attitude to market capitalism manifested by 'new left'
theorists, their postmodern successors and 'new right' advocates, they all share a hostility to the welfare state as the
embodiment of claims of social citizenship. Ultimately, each
group of writers is operating in relation to a 'core' theory of
capitalism whose basic categories are at odds with current
social arrangements. For each, developments within the
societies to which they believe that theory to have been relevant have not confirmed the processes of the theory. However,
there is an asymmetry in their relation to this situation. For
'new left' theorists, current circumstances deviate not only
from their core understanding of capitalism, but also from the
conditions necessary to the realisation of socialism. For 'new
right' theorists, however, a similar lack of fit is a 'policy opportunity'. Their theory of capitalism provides a series of policy
prescriptions by which 'deviant' social arrangements can be
returned to the 'order' of their theoretical constructs. The
issue, apparently, can be one of a choice of values, of 'market'
disciplines over 'bureaucratic statism'. By arguing that the
non-application of a theory does not call into question its rationality, 'new right' theorists represent the theory of capitalism as not the case, but capable of being the case, if chosen.
Since its non-application, apparently, is not an issue in deter-

mining the coherence of its categories, coherent policies could be derived from it. But the only coherent policy would be one designed to bring 'non-market' forms under market determination.

Over the last decade – especially, perhaps, in Britain and the United States – we have been living the consequences of that understanding. Yet, as I have shown, it is an understanding which conforms with standard social scientific epistemology, including that of postmodernism. The 'new consumer society' poses us with a challenge. If we accept that it is grounded in heterogeneity, the incommensurability of ends and the primacy of choice, we seem to favour the market as its institutional expression. But, wherever the scope of the market is expanded against the state as an expression of collective requirements, we find that inequality and poverty also grow. The challenge is to identify the basis for defending welfare services and social citizenship. I have argued that to meet this challenge requires a fundamental address to the nature of the sociological undertaking itself. Issues of 'inclusion' and 'exclusion' in social citizenship cannot be separated from issues of 'inclusion' in sociological theory. It is precisely because postmodernism eschews inclusive social theory that, rather than transcending 'grand narrative', it converges with the neoliberal 'narrative' of the 'new right'.

## Notes

1.  For example, Baudrillard refers to 'resistance' (in other words, conformity) as a subversive activity, writing that, 'the hyperconformist simulation of the very mechanisms of the system ... is another form of refusal by over acceptance. It is the actual strategy of the masses' (1988, 219). But it is the social theorist's claims about the masses which is being refused.

2.  A number of feminist writers have seen parallels, or 'elective affinities', between feminism and postmodernism (Hekman, 1991; Gross, 1986; Flax, 1986; Fraser and Nicholson, 1988). The feminist representation of social theory as constituting a male perspective is one of the major reasons for the current unease concerning the claims of any reconstructive sociology. From another perspective a feminist argument must be that inclusion could not be a simple issue of the mere extension of existing forms of citizenship to women, but requires a transformation of those forms (Thompson, 1986; Benhabib and Cornell, 1987). However, postmodernism seems to deny that

there could be an inclusive citizenship at all. (For further discussion see Holmwood, forthcoming.)

3. The classic statement of 'ideal types' is Weber (1949). For a more detailed discussion, see Holmwood and Stewart (1991).

4. This is not as far-fetched as it might seem. Flax, for example, describes the aims of postmodern feminism thus: 'if we do our work well, "reality" will appear even more unstable, complex and disorderly than it does now' (1986, 213). The problem of distinguishing a real 'disorder' of the social world from the appearance of disorder created by the inadequacy of our theoretical schemes is evident, if only implicitly, in the following comment by Harding:

> I am not suggesting that we should try to produce incoherent theories, but that we should try to fashion conceptual schemes that are more alert to the complex and often beneficial ways in which the modernist world is falling apart. (1986, 164)

Quite obviously, if social theory is 'falling apart', the world will appear to be 'falling apart'. It must be stressed that what I am arguing does not involve a denial of 'difference'. Any elaborated scheme is necessarily a scheme of differentiated entities. The issue is not one of the acceptance or denial of 'difference', but the coherence, or otherwise, of the scheme in which difference is expressed and accounted.

# References

Alexander, J. C., 'The new theoretical movement', in Smelser N. J. (ed.), *Handbook of Sociology* (London: Sage, 1988).

Barry, N., *Welfare* (Milton Keynes: Open University Press, 1990).

Baudrillard, J., *In the Shadow of the Silent Majorities. Or, the end of the social and other essays* (New York: Semiotext[e], 1983).

Baudrillard, J., 'The Masses: the implosion of the social in the media', in Baudrillard, J., *Selected Writings* (Cambridge: Polity Press, 1988).

Bauman, Z., 'Sociology and Postmodernity', *Sociological Review*, 36(4) (1988).

Bell, D., *The End of Ideology: On the exhaustion of political ideas in the fifties* (New York: Free Press, 1960).

Benhabib, S. and Cornell, D. (eds), *Feminism as Critique* (Cambridge: Polity Press, 1987).

Block, F., *Postindustrial Possibilities: A critique of economic discourse* (Berkeley: University of California Press, 1990).

Bohman, J., *New Philosophy of Social Science: Problems of indeterminacy* (Cambridge: Polity, 1991).

Crook, S., Pakulski, J. and Waters, M., *Postmodernization: Change in advanced society* (London: Sage, 1992).

Eder, K., *The New Politics of Class: Social movements and cultural dynamics in advanced societies* (London: Sage, 1993).

Esping-Andersen, G., *The Three Worlds of Welfare Capitalism* (Cambridge: Polity Press, 1990).

Featherstone, M., 'In Pursuit of the Postmodern', *Theory, Culture and Society*, 5(2) (1988).

Featherstone, M., *Consumer Culture and Postmodernism* (London: Sage, 1991).

Flax, J., 'Gender as a Problem in and for Feminist Theory', *American Studies* (1986).

Fraser, N. and Nicholson, L., 'Social Criticism without Philosophy: An encounter between feminism and postmodernism', *Theory, Culture and Society*, 5(2) (1988).

Ginsburg, N., *Class, Capital and Social Policy* (London: Macmillan, 1979).

Gough, I., *The Political Economy of Welfare* (London: Macmillan, 1979).

Gouldner, A., 'Editorial', *Theory and Society*, 1 (1974).

Gray, J., 'Classical Liberalism, Positional Goods and the Politicisation of Poverty', in Ellis, A. and Kumar, K. (eds), *Dilemmas of Liberal Democracies: Readings of Fred Hirsch's social limits to growth* (London: Tavistock, 1983).

Gross, E., 'What is Feminist Theory?', in Pateman, C. and Gross, E. (eds), *Feminist Challenges: Social and political theory* (Sydney: Allen & Unwin 1986).

Habermas, J., *Legitimation Crisis* (London: Heinemann, 1976).

Hebermas, J., 'Modernity versus Postmodernity', *New German Critique*, 22(1) (1981).

Harding, S., *The Science Question in Feminism* (Milton Keynes: Open University Press, 1986).

Hekman, S., *Gender and Knowledge* (Cambridge: Polity Press, 1991).

Held, D. and Hall, S., 'Citizens and Citizenship', in Hall, S. and Jacques, M. (eds), *New Times* (London: Lawrence & Wishart, 1989).

Hesse, M., *Revolutions and Reconstructions in the Philosophy of Science* (Brighton: Harvester, 1980).

Holmwood, J., 'W(h)ither Welfare?', *Work, Employment and Society*, 5(2) (1991).

Holmwood, J., 'Feminism and Epistemology: What kind of successor science?' *Sociology*, 29(3) (1995).

Holmwood J. and Siltanen, J., 'Gender, the Professions and Employment Citizenship', in Boje, T. P. (ed.), *A Changing Europe: Trends in welfare state and labour market* (New York: M. E. Sharpe, 1995).

Holmwood J. and Stewart, A., *Explanation and Social Theory* (London: Macmillan, 1991).

Holmwood J. and Stewart, A., 'Synthesis and Fragmentation in Social Theory: A progressive solution' *Sociological Theory*, 12(1) (1994).

Kuhn, T. S., *The Structure of Scientific Revolutions* (Chicago: University of Chicago Press, 1962).

Lakatos, I., 'Falsification and the Methodology of Scientific Research Programmes', in Lakatos, I. and Musgrave, A. (eds), *Criticism and the Growth of Knowledge* (Cambridge: Cambridge University Press, 1970).

Lash S. and Urry, J., *The End of Organised Capitalism* (Cambridge: Polity Press, 1987).

Lemert, C., 'Sociological Metatheory and its Cultured Despisers', in Ritzer, G. (ed.), *Metatheorizing* (London: Sage, 1992a).

Lemert, C., 'General Social Theory, Irony, Postmodernism', in Seidman, S. and Wagner, D. G. (eds), *Postmodernism and Social Theory* (Oxford: Blackwell, 1992b).

Lyotard, J.-F., *The Postmodern Condition: A report on knowledge* (Minneapolis: University of Minnesota Press, 1984).

Marshall, T. H., *Citizenship and Social Class and Other Essays* (Cambridge: Cambridge University Press, 1950).

Newton-Smith, W. H., *The Rationality of Science* (London: Routledge & Kegan Paul, 1981).

Offe, C., *Disorganised Capitalism* (Cambridge: Polity Press, 1985).

Papineau, D., *Theory and Meaning* (Oxford: Clarendon Press, 1979).

Rorty, R., *Contingency, Irony, and Solidarity* (Cambridge: Cambridge University Press, 1989).

Smart, B., 'Modernity, Postmodernity and the Present', in Turner, B. S. (ed.), *Theories of Modernity and Postmodernity* (London: Sage, 1990).

Taylor-Gooby, P., 'Postmodernism and Social Policy: A great leap backwards?', *Journal of Social Policy*, 23(3) (1994).

Thompson, J., 'Women and Political Rationality', in Pateman, C. and Gross, E. (eds), *Feminist Challenges: Social and political theory* (Sydney: Allen & Unwin 1986).

Turner, B. S., *Status* (Milton Keynes: Open University Press, 1988).

Turner, B. S., 'Periodization and Politics in the Postmodern', in Turner, B. S. (ed.), *Theories of Modernity and Postmodernity* (London: Sage, 1990).

Turner, S. P., 'The Strange Life and Hard Times of the Concept of General Theory in Sociology: A short history of hope', in Seidman, S. and Wagner, D. G., *Postmodernism and Social Theory* (Oxford: Basic Blackwell, 1992).

Weber, M., *The Methodology of the Social Sciences* (New York: Free Press, 1949).

# Part II
# New Codes of Happiness

# 5 The Genealogy of Advertising[1]

## Pasi Falk

Advertisement, in its modern and proper meaning (Leiss *et al.*, 1986), originated with the massive breakthrough around the turn of the century of consumer society and its huge markets for consumer goods in the major European centres and particularly in the United States (Fraser, 1981; Hayes, 1941). The step from *announcement* to *advertisement* came with the recognition that making the product known to people formed an integral part of sales; or, to paraphrase Clausewitz, when this was recognised as a continuation of sales by other means. An early formulation of the idea was presented in 1904 by American advertising guru John E. Kennedy, whose simple but ingenious thesis was: 'advertising is salesmanship in print' (Pope, 1983, 238).

As well as a particular mode of production (Marx), modern advertising required a particular 'mode of information' (Poster, 1990) that made possible the transformation of concrete products into representations, into complex meanings carried by words and images.

This connection between mass markets and mass communication is crystallised in modern advertising. In the mass production of consumer goods, the target, on the one hand, is an anonymous 'mass'; on the other hand, that mass is recognised as consisting of individual buyers. The same duality is repeated in the sender–recipient logic of the mode of information: the message is sent out equally to the whole body of recipients, but it is received individually by each one of them.

This paradoxical duality helps to explain the image of a Janus-faced consumer that unfolds not only in marketing philosophies but also in theories of modern consumption since the late nineteenth century: the mass of consumers was represented as more or less irrational 'adult children' – as it was put in the *Printer's Ink* magazine in 1897 (Lears, 1984, 376) – and on the other hand as consisting of individuals

81

who were capable of making sensible decisions and choices (even though the conduct would not be considered as strictly rational in economic terms).

What really lies behind this dual consumer role is a confrontation of two antithetical perspectives. On the one hand, the producer's concern is to realise the material mass of similarity (mass product) on what is regarded as a homogeneous consumer market. This is supposed to happen with the help of marketing to make sure that the correspondence between the two masses is established. On the other hand, the producer and the marketing apparatus must recognise the individual consumer's inalienable freedom of choice.

## NEED, DESIRE, WILL

Even though the (somewhat problematic) distinction between *needs* and *desires* (see Falk, 1994, 93–150, 182–3, n. 1) is crucial in the deconstruction of the Janus-faced consumer, this distinction appears to have only marginal relevance from a marketing and advertising point of view. At the point where a willingness or readiness to sell is transformed into an active intention to sell, every product that is for sale becomes necessary ('you need this'), desirable ('this is what you desire'), missing ('you still lack this'); in a word, it becomes something that is *good* ('for you'). As far as the intention of selling is concerned it is of course a basic condition that the product is realised in the transaction of exchange, which from the buyer's (consumer's) point of view is defined as a choice, as a realisation of a definite *will* to buy a certain product.

Because of its strategic significance, will becomes a key concept that supersedes both needs and desires. This reformulation is also found in the neo-classical economics of the late nineteenth century: the discourse on needs and desires is replaced by theorising of the consumer's 'wants' and 'preferences' (cf. Falk, 1994, Chapter 5). As far as the business transaction is concerned, the most important thing is what the buyer wants, regardless of how the underlying motives are described.

However, the situation appears in a somewhat different light when it is approached from the marketing theorist's or the advertising psychologist's point of view. In an attempt to establish what sort of representation most effectively attracts the will and attention of the consumer to the product, the advertising expert will need to go beyond the surface and probe into the possible motives that lead to the act of will to buy. At the same time, the advertising expert is confronted, time and time again, with the problem of the multitude of these motives. The solution to that problem lies (seemingly) in the Janus-faced consumer, in its different variants. One of the most interesting versions was presented back in 1926 in the American journal *Advertising and Selling*, which said that 'consumers made purchases on emotional impulse and then justified them with "reason-why" rationalisations' (Marchand, 1986, 153). Later a different approach was adopted to the problem of the Janus-faced consumer: the analysis was now based on a classification of different types of consumer goods – a theme that nowadays occurs mainly in the discussions on the dimensions of 'high and low involvement' in consumer behaviour (for example, Rajaniemi, 1992) – and on different types and groups of consumers ('market segmentation'; see Pope, 1983, 291 ff.).

THE GOOD THINGS OF LIFE

But no matter what approach they adopted to arranging and classifying motives, marketing theorists and advertising psychologists still remained captive to the seller's point of view. That is, no matter what words or images beyond the simple statement of availability were attached to the product, they had to promote a positive expression of want, a positive decision to buy. There are various different ways to argue in favour of a product; you may say it is 'useful', 'comfortable', 'healthy', that it brings 'social prestige' or simply that it 'makes you feel good'. The crucial thing is that an image is created of a 'good object' – to use the psychoanalytical concept introduced by Melanie Klein (1932) – that *you* do not yet have.

Some of these arguments may of course appear as more 'rational' than others, but even so their function remains the same. Even the rational argument serves to provide a representation of the (good) thing you are lacking, and in this capacity it often boils down to straightforward rationalisation (in the psychological sense of the term). An example is provided by an American advert where the argumentation for a 'completely new type' of deodorant bottle says it saves time, thanks to the new wider ball; you need just one stroke instead of two (Wills, 1989). Gary Wills demonstrates in his analysis that this 'advantage' – 'rolls on fast dries fast !', as the slogan goes – is in fact an imaginary product quality, the 'rationality' of which lies in your saving a few minutes of time per year.

Arguments attached to the product and/or its consumption may even exploit the register of negative images, but the overall effect must be positive, otherwise people are not going to come in and buy the product. The idea that both the positive and negative register could be used was formulated by Roy Johnson, father of the 'impressionistic principle' of advertising, in 1911 as follows:

> we suggest the comfort or profit which results from the use of the product, or the dissatisfaction, embarrassment, or loss which follows from its absence. (*Printer's Ink*, 75 (25 May 1911), 10–11; cited in Lears, 1984, 382)

In other words, even where indirect or inverted means are applied, these must help to transform the product and its context into a representation of 'good'. The negative register is used for depicting the state of deficiency that follows with the absence of the product and/or its use.

First, a negative image may be linked up with an identifiable moment in the present time, in which case it will appeal to the buyer's actual experience of deficit (the classical 'before–after' scheme); alternatively, it may interpret the consumer's current situation as 'relative deprivation' in comparison with the better situation that will (should) follow with the purchase and/or use of the product. This type of advert played an important role not only in the advertising of patent medicines towards the end of the nineteenth century, but also in the socially stigmatising, 'anxiety format' adverts of the 1920s and 1930s (see Leiss *et al.*, 1986, 52–3; Marchand, 1986, 18–21). The latter appealed to the glances of reproof from neighbours and significant others and in general depicted the evil, the deficit that the absence and non-use of the product would cause to social relations, career prospects, and so on. This type of advertisement was used in the marketing of mouthwash, for instance, a product which promised to resolve once and for all the problem of bad breath and at once the distress, discrimination and loneliness that followed. It promised a completely different world of happiness, a world that was to be later outlined by Dale Carnegie in his famous guidebook for those who wanted to win friends and money and influence people. It is symptomatic that the marketing of this particular product named not only the product itself (*Listerine*) but also the deficit it promised to do away with. Discovered in an old medical dictionary, 'halitosis' was defined as a condition that could be cured by *Listerine*, opening the doors to a happy (social) life: 'For Halitosis use Listerine!' (Marchand, 1986, 19).

In modern advertising one is hard put to find such uses of the negative register, although it may sometimes occur in the form of self-irony, with parodic repetition of 'outdated' advertising jargon and 'old' styles and patterns appealing to a sense of anxiety and guilt. Modern advertising operates almost exclusively with the positive register, depicting the happy and content soap user for whom there is always room even in a cramped lift rather than the distressed non-user who is left out.

Secondly, a negative image may be projected into a conceivable future as a threat or as an otherwise undesirable state of affairs – loss of health, loss of face – that the product promises to keep at bay. Whereas negative images referring to the present time have more or less disappeared from advertising, images of threats projected into the future continue to occupy a quite firm position in present-day advertising jargon. This is most particularly true of adverts for beauty and health products, which do not portray horror scenes but rather hint at the prospect. Here, too, the negative is excluded from the frame of representation.

The strategy is applied most notably to selling today's 'patent medicines'; that is, the various vitamin products, the consumption of which has been increasing significantly in the Western world during the last two decades (Klaukka, 1989).

Unlike their precursors in the nineteenth century, these products do not need to make promises that they have curative effects because their 'use value' is located in a possible future – and in the threat contained therein – rather than in the present time and its verifiable effects. In this sense these products make for an ideal marketing item: no one can say they don't work because there is no argument that the effects are visible here and now. The promises of future health and longevity cannot be falsified unless one lives one's life all over again in a 'control group'. This has to do with more than just the placebo character of a product (cf. Richards, 1990, 193): the utility of this product is equally verified by the presence and absence of any effects; after all things could have been worse if ...

## MODERN ADVERTISING: DIMENSIONS OF CHANGE

Whether the advertisement uses the positive or the negative register of representation, the outcome must establish a positive link between the identified product and the 'good' that characterises it. The building of this link implies a metamorphosis in which the product transforms into a representation – and it is this that modern advertising is basically about. The basic pattern has remained unchanged through the century-long history of modern advertising, but the modes and methods of creating representations of 'good' have changed. These changes can be roughly outlined in three stages of development:

1. The shift from product-centred argumentation and representation to a thematisation of the product – user relationship and further to the depiction of scenes of consumption which emphasise the *experiential* aspect of consumption;
2. The shift from the emphatically rational mode of argumentation supported by essentially falsifiable 'evidence' of product utility towards representations of the satisfaction that comes with using the product – again emphasising the experiential aspect of consumption; and
3. The shift in communication from verbal and literary means to audio-visual means, based on the development of com-

munications technology that is closely related to the two former dimensions. Pictures were introduced to printed advertising in 1880s, photographs in 1890s and the next century offered the new powerful medias of cinema, radio and television.

These trends in development would seem to be heading towards a form of representation which has increasing independence *vis-à-vis* its point of reference, that is, the product, and which increasingly operates with expressions of the positive register. In other words, the language and argumentation of advertising is moving towards a pure 'good', towards a true positive experience. Of course, this argument needs to be backed up with a closer definition of what is meant by representation of 'good', and this is in fact one of the chief concerns of the discussion that follows. Suffice it to note at this point that the shifts identified above characterise not only the history of modern advertising, but more generally the completion of the modern world of consumption, particularly in its emphasis on the *experiential nature of consumption.*

The story to follow is primarily about how this world of goods becomes visible to the consumer and how this visibility constitutes a direct consumer–product relationship.


NAMING THE NAMELESS

Modern advertising identifies and singles out products as representations which are intended to appeal to the consumer at once as an individual and as a mass. Or, as Leo Lowenthal puts it: the individualising 'for you' actually addresses 'all of you' (Marchand, 1986, 108). On the other hand, each argument and quality that is attached to the product identifies it precisely as a positive thing or 'good object' which in one way or another promises to fill in the 'empty space' that consumers feel is there, *even though they do not know how to name it.*

What could the identification of this unnameable deficit mean? If hunger were plain hunger and bread just plain bread, then the whole problem of anonymity wouldn't even exist. The naturalist theory of needs has a name both for the deficit (hunger) and for whatever it is that fills the stomach (bread). However, a fundamental thesis of modern advertising is that 'bread is not only bread', which necessarily means that the same applies to the other side of the equation; 'hunger is not only hunger'. In other words, both are (also) something else and more; but what? This leads us inevitably to the problem of namelessness, which has two addresses – but which as we shall soon discover are just different entrances to the same house.

First, on the one hand there is the problem of the nameless *product*, which is resolved by naming and individualising the product and by setting it apart (in positive terms) from other products by means of marketing (packaging, adverts, and so on). A paradigmatic case of product identification is the pioneering work that was done by the American Quaker Oats Company (renamed as The American Cereal Company in the early twentieth century) towards the end of the nineteenth century (Marquette, 1967). In 1880, an oat producer by the name of Schumacher started packing his produce – which so far had been known simply as 'oats' – into sacks that had the producer's name printed on them (Marquette, 1967, 16). This was the first step in creating a brandname, which was soon to be followed by a technological innovation (steam mill) that made possible the processing of oats into a specific, identifiable form (rolled oats) and finally by the packaging and naming of this product: Quaker Oats.

Hence the transformation of plain oats into a potential *brand*; a potential that in this case was well exploited. The relationship of people to oats was of course nothing new, but the individualised (albeit imaginary) relationship of the (mass) consumer to Quaker Oats very definitely was. It was in this particular packaged, identified form – as a representation – that the product became more than just 'plain oats'.[2] The making of the product did of course require some real effort in terms of product development (from flour into flakes), which changes the sensory qualities of the raw material. However, the crucial thing here is that all the characteristics that emphasise the distinctive identity of the product are packaged together in the form of a representation. And if the physical characteristics no longer suffice to support the unique identity of the product, the other elements of the representation, the surplus 'goods' will have to take their place.

No product can expect to have the market all to itself for very long. Quaker Oats was soon followed by Kellogg's Company, Postum Cereal Company and many others who went after the consumer with cornflakes and rice krispies, which by now have become the staple food of breakfasts the world over. Therefore a positive character must be continuously created and re-created for a named product.

Secondly, on the other hand, as a message to the potential consumer, the building of a positive product identity implies a representation of that product as a *complement*. It is in this function that the advertisement has to name something that is fundamentally nameless, the negative form of which is the consumer's *deficit* (which is eliminated by the complement) and the positive form of which is the *wholeness* that buying the product and/or using it promises to bring. 'It' is fundamentally nameless, not representable, and that is why it is always given new names, over and over again.

But regardless of whether the naming of 'it' focuses on the negative (deficit) or on the positive (wholeness), the role of the product as a *complement* is always and necessarily positive. As a representation appealing to the potential consumer, it promises something good, either in terms of eliminating the evil or in terms of offering surplus good; in this latter case the state preceding the surplus good is necessarily redefined as a deficit. In other words the duality of deficit (negative) and wholeness (positive) is present in the representation either explicitly or implicitly, on the reverse side of either deficit or wholeness. In any event the role of the product as a complement remains positive, as Roy Johnson (see p. 84 above) clearly understood.

So in the end the two addresses of identification or naming in modern advertising – the singularisation of the product and its representation as a complement to an identified deficit and/or as a surplus which produces the wholeness identified – lead to exactly the same place. Transformed into a representation, the product must stand clearly apart from other similar products, in which case it will also be individualised to the potential consumer as a party to a bilateral (albeit imaginary) relationship. All the attributes of 'good' attached to the product in its representation fulfil both of these functions. In fact the full range of 'goods' – which has since been repeated in various combinations by modern advertising – was already in use in the marketing of selected pioneer products (that is cereals) in the late nineteenth century:

> Every device of the Advertiser's art was used by *American Cereal Company* between 1890 and 1896. Techniques later men claim to have innovated were tested by Crowell as early as 1893. In his ads he appealed to love, pride, cosmetic satisfactions, sex, marriage, good health, cleanliness, safety, labour-saving, and status-seeking. His boldness, at the height of prudish Victorianism, reached its peak in 1899 in an advertisement in *Birds* magazine and several other periodicals of the day. The illustration was a voluptuous, bare-breasted girl, her torso draped in Roman style, sitting on a *Quaker Oats* box. (Marquette, 1967, 51)

If for reasons of distinction or competition advertising has to resort to the positive register ('our' product is better than 'theirs', or 'better value for money'), the situation is somewhat more complex as far as the building of a product–consumer relationship is concerned. This is because the naming may concern both the deficit that the product 'promises' to make disappear and the 'good' that is secured by ownership and use of the product. It is on this dimension of duality that we can follow the development of the modern advert towards the positive. This process is made visible by the history of patent medicines, which in effect lies at the very root of modern advertising. Indeed, the thematic shift from the novelty products of the foodstuffs industry to patent medicines is not all that dramatic; most of the former were introduced to the general public precisely as 'health' products (see, for example, Levenstein, 1988; Young, 1967; Porter, 1989), such as one particular successor of patent medicines called Coca-Cola.


PATENT MEDICINES

Patent medicines have played a central role in the history of modern advertising. These cure-alls were first 'advertised' in announcement or public notices, in the mid-seventeenth century in England (Wright, 1991), but the product group was still going strong when modern advertising made its break-through around the turn of the nineteenth and twentieth century (Holbrook, 1959; Schudson, 1986; Young, 1961).

Given the special nature of the product – a 'medicine' (+) that cured many different 'illnesses' (–) – patent medicines had no choice but to try and build up a positive image for themselves. It was a magical substance which affected change, so it had to inform people not only about its availability but also about its effects and efficiency. The announcement that was published in the London *Perfect Diurnall* in 1652, for instance, contained not only information on where the medicine could be obtained ('at the Physitians house in Flying Horse Court in Fleet Street'), but also an assurance on its effectiveness:

> a water for 3sh the ounce that will purify the face to an exact clearness and fresh colour, keep it from wrinkles, take off freckles, morphew, sunburn, and so on. An oil for 4sh an ounce that will change red hair brown or black. A powder and a plaster for 20sh that in 6 weeks time will cure the Kings Evil perfectly. (Cited in Wright, 1991, 8)

The very same distinctive characteristics make the advertising of patent medicines, especially upon entering the nineteenth century, a paradigmatic case of the *naming of deficit*. In these adverts not only known diseases were named but also vaguer psychosomatic syndromes which effectively boiled down to anxiety and not feeling well. Patent medicines entered this vague domain of deficit as a saviour by naming known ailments but also by inventing new ones so that potential users could easily identify their very own deficiency and neediness.

The wider (and vaguer) the range of deficits that patent medicines came to identify, the more closely their promises of complementation began to resemble religious conversion. The favoured self-representation of patent medicines was indeed one of saviour: they could get rid of all evil and replace it with good. The affinities between religious conversion and advertising for patent medicines extend all the way to the individualising mutuality of the (object) relationship that is aimed at – insofar as the salvation of the religious convert is based on an individualised 'god-relationship'. However, the crucial difference here is that the salvation of the convert requires subordination to a larger whole (whole = holy), that is, a partial rejection of the (individual) self, whereas the happiness of the consumer (wholeness) presupposes the maintenance of the individual self in which the good (object) is internalised. In the former case wholeness requires self-denial, subordination as 'lamb of the Lord', but in the latter case the attachment to oneself of an object that exists 'just for you'. Nonetheless, 'it' still remains nameless and the same in both cases: salvation, healing, freedom and happiness.

However, this correspondence with religious conversion in the identification of deficits is found not only in adverts for patent medicines in the nineteenth century; it is still evident in modern marketing during the early decades of the twentieth century. For example, in a psychology textbook published in early 1920s and intended for the training of salespeople, the model of religious conversion is applied with the aim of getting the potential buyer to recognise the deficit, which will be complemented by the product sold:

> For an excellent example of tactics to pursue at this stage the seller may profitably study the methods used by a professional evangelist in 'selling' religion. He begins by showing the prospective convert (buyer) *how great a lack there is in his life.* (Kitson, 1921, 180, my italics)

But the message of salvation only makes sense if there exists a threat of damnation, and it was in this domain that nineteenth-century advertising for patent medicines operated, all the way till the turn of the century. Advertisers did not even have to go to too much trouble to identify illnesses; physicians and 'alienists' (now known as psychiatrists) had plenty of names in stock, especially of vague syndromes that seemed to cover virtually every form of 'not feeling well' known to modern man. For example, one of the mid-nineteenth-century patent medicines, Helmbold's Buchu, promised in its announcement–advertisement (1860) that it would cure at least the following ailments:

General Debility, Mental and Physical Depression, Imbecility, Determination of Blood to the Head, Confused Ideas, Hysteria, Absence of Muscular Efficiency, Loss of Appetite, Dyspepsia, Emaciation, Low Spirits, Disorganisation or Paralysis of the Organs of Generation, Palpitation of the Heart, And, in fact, all the concomitants of a Nervous and Debilitated state of the system. (Cited in Young, 1961, 117)

The lists of ailments were longer for some patent medicines than for others, but as a rule (with only few exceptions) the list contained at least one ambiguous psychosomatic syndrome which meant that the series of ailments remained open ended – towards all possible variations of the theme 'not feeling well'. The Helmbold's Buchu advertisement, cited above, does this in explicit terms ('all the concomitants of a Nervous ...'), but the same applies also to the patent medicine advertisements which referred to a civilisation-illness diagnosed and named by the American neurologist George M. Beard as 'neurasthenia' (nervous exhaustion) in the late 1860s. Beard characterises the illness of neurasthenia with a page-long list of symptoms ranging from insomnia to different kinds of fears and from 'desire for stimulants' to 'dryness of the hair' – a list which according to Beard is by no means exhaustive (Beard, 1881, 7–8) and remains thus open to ailments yet to be discovered or invented and named.

The same applies more generally to lists of ailments that can be cured by patent medicines; just about any ill(ness) was acceptable. While adverts for patent medicines in the late nineteenth century utilised the entire register of the mythical to produce powerful images of the ill and the evil – with dragons (Swaim's Panacea), skeletons (W. M. Radams Microbekiller, 1887), and alike – and dramatised the scene as a struggle between good and evil (Pilules Pink, 1899), the endless lists of all sorts of ailments actually served to expand the evil into a category of general ill-being or not-feeling-well that accommodated just about every expression of deficit.

In other words, the generalised ill (deficit) became the inverse image of generalised 'good' (wholeness); and that was what the patent medicine promised to achieve in its capacity as an agent for good. So by the late nineteenth century adverts for patent medicines were already operating in the good (feeling) world[3], albeit indirectly through its inverse image ('deliver us from evil ...'). Even though the 'before–after' format of advertising, as a typical intermediate form was still commonly used, the argumentation for and depiction of the products had by now come fairly close to using a purely positive register of representations. But obviously a more in-depth explanation is required of this shift towards plain good in which the nameless 'it' appears as variations of wholeness with different names. To resolve the mystery we have to continue our journey for a while through the wonderful world of patent medicines.

## THE METAMORPHOSIS OF PATENT MEDICINES

One reason for the move to using the positive register in representations of patent medicines was that the producer wanted to expand his markets to include not only people who were (or felt) ill but also those who were (did) not. By the end of the nineteenth century all patent medicines had redefined themselves not only as a cure for the sick and frail, but also as a preventive elixir for the healthy. A patent medicine called Pure Malt Nectar, for instance, was advertised under this slogan in the United States: 'invigorating tonic, alike for invalids and those in health' (Petersen, 1969, 321). At the same time, advertisements started to identify and visualise the 'good' that followed for those who decided to use the product, defined either as a succession of specific 'goods' or in more ambiguous terms, as in this slogan for a very popular patent medicine: 'HADACOL – for the better tomorrow!' (Brigham and Kenyon, 1976). This advert no longer includes the negative condition which remains behind; from the identification of a deficit, it has moved on to naming the desired (good) state of being that can be attained by the goods (that is the products) specified.

The redefinition and expansion of the identity of patent medicines was instrumental in pulling down the barriers between different categories of oral consumption: the line between preventive medicines and foodstuffs was blurred. Preventive medicines promised to keep the evil (illness, ageing and ultimately death) away and turn the 'normal' life into a better one by providing extra energy, happiness, beauty, and so on. The same arguments were used also in the marketing of cornflakes, rice krispies, and so on, in the name of 'good health'. This trend was very much reinforced by innovations in organic chemistry and nutrition science, which shifted the focus of attention somewhat away from invisible enemies, the bad 'microbes', to the good invisible helpers, that is vitamins and other 'protective foods' (Levenstein, 1988, 147–8).

Another factor with dramatic effects on the identity and advertising of patent medicines is a less modern aspect of how they were promoted, that is their direct *promises* of 'good' that, in principle, were falsifiable. It was these 'empty promises' that inspired rather heated debate in the early twentieth century, first in the United States and later elsewhere, on the ethical principles of advertising. Soon after it was established in 1911, the Associated Advertising Clubs of America launched a 'Truth-in-Advertising' campaign in order to drive through legislation to stop untruthful and misleading advertisement (Lears, 1984, 366). This proved an important impetus for consumer protection legislation both in the United States and in other western countries.

All this promoted the 'rhetorical turn' of advertising for patent medicines (the single biggest product category advertised at that time), that is its reorientation to assurances of 'good' and particularly to such forms of representation that precluded any risk of breaking promises. It is easy to retrace this process of transformation by looking at how the slogans for an early wonder drug called Coca-Cola have changed with time: in the 1890s it was marketed as a remedy for headache and as a brain tonic (1893, 'The ideal brain tonic'); in the early twentieth century (1906) the product was associated both with good health and with happiness ('A toast to health and happiness'); and ten years later the deficit (thirst) had become plain fun (1916, 'Fun to be thirsty'). This process is not just a case of Orwellian Newspeak where the negative is redefined as positive, but of a fundamentally new formula in which the 'good' offered by the product (wholeness) is associated with a positive *experience*, which covers both thirst and its satisfaction. As it is put in the longer slogan from the same year: 'It's fun to be thirsty when you can get a Coca-Cola'. The same pattern could hardly be applied to a medicine ('It's fun to be sick'.).

The more recent slogan from 1982 for the same product: 'Coke is it!', is perhaps the most simple and straightforward expression of the positive form of 'it', of the secularised state of wholeness which acquires ever new names: Americanism, youth and beauty, sunny beaches, partying people, anything *good* that can be imagined in this world.

The transformation of Coca-Cola from a patent medicine into a stimulant and soft drink is an obvious step towards plain good, but does it really tell us anything important about the development of modern advertising in a more general sense? In the case of Coca-Cola the shift to the positive register of representation is closely linked up with the change in the identity of the product. Many other patent medicines of the late nineteenth century went through a very similar metamorphosis. Some of them became food (Kellogg's Cornflakes), others were redefined as spices and seasonings, such as (Heinz) ketchup (which was preceded by Dr Miles Compound Extract of Tomato: 'a sovereign remedy for mankind's ills'; Young, 1961) and peppermint (Essence of Peppermint; Jones, 1981); and one became a scented skin cleansing agent for external use: Eau de Cologne, brandnamed as *4711*, was also originally a patent medicine for internal use (Bongard, 1964).

TOWARDS PURE EXPERIENCES OF GOOD

While patent medicines and their successors had clear reasons to move towards the positive register of representation, there was also under way a more sweeping process of change in advertising. That is, the language of *modern* advertising was now beginning to take shape, a process which clearly highlights the connections between the dimensions of change mentioned earlier. As naming and representation begin to move away from the actual product and its qualities and towards the act and context of consuming the product, the fundamentally nameless 'it' becomes thematised in the domain of satisfaction and wholeness. This means that the building of the connection between the product and 'goods' turns round: the positive elements no longer refer (primarily) to the qualities of the product (for example to the efficacy of the patent medicine, which may turn out to be an embarrassing fraud), but the product is associated with representations of wholeness. The first (negative) part is wiped out of the 'before–after' scheme, but so is the obligation to meet 'use value promises' (Haug, 1980) because the depicted 'good' has gained independence from the product and its qualities.

Insofar as this process of change boils down to a change of identity from medicines to foodstuffs and stimulants (a change paradigmatically represented by the case of Coca-Cola), there is no need to explain the shift to the positive register of representation: pleasing experiences are obviously marketed by means of pleasing images. However, the trend towards the experiential good cannot be fully reduced to the identity of the product because positive representations cut across different product groups. This is clearly seen if we compare the destinies of Coca-Cola and another mythical product, that is, Aspirin, as product types and on the other hand as advertised representations. Both originated towards the end of the nineteenth century; the former as a classical patent medicine that in the early decades of the twentieth century is transformed into a soft drink, and the latter as a modern painkiller that in spite of its cure-all character is intended for specific uses (unlike traditional patent medicines).

In the late nineteenth century the identities of the two products were still more or less indistinguishable; Coca-Cola was emphatically represented as a brain tonic and a medicine that would cure headaches. Even their announcement-advertisements were very similar – both in their (typo)graphical layout and in their use-value-oriented argumentation. But then their ways parted. In the new division of labour, Coca-Cola's role was to produce surplus 'good' (pleasure), while the job of Aspirin was to exorcise the evil, the ill being, the (head)ache. This division of labour is repeated in the representations of their adverts: Coca-Cola depicted the world of pleasure and Aspirin the pain to be eliminated. Coke has persisted with its positive line-up until the present day, whereas Aspirin (not the product but the representation) has recently undergone a transformation. From the late 1980s onwards the Aspirin adverts have operated exclusively on the positive register of representation. A recent Aspirin advert links the brand (name) to a woman's smiling face – a picture which could easily be used to sell a whole range of pleasurable products, for example some perfume or a certain soft drink, such as Coke. What is it that makes possible this interchangeability? True, we have seen a shift from product orientation (qualities and effects) to the contextual representation of consumption, but on the other hand this shift itself requires the redefinition of consumption as an *experience*. In its capacity as producer of a consumption experience, the product must be located within a scene of consumption acts that allows for positive identification and imagining oneself in different situations. This is why the painkiller must adopt a different strategy and begin to represent a world in which pain does not exist (any more). Consumers do not need to be reminded about the experience of headache; they know enough about headaches as it is and they don't really want to imagine themselves in that situation. On the other hand, there is no way in which the *absence* of headache can be represented, for that is just an empty place. Therefore the representation must be based on the elements of a good (full) life, on the fun and pleasure that the medicine makes possible and with which consumers want to identify themselves.

This points at an important principle of representation where the depiction of the good world has assumed full independence as a process of building an experiential target for identification and to which the product is attached retrospectively, as it were. As already noted, the product (name) is attached to 'good' rather than the other way round, as was the case during the early stages of modern advertising (in terms of explicit promises and rhetoric assurances of surplus good). This crucial step towards irreferentiality does not occur until the representation of 'good' focuses on the act of consumption and (later) on the scenes of consumption that make possible an experiential identification with the users and the use of the products and in general with the good world that is represented.

So the move towards the positive register of representation and the shift towards irreferentiality are actually two aspects of the same transformation process which surely is something more than a mere change of advertising language. Rather it is a symptom of a more profound cultural change where the experience of consumption and the consumption of experiences appear as mutual prerequisites for each other.

A perceptive analysis of this broader cultural change has been offered by the American historian Jackson Lears (1981, 1983, 1984) by relating (perhaps somewhat surprisingly) two rival concepts of 'therapy' (in the broad sense of care of both body and mind) from the turn of the century to the massive breakthrough of 'consumer society' (Falk, 1994). The receding concept of caring, 'scarcity therapy', stressed the importance of asceticism, withdrawal and rest and the avoidance of stress and overstimulation (characteristic of 'modern times'), while the emerging 'abundance therapy' favoured the opening up to new stimuli in the modern individualised project of self-realisation and self-expression.

In relation to the receding therapy concept, this implied giving moral permission to accept the goods of the expanding mass consumption and mass culture. The new 'therapeutic ethos' rejected the principles of ascetic self-control promoting instead the ideals of psychic growth and perpetual education of the personality capable of enjoying the gifts (goods) of the civilisation. This was the 'new basis of civilization' – as the economist Simon Nelson Patten put it in the title of his book from 1907 – implying 'a new morality' which 'does not consist in saving but in expanding consumption' (Patten, 1968, 143; cited in Lears, 1981, 54). Against this background it is hardly surprising that by the turn of the century, as Jackson Lears has shown, the latter therapeutic principle had won a firm position also in advertising psychology.

In this broader context of cultural change, modern advertising as a whole had a key role not only in the marketing of certain products but more generally in creating more permissive attitudes towards consumption. Advertising has an 'historical mission' which was later formulated by advertising psychologist Ernest Dichter as follows:

In the promotion and advertising of many items, nothing is more important than to encourage this tendency to greater inner freedom and *to give moral permission* to enjoy life through the use of an item, whether it is good food, a speed boat, a radio set, or a sports jacket. (Dichter, 1960, 189; my italics)

Modern advertising is born with one foot in the world of goods and the other in mass culture. The precondition for the birth of modern advertising, as we have seen earlier, was the expansion of consumer goods markets as well as the formation of a specific mode of information, in which entertainment, and more generally, the 'spectacular' was to assume an important role. At the beginning of the century figures for the consumption of mass culture and the world of goods skyrocketed: films, magazines, department stores, and the advertising that links all these together. Mass culture transformed experiences into marketable products and advertising turned marketable products into representations, images and, with time, into experiences again. In other words, the consumption of experiences and the experience of consumption (in its elementary form) have been interlinked from the very outset, as it were (see Eckert, 1978, 1–21; Lears, 1984, 351; Mayne, 1988, 69).

In the world of representations, the issue of 'truth' is replaced by 'credibility' (Jackson Lears, 1984, 361) and 'believability' (Boorstin, 1962, 226), which are tested against the *verisimilitude* of the experience rather than in terms of its veridicality. This concept of the experiential 'real' can hardly be expressed more succinctly than in the American pop song I happened to hear some time ago, in which the intoxicating state of being in love is described by the words: 'I feel so real!'

The question of the 'truthfulness' of advertising is accordingly pushed into the background. An illuminating case is the justification for an acquittal in a hearing against misleading advertising in the United States in 1963:

A representation does not become 'false and deceptive' merely because it will be unreasonably understood by an insignificant and unrepresentative segment of the class of persons to whom representation is addressed. (Cited in Pope, 1983, 279)

So you need to know how to read adverts, just as you need to know how to read the fiction (of) film. But an advert is not just entertainment, except perhaps to the Parisian intellectuals who gather once a year to watch advertisements through the night in a cinema theatre. The advert is still a representation of a product even if it no longer is product-centred but focuses on the experience of consumption. The advert attaches a meaning to the represented product, which is then not merely adopted but also transformed by the other party to the bilateral relationship, that is by the potential consumer. But in spite of the freedom that the consumer enjoys in the 'productive' act of (re)interpretation (de Certeau, 1984) – which marketing tries to anticipate the best it can[4] – the building of representations has a special logic of its own. In entering the experiential world of consumption, the advert begins to operate with the positive images of wholeness.

It is hardly a coincidence that the representation of the good world begins with stimulants and other oral goods, which are the most basic areas of experiential (sensory) pleasure. But the representation of the world of wholeness does not remain within the boundaries of certain product types. If Coca-Cola invented the 'pleasure of thirst' in 1916 ('Fun to be thirsty'), just three years later the American markets saw the appearance of a car advert that stressed the 'pleasure of driving'. In 1919 the Jordan Motor Car Company launched an erotic–experiential car advert:

> In a motor car youth will have its fling. The road skims beneath you, winds before you, and unless a man is bloodless he cannot but surrender himself to that fine intoxication that comes of such motion in the open air. It begins in a sort of breathless sensation and ends with that pleasing drowsiness – a silence in which two people need exchange no words to understand. (Cited in Lears, 1984, 394–5)

In today's advertising shaving is no longer just efficient and easy; it opens the way to the world of (erotic) sociability (Gilette) and finally re-defines shaving as a pleasurable experience in itself (a Philishave advert). And if you have happened to see the erotically-tinged fantasy-like television advert for Whirlpool household appliances, which begins with a symptomatic 'Imagine!', it must be clear that even these

fundamentally 'sensible' goods have entered the realm of experiential representation. Ernest Dichter's thesis gets down to
the essence of this logic of representation, rather by intuition
than due to theoretical insight:

> Strictly speaking, a new car, a colour TV-set, cigarettes, beer,
> or French wine are not necessities. *But they all represent
> aspects of a full life.* (Dichter, 1960, 14; my italics)

### EPILOGUE

The overall shift towards good experiences, characteristic of
modern advertising specifically during the last decades, does
not, however, imply that the representations produced operate
solely within the positive register. The scale of positive experience goes far beyond unambiguous images of pleasure and
happiness (beautiful bodies, smiling faces, sunny skies, and so
on). Contemporary adverts – posters and especially TV-spots –
are filled with dramatic and spectacular elements, touching
mini-stories of life which may bring tears to one's eyes and, of
course, spiced with humour of different kinds. In other words,
today's advertising exploits the same themes as other contemporary experiential goods such as fiction film and music
videos. The advert is located at the same continuum, more
precisely, in the 'compressed' end of the line not so far from
film trailers and music videos (the duration of a TV-spot is
about 30 seconds compared to the 3- to 4-minute music videos
and slightly shorter film trailers).

The common ground of these categories becomes the more
obvious as the advert's autonomy as an experiential product
strengthens. Nevertheless, even though the advert is turned
into entertainment and perhaps even art, it still has to refer to
the product it wants to sell and, consequently, the advert
should leave a positive impression on the potential consumer
– an impression which is associated with the product. So, even
if the mini-story contains representations of negative feelings –
sadness, aggression, fear, and so on – it still must have a 'happy
ending', a positive effect which (as hoped) associates with the
marketed product. It may well be that an 'average' consumer
of experiential goods (fiction novels and films) prefers happy

ends to tragic ones but in the case of adverts the necessity of a positive end effect is already defined by the basic function: advertised goods must be positively charged in order to act as objects of desire for the potential consumer.

The point is, however, that the positive charge may be produced by many other means besides a straightforward display of happy faces, etc. The advert may evoke a whole range of feelings provided the overall effect – the after-image or aftertaste – remains in the positive side. A compressed 30-second version of a happy-end story is one way to do it but the aim may be reached also by various combinations of metaphoric, comic, dramatic, aesthetic and spectacular elements. So, returning for a while to the advertisement for pain-killers, if the Aspirin advert discussed on p. 97–8 above is a paradigmatic case for the shift towards the positive register displaying a world without pain (representing merely the happy end), it should not be too difficult to come up with counter-examples which disregard this simple formula of the positive. The negative – the pain to be cured – may still be represented but this is done, as a rule, in a way in which the negative is given a secondary role in relation to the positive value of the style of representation.

This principle of stylistic elaboration could be illustrated by two Finnish TV-ads for pain-killers: the first one (Nurofen) shows two fighting yaks charging each other, their horns and heads crashing together with an impressive bang, and the other (Orudis) is a scene of miners working with their drills in a coal mine accompanied by dramatic opera music. In both examples the negative element of pain is actually reduced into a sign (bang, drills) contextualised in a metaphorical scene giving priority to the positive experiential aspects of the aesthetic (both cases), the comic (former case) and the spectacular (latter case). The negative (pain) enters the representation only as a sign subordinated to positive experiential (aesthetic and so on) values and not as a figure inviting identificatory experience – thus affirming the dominance of the positive register.

But what about Benetton's line of advertising launched in 1991–2? How should we interpret the documentary genre of photograph-posters and prints which is indistinguishable from the 'catastrophe aesthetics' so characteristic of contemporary network news? A ship packed full of Albanian refugees, some of them falling over the rail, an exploded car burning, a dead man lying in a pool of blood and a AIDS victim and his family by the bed just three minutes after the death.

Surely these images do not respect the representation code of advertising as characterised above. These Benetton adverts transgress not only the boundaries of more traditional advertising depicting the 'good things of life' but they also break the rule of the contemporary ad-language by disregarding the principle of the positive end effect. These adverts evoke anxiety rather than some version of 'feeling good'. Nevertheless, the effect is undoubtedly strong, evoking not only strong emotional reactions in the big audience but also among the authorities guarding the code of public representation, that is, defining what may be shown to people, where and how.

Sr Benetton himself stated in an interview (*The Independent*, 1992) that it would be pure waste of money to 'speak about the products' (clothes) in the adverts and that he wanted to create adverts (with his art director Oliviero Toscani) that would 'touch people', and make them *feel* the reality of today's world. Perhaps in order to heighten the awareness of the people and to make them realise their responsibility in building a better tomorrow? Fighting against inequality and human suffering – clothed in the 'united colours of Benetton'?

This is, of course, a noble intention. Nevertheless, it cannot override the fact that the documentary posters should still function as adverts selling the goods of Benetton and appealing to the individualised consumer. Thus we have to take a closer look at the 'special effect' of these adverts. First of all, these adverts function very efficiently in promoting the brand and distinguishing it from the others clinging to the conventional modes of advert representation. And, as many marketing theorists have claimed, this may be the most important function because the negative images associated with the product will fade away with time and all that will be left will be a recognised name occupying a firm place in the consumer cosmology.

On the other hand, these Benetton ads certainly succeed in making people *feel* something, and thus themselves. The experience effect is strong even if it does not fit very well in the 'feeling good' scheme. So, could it be possible that the 'society of the spectacle' (Debord, 1977) should also be conceived of as a 'society of experience' (*Erlebnisgesellschaft*; Schulze, 1992) where emotional and bodily experiences in general are charged positively in relation to the state of 'not feeling anything'. Even the anxiety experienced in front of a photograph of an AIDS victim in the 'act' of death makes one feel oneself – alive – as long as it remains in the regime of 'co-suffering' (*Mitleiden*) and does not mirror one's own fate. From this point of view, the Benetton adverts are not primarily about 'social concerns' but exemplify a strategy in which the spectacular effect is taken to the limits of representation towards the illusion of 'real presence' ('Look. this is really happening!') which is not too far from the pornographic 'live acts' based on the illusion of 'realness' (Falk, 1993, 1994).

## Notes

1.  A more extensive version of this article was published with the title 'Selling Good(s) – on the genealogy of modern advertising', in Falk (1994), *The Consuming Body*. Sage Publications, Theory, Culture & Society book series, London 1994, ch. 6, 151–85, by permission of Sage Publications Ltd.

2.  Haug (1980); the 'commodity aesthetics' theorist would say that this represented a transition from real use values to empty promises of use value. However, the problem cannot be brushed aside as easily as that, as I have tried to demonstrate elsewhere (Falk, 1982). It is also interesting to note that in her critique of the world of goods, Susan Willis (1991) uses precisely the case of Quaker Oats as an example of how marketing (naming and packaging) distorts people's 'natural' relationship to oats.

3.  Many of the patent medicines did in fact live up to their promises of 'good feeling', at least in the short term: they contained intoxicating substances. A typical patent medicine of the nineteenth century (Laudanum, Hoffman's drops, and so on) contained alcohol as well as some hard drug (opium, cocaine).

4.  The (problem of the) active role of the audience was recognised already by Roy W. Johnson (1911). According to Johnson,

> The meaning of a word isn't determined by the dictionary, but by the thoughts and feelings and sentiments of the man who reads it. In other words, it requires constant study to make sure that the reader will get out of our ads precisely what we put in. He will read

between the lines in spite of us. Let's try to see that he reads the right things there. (*Printer's Ink*, 75 (25 May 1911), 8; cited in Jackson Lears, 1984, 382)

# References

Beard, G. M., *American Nervousness* (New York: G.P. Putnam's & Sons, 1881).

Bongard, W., *Fetische des Konsums* (Hamburg: Nannen-Verlag, 1964).

Boorstin, D., *The Image* (New York: Atheneum, 1962).

Brigham, J. C. and Kenyon, K. K., 'HADACOL – The Last Great Medicine Show', *Journal of Popular Culture*, 10 (3) (1976), 520–33.

de Certeau, M., *The Practice of Everyday Life* (Berkeley: University of California Press, 1984).

Debord, G., *Society of the Spectacle* (Detroit: Black & Red, 1977).

Dichter, E., *The Strategy of Desire* (London: T. V. Boardman & Co Ltd, 1960).

Eckert, C., 'The Carole Lombard in Macy's Window', *Quarterly Review of Film Studies* 1 (1978) 1–21.

Falk, P., 'Tavarametafysiikkaa' (Commodity Metaphysics), *Tiedotustutkimus*, 5 (3) (1982), 78–84.

Falk, P., 'The Representation of Presence: Outlining the anti-aesthetics of pornography', *Theory, Culture and Society*, 10 (2) (1993) 1–42.

Falk, P., *The Consuming Body* (London: Sage TCS, 1994).

Fraser, W. H., *The Coming of the Mass Market, 1850–1914* (London: Archon, 1981).

Haug, W. F., *Warenästhetik und kapitalistische Massenkultur: Systematische Einführung in die Warenästhetik* (Berlin: Argument Verlag 1980).

Hayes, C. J. H., *A Generation of Materialism, 1871–1900* (New York: Harper & Bros., 1941).

Holbrook, S. H., *The Golden Age of Quackery* (New York: Macmillan, 1959).

Jones, O. R., 'Essence of Peppermint: A history of the medicine and its bottle', *Historical Archaeology*, 15 (2) (1981), 1–33.

Kitson, H. D., *The Mind of the Buyer: A psychology of selling* (New York: Macmillan, 1921).

Klaukka, T., *Lääkkeiden käyttö ja käyttäjät Suomessa* (*The Use and Users of Medicine in Finland*) (Helsinki: Kansaneläkelaitos, 1989).

Klein, M., *The Psycho-Analysis of Children* (London: Hogarth Press, 1932).

Lears, J. T. J., *No Place of Grace* (New York: Pantheon Books, 1981).

Lears, J. T. J., 'From Salvation to Self-realization', in Fox, R. W. and Lears, T. J. J. (eds), *The Culture of Consumption* (New York: Pantheon Books, 1983), 1–38.

Lears, J. T. J., *Some Versions of Fantasy: Toward a Cultural History of American Advertising, 1880–1930, Vol. 9. Prospects*, in Salzman, J. (ed.), *The Annual of American Cultural Studies* (New York: Cambridge University Press, 1984).

Leiss, W., Kline, S. and Jhally, S., *Social Communication in Advertising* (Toronto: Methuen, 1986).

Levenstein, H., *Revolution at the Table* (New York: Oxford University Press, 1988).

Marchand, R., *Advertising the American Dream* (Berkeley: University of California Press, 1986).

Marquette, A., *Brands, Trademarks and Good Will: The story of the Quaker Oats Company* (New York: McGraw-Hill, 1967).

Mayne, J., *Private Novels, Public Films* (Athens, Georgia: The University of Georgia Press, 1988).

Patten, S. N., *The New Basis of Civilization* (Cambridge, Mass.: John Harvard Library, 1968 [1907]).

Petersen, W. J., 'Devils, Drugs, and Doctors: Patent medicine advertising cards', *Palimpsest*, 50 (6) (1969), 317–31.

Pope, D., *The Making of Modern Advertising* (New York: Basic Books, 1983).

Porter, R., *Health for Sale* (Manchester: Manchester University Press, 1989).

Poster, M., 'Words without Things: The mode of information' *October*, 53 (1990), 63–77.

Rajaniemi, P., 'Conceptualization of Product Involvement as a Property of a Cognitive Structure', Vol. 29, in Mikkonen, K. (ed.), *Acta Wasaensia* (Vaasa: University of Vaasa, 1992).

Richards, T., *The Commodity Culture in Victorian England: Advertising and spectacle, 1851–1914* (Stanford: Stanford University Press, 1990).

Schudson, M., *Advertising: The uneasy persuasion* (New York: Basic Books, 1986).

Schulze, G., *Die Erlebnisgesellschaft: Kultursoziologie der Gegenwart* (Frankfurt am Main and New York: Campus Verlag, 1992). (Appearing in English as *The Experience Society*, London: Sage, 1995.)

Willis, S., *A Primer for Daily Life* (London: Routledge, 1991).

Wills, G., 'Message in the Deodorant Bottle: Inventing time', *Critical Inquiry*, 15 (3) (1989) 497–509.

Wright, A., 'Early Advertising and Media', *Pharmaceutical Historian*, 21 (1) (1991) 6–8.

Young, J. H., *The Toadstool Millionaires: A social history of patent medicines in America before Federal regulation* (Princeton: Princeton University Press, 1961).

Young, J. H., *The Medical Messiahs: A social history of health quackery in Twentieth-Century America* (Princeton: Princeton University Press, 1967).

# 6 Producing the Body: Jane Fonda and the New Public Feminine[1]
## Hilary Radner

### INTRODUCTION

In the 'Style' section of the New York *Time Magazine* an autobiographical vignette titled 'True Romance' recounting a young woman's first date with a young man ends with the following statement: 'It had been a grand and fulfilling success: a date with my dress' (Schwartz, 1994, 63). This piece revolves around the memory not of the young man but of 'the caress of the dress; satiny, clinging, transforming'. It embodies one of the current contradictions of feminine culture in which two narratives collide – in the first, feminine consumer culture operates in the service of a dominant heterosexist paradigm in which feminine agency is subjugated to masculine desire; in the second, feminine culture revolves around a narcissistic feminine subject for whom heterosexuality serves as a 'cover', the 'alibi' that legitimises its covert pleasures.[2]

In elucidating this contradiction of feminine culture it has become commonplace in feminist criticism to draw upon Michel Foucault's account of the production of the docile body in the eighteenth century to discuss the representation and production of a feminine body within contemporary feminine culture (Foucault, 1979). Susan Bordo, in particular, mobilises Foucault's argument to articulate a concept of the feminine body as a

> site of struggle where we must work to keep our daily practices in the service of resistance to gender domination, not in the service of 'docility' and gender normalisation. (Bordo, 1989, 28)

If, as Bordo (1988, 90) asserts, 'Our bodies, no less than anything else that is human, are constituted by culture', how, then, is resistance 'constructed' within a cultural formation which must produce a docile body? From a Foucauldian perspective, the 'resistant' body, in Bordo's terms, is no less a product of cultural discipline than the 'dominated' body, of 'gender normalisation'. Similarly when Sandra Bartky (1988, 64) criticises a social structure because it generates a series of 'disciplinary practices that produce a body which in gesture and appearance is recognisably feminine', she seemingly overlooks that femininity is never any more or less than the disciplinary practices that produce it. To write a history of the female body as the univocal expression, the sign, of a pure 'domination' is fundamentally to misread the complexities of feminine culture reducing it to the terms of a homogeneous systematicity – rather than to understand it in terms of 'a multiplicity of discourses produced by a whole series of mechanisms operating in different institutions', to borrow from Foucault's discussion of sexuality (Foucault, 1985, 33).

By concentrating exclusively on the notion of the 'docile body' of *Discipline and Punish*, Bordo and Bartky pass over the specificity of the production of the female body within the private sphere, which has been governed by its biological reproductive function. In so doing, they can privilege the female body as the dominated body, from a traditional feminist perspective. Though the male body is similarly dominated, it is always posited as subject to less domination than the female body. Feminists have been criticised for upholding the position in which gender is seen as the primary determinant of social oppression. Such criticisms are always with the purpose of staking out another hierarchy of more or less dominant, more or less subjected, in which the position of the white bourgeois feminist is compared unfavourably, or rather favourably, with that of some other population – African–Americans, lesbians, and so on. This hierarchy is measured against a humanist utopian model in which perfect equality and liberty might be achieved, in which the 'white male' citizen is held up as the liberated ideal, the norm. The goal of this politics then becomes the production of parity between the 'white male' citizen and the population of the aggrieved. For example, the fight for equal wages is always determined by measuring how much less a woman, a black, a latino, and so on, might earn in comparison with a white male.[3]

If one does indeed want to adopt a Foucauldian perspective, the well-documented discrepancy between men's and women's wages in the United States does not produce in itself relations of power; rather it is a product of the articulation of power within US culture. This discrepancy is not so much a measure of Man's domination over Woman but of the technologies of discipline such as education that produce masculinity and femininity as discursive categories. A Foucauldian methodology renders problematic a politics based on a hierarchy of 'aggrievements' in which privilege is accorded, as it were, in mirror image to that culture it purports to critique. To generate a feminist agenda that is based on such a hierarchy, that is to say based on the assumption of a hierarchy of the more or less dominated, will eventually only serve to preserve that hierarchy in one form or another.

What I wish to suggest here is that perhaps such feminist criticisms are asking the wrong questions. The discipline of the body is given within any social formation. The questions then become: How do we articulate the stakes of the historically specific forms of a given discipline? In the service of what larger discursive structures does it operate? And finally, What are the profits and losses of this discipline as opposed to some other procedure or technology? I want to focus on the 'aerobics craze' in the United States during the 1980s as a specific formulation of public discipline – in which both the panoptical model of 'docile bodies' and a new 'culture of the self' converge to produce a feminine body. This formulation of the public body occurs precisely at that moment in US history in which the majority of US women work outside the home. The shift from a body in which the woman's primary function was constructed in terms of biological reproduction within the private sphere, to a body that 'works' within the public sphere, demanded a new form of discipline. As she spends less of her time caught up in the process of biological reproduction, and more of her time within the public sphere, the discipline of the female body could no longer be left in the hands of the family as the primary institution regulating the private sphere.

## PRODUCING THE FEMININE SELF

*Jane Fonda's Workout Book*, published in 1981, serves as a handbook that seeks to assist the new citizen in the production of a public body. As a text, the book provides a 'document' that is both produced by and productive of a public body, the body of a citizen designated as feminine. 'Citizen Jane' (a soubriquet attached to Fonda by one of her biographers), marks the place of a 'gendered' citizen that challenges apparently neutral images of the citizen, which in reality imply masculine by default. *Jane Fonda's Workout Book* documents an exemplary moment in which exercise, previously simply a general programme of fitness and good health, becomes a central discourse of feminine culture. An activity ('physical fitness') previously on the edges of ideology (dependent on a masculine ideal of athletic activity) is reformulated as a critical practice in the production of a feminine 'self'. The book constitutes a meta-critical text in which procedures are situated in larger discursive structures. *Jane Fonda's Workout Book* parallels the type of texts that Foucault has used to define 'the culture of the self', which offers instruction in the production of a 'self' to a 'subject' that willingly engages in its discourse and practice. This notion of discipline contrasts with that defined in *Discipline and Punish*, in which subjectivity is theorised only through the production of a 'docile body' (McNay, 1992, 61).

As Sandra Bartky remarks, 'no one is marched off for electrolysis at gunpoint' (Bartky, quoted in McNay, 1992, 33). A theoretical conception of a subject that takes an 'active' part in his or her production, though a deliberate cultivation of the 'self', offers not simply an explanation of why women engage in a process of self-discipline without being threatened at gunpoint. It also offers a model of resistance that does not fall back on some form of the repressive hypothesis (McNay, 1992, 61). If feminine culture has as its sole goal to turn women into 'the docile and compliant companions of men just as surely as the army to turn its raw recruits into soldiers'

(Bartky, quoted in McNay, 1992, 33), how then would Bartky herself come to occupy a position from which she might speak against such a system? Rather, it seems more accurate to see the subject as produced heterogeneously in which a degree of choice is offered her. Foucault, himself, suggests this possibility in the very concept of a deliberate culture of the self.

Fonda offers, signalled through the use of the possessive in the title, a specifically feminine 'model of self-mastery', which preserves the dichotomy masculine–feminine but reformulates the terms of this opposition. It is 'her' self-mastery that Fonda 'works out'. In this production of 'mastery', the subject resists the domestic disciplines of the family by submitting to a public discipline, or another technology or procedure of 'domination'. The question that Fonda's practices pose centres around this issue of resistance. In the articulation of a public practice that is linked to the discourses of consumerism and nationalism, does the workout transform tactics of resistance into strategies of domination?

## THE MUTABILITY OF FEMININE REPRESENTATION

The social and cultural position enjoyed by Fonda is important to an understanding of the status of these practices. For more than three decades, in a range of media, Fonda has maintained her social and popular prominence. She is, in Henri Lefevre's terms, one of the 'Idols':

> whose outstanding advantage is that they are perfectly unremarkable (neither too ugly nor too beautiful, too vulgar nor too refined, neither too gifted nor without gifts), that they lead the same 'everyday' life as anybody else and that they present to everyone an image of his (everyday) life transfigured by the fact that it is not his but that of another (an Idol, therefore rich and famous). Thus it is absolutely fascinating to watch an Idol amid his satellites having a bath, kissing his children, driving his car or doing any one of these things that everybody does but as if nobody had ever done them before. (Lefevre, 1984, 175)

In addition to representing a transition point between the exigencies of everyday life and the glamour of an Olympian existence, Fonda articulates the mutability of feminine representation. In contrast with stars of only one image such as Brigitte Bardot, Fonda's ability to transform the perimeters of her star iconography lent a peculiarly feminine cast to the construction of Jane. But Fonda's presence is, paradoxically, also fixed. Unlike Madonna, who foregrounds mutability as a sign of post-feminist femininity, she would always evoke an essential Americanness. If Madonna is frequently analysed as 'problematising the bourgeois illusion of "real" individual gendered selves (there is nothing but masks)' (Kaplan, 1993, 149), Fonda represents the integrity of the 'bourgeois' gendered self despite its transformations. As an icon she embodies a narrative of transformation grounded in an ideology of identity, of a fixed self – a serial authenticity and sincerity. It is precisely for the changes in the perimeters of this category of American femininity that Fonda provides a narrative of cohesion, which assumes a self in control of its transformations.

Though Fonda fostered a privileged position in the public eye that she literally inherited from her father, the Hollywood actor Henry Fonda, she self-consciously identified with her public and invited them to share with her the now demystified process of the production of glamour and beauty. Part of Fonda's status as a star is that her public recognises her status and her function as both producer and product, as a star who self-consciously represents both to her public.

*McCall's*, a women's service magazine, describes Fonda as:

> The original zeitgeist woman – a sex kitten in the 1950s, antiwar radical in the late 1960s, feminist in the 1970s, successful entrepreneur in the 1980s, (Ball, 1992, 96)

The magazine emphasising her identity as one that represents the concerns of a given moment rather than a constant, a narrative that embodies recent feminine history and culture. This identity, both transformable and cohesive in the sense that Jane is still Jane from one incarnation to the next, represents the possibility that the woman takes control over the 'selves' that she produces and transforms according to a given context. This transformability as feminine empowerment is most palpable in the emphasis placed on Fonda's body, with which her public is invited to identify and which serves as the sign of an authentic underlying 'self'.

Fonda fosters her identification with her public by downplaying her role as an 'authority', underlining her image as a form of celebrity counter-transference with the women who purchase her tapes. Thus she confesses to *Redbook*, another women's magazine directed towards a general readership:

> People listen to me because I've had the kind of warfare with food that they are having. I thought I was fat, and so I became anorexic for a long time. It took me years to recover from that. Then, around 1957, I discovered the benefits of exercise. I want other people to share in this knowledge – and they have, thanks to me and my big mouth. ('Jane Fonda', *Redbook*, 1988, 77)

Critical to the discursive function of the workout is the process whereby Fonda as a popular icon reproduced herself through ancillary texts such as the women's magazines quoted above. They articulate 'doing Jane' as a process of self-control or self-production representing an economic and political agency integral to the practice of working out.

> It's very gratifying to me that 'doing Jane' has had such a positive effect on so many people's lives. And as I had hoped, the results reported back to me person-to-person or in letters demonstrate not only weight loss, but also reduced stress, increased energy, more interest in nutrition, more motivation to become involved in sports, less need for medication and many other life-enhancing benefits. (Fonda, 1986, 89)

Important here is the distinction between 'doing Jane' and 'being Jane'. Rather than encouraging a passive identification with an image or Idol, the expression suggests an active choice and mode of reproduction. 'Doing Jane' resolves the dichotomy between a public femininity, political and economic agency, and a private femininity, sexual identity. The workout phenomenon derives from the conjunction between Fonda as a totemic representation of a new public feminine and the generalised pursuit of a feminine body constructed through agency rather than passivity. The production of an 'undocile' body does not disrupt existing heterosexual institutions in which a woman 'appears' for a man. 'In a world that is increasingly out of control', Fonda says, 'it's something you can control. I may dress for a man, but I exercise for myself' (quoted in Ball, 1992, 143). The 'it' that Fonda 'controls' is her body – not the body constructed when she dresses 'for a man', but the bod(ies) produced in the process of exercise, a discipline that she controls as a sign of 'agency' and finally of subjectivity and of citizenship.

## YOUR PLEASURE IN YOUR OWN DISCIPLINE

*Jane Fonda's Workout Book*, Fonda's first workout book, under-lines the manner in which the workout engenders, in Timothy Reiss' words, a set of 'conceptual tools that make the majority of human [here, feminine] practices meaningful' (Reiss, 1982, 11). The significance of the book lies not only in its documen-tation of the exercises as a technology of the body, but also in the manner in which these exercises are situated through metonymic and metaphoric relationships to larger ideological categories such as humanism or nationalism. The book is divided into five parts: Lessons Learned (I), Wholly Health (II), Being Strong (III), The Workout (IV), The Body Besieged (V). The longest section (Part IV) is devoted to de-scriptions of the workout exercises revolving around photos of various women performing these exercises, which isolate dif-ferent body parts (arms, waist, hips, and so on). The descrip-tion of the workout itself fills 141 out of the 254 pages in the book. The rest of the book (parts I–III and V) constructs an autobiographical apologia in the style of Saint Augustine's confessions legitimating the workout as the manifest practice of a larger discursive category – or moral and philosophical position. As the titles of the sections themselves suggest, the book leads the reader to a position from which she may reclaim her body as 'a body abused' and 'hold' it against further attack in a social context in which, to quote Bordo, the body will always be 'a site of struggle' – or in Fonda's terms, 'the body besieged'. The apologia defines how the workout functions as part of a way of life – it calls forth the subject of the workout, which itself as a technology defines the body as object. Thus, the book reproduces the process by which a woman is constituted as both a subject and an object within a given context, whereby a woman may aspire to a limited sense of 'control' over the troubled terrain of her own body.

In the detailed enumeration of the positions of the body, the discipline of the workout does in fact recall Foucault's description of the development of a military discipline in the eighteenth century, which he describes as follows:

> it was a question of not treating the body, en masse, 'wholesale', as if it were an indissociable unity, but of working it 'retail', individually; of exercising upon it a subtle coercion, of obtaining holds upon it at the level of the mechanism itself – movements, gestures, attitudes, rapidity: an infinitesimal power over the active body. (Foucault, 1979, 136–7)

The details of the actual disciplinary procedure are less important than the conceptualisation of a technology of power founded on a discipline of the body as a segmented and thus controlled and controllable entity, which initially suggests a marked parallel between the discipline of the workout and of military procedures. The procedure of control effected through the workout is formulaic and depends upon a regimentation and articulation of the body as an incremental process. Implied in this same description are the major elements that distinguish Jane's discipline from the military discipline described by Foucault. First, the practitioner 'does' the exercise; she disciplines herself as an individual rather than moving in a body as does the military unit. The body is very clearly her body, just as it is Jane's workout. Though women exercise in groups, they remain autonomous individuals who discipline themselves. The instructor offers herself as an example (as does Jane in her book) rather than an as authority. If it is Jane who 'authors' the book, her authority is generated by her membership within the group to whom she speaks. She is not a professional physiologist – rather, like her reader, she is simply a subject in search of an adequate practice, a culture of the self.

This possession of the body by its 'self', is complicated by the fact that, as has been pointed out by Margaret Morse (1987–8) and Susan Willis (1991), the exerciser possesses her body through her identification with an image that is not her own but that of the exemplary bod(ies) offered her. When exercising in a group she compares her body, which she sees in the mirror, with those bodies previously offered her in books, or on video, or in magazine spreads. When exercising with a video tape, this disjunction is further marked by the video image that appears to mirror her, but which effectively elides her own image such as she would see it in the studio mirror. Finally, the projection of an adequate image guarantees the production of the 'self' through a topology in which she measures her image against the image of the exemplar. The proliferation of images in the workout book, the detailed delineation of the body as image, serves to reiterate this specular relation. In order to ensure this relationship, to fix the relationship between body and image as a controlled pattern, aerobic workouts follow a highly ritualised and formulaic procedure that rarely varies except in details. It is necessary to 'know' the pattern in order to properly perform the exercise in which alignment, balance, position, signal accomplishment. This aspect of the workout is carried over from dance techniques. It is not insignificant that Fonda studied ballet for many years before evolving the workout (Fonda, 1981, 21).

The Fonda workout is characteristic of aerobic workouts in general, of which it is the most publicised, but neither the first nor the most prevalent. The formula for all workouts is similar, but certain sections, the aerobic sections in particular, are extended in advanced classes or modified in low-impact classes or other variations such as 'step' or 'hip-hop'. The practice of the workout, at the studio or on the cassette, is extremely repetitive. In fact, there is very little variation from studio to studio regardless of the 'method' employed. All the studios where I did research for this article (in Berkeley, California, San Francisco, New York City, Pittsburgh, Pennsylvania, South Bend, Indiana), whether Jazzercize or more personalised instruction, follow the same basic format detailed here, popularised as 'doing Jane'. Regardless of these variations, the workout is always framed by a warm-up and cool-down. These sections function as a means of calling into play the body and defining the liminal space of the workout itself in which the body will function differently than in everyday procedures. The description of the workout in *Jane Fonda's Workout Book* begins with an invocation: 'Concentrate on what you are doing – no distractions – centre yourself – this is your time' (Fonda, 1981, 74). Women variously describe the pleasure of working out in terms of this evasion from their everyday life, a return to a level of visceral involvement with the body. The workout provides the woman an opportunity to enjoy narcissistic involvement in her own body, but under circumstances protected by a methodology of discipline and social regulation, signalled by the moment of interpellation. 'Doing Jane' or any other aerobic workout, appears to give women a certain type of pleasure through movement that until very recently was denied them. The constrictions imposed by certain garments as well as modes of behaviour have prevented mature women of the middle classes from enjoying sustained physical activity (Banner, 1983, 202–3). Though exercise was initially popularised in the early twentieth century aerobics represents an extension and systemisation of this phenomenon for a wide demographic segment of the female population.

As the initial moment of interpellation, the warm-up designates a series of body parts. It codifies the body by designating various areas that will be repeated in the rest of the workout – head, shoulder, side, waist, hamstring, spine, calf, inner thigh – and then returns the body to an upright position. This section culminates in another brief series of stretches – back, knees, tendons, back. After this preparation or induction, the body is ready to move into a phase in which it is broken down into component parts that are isolated and disciplined and finally reassembled into the workout body.

This breakdown into body parts corresponds to a similar breakdown effected in terms of product usage in feminine culture, as Mary Ann Doane (1987) points out

Commodification presupposes that acutely self-conscious relation to the body which is attributed to femininity. The effective operation of the commodity system requires the breakdown of the body into parts – nails, hair, skin, breath – each one of which can constantly be improved through the púrchase of a commodity. (Doane, 1987, 32)

Each group of exercises concentrating on a specific area of the body is introduced by a photograph of Fonda, which functions as a template of physicality that is reproduced by the models who actually demonstrate the exercises. Their bodies do not conform to the norms most generally propagated by the media – the pencil thin fashion mannequin or the voluptuous swimsuit model. Instead they represent a certain type usually associated with professional dancers. All are fit, slim but not thin, small-breasted with small pelvises, taut without being muscular. Thus these bodies are reproduced as a sign that signifies femininity, but a femininity that is de-eroticised and rendered as fragile rather than fecund. It signifies a body suited to public life, neither the obvious object of an eroticised masculine gaze nor a body defined by its reproductive potential. Further, a diversification of age, race, and body type creates a heteroglossic subject, which is rendered homogeneous through the ritual of the exercise process as a rigid formula. Exercise produces the feminine body as a cohesive moment within the multiplicity of other forms of identity, such as race, class, age, and so on that articulate social structure. The rigid formula (its 'sameness') invites the practitioner to appropriate this culturally produced category as her 'body' – a moment which confirms her identity as 'self' but also her 'identification' with women.

The progression of the exercises defines the perimeters of this body by routinely moving it from an upright position to a supine position. The process that initially isolates various areas of the body ends with a 'cool-down', which leaves the body stretched full length upon the floor. The final position in which the relaxed body gives itself over to gravity constitutes a release from the constraints of discipline. This architectured release permits an identification with the body as fully itself within the protected arena of discipline. The workout gives a carefully orchestrated balance of constraint and release, of pain and pleasure – or what Fonda calls 'your pleasure in your own discipline' (Fonda, 1981, 56). She elaborates in another chapter:

afterwards [after working out] I would feel alive and revitalised. It was hard to explain this or to describe how good I felt about being disciplined. (Fonda, 1981, 21)

We note that Fonda talks about 'being disciplined' as though she were not the 'author' of her discipline. Yet it is precisely the power to control the body that the workout offers its practitioners. Fonda's own body, in the process of constructing a 'self' that is simultaneously both 'master and slave', becomes that which is to be disciplined – an 'it' in opposition to the 'self' that controls 'it'.


WE ARE THE PIONEERS

This issue of control, in which Fonda represents a doubled figure of master–slave, coupled with that of the family, forms the governing thematic of the Fonda narrative. Fonda opens her story, recounted in the first person, with the remark that she is 'the product of a culture'. 'Like a great many women, I am a product of a culture that says thin is better, blond is beautiful and buxom is best' (Fonda, 1981, 9). By representing herself as a product, she places herself initially in a passive position. She is an object, acted upon rather than acting. However, the workout as a technology of the body transforms looks into accomplishment, thus articulating a femininity (and a feminism) that retains its identity by retaining its 'looks', but that also accords agency and accomplishment to the subject that produces the 'looks'. It is not he who 'looks' but she who incites those looks, produces them, who becomes the agent of exchange. Working out becomes an assertion of control that a woman makes over her looks, though her work is still her body. Fonda titles one section of the book 'We Become What We Do' (Fonda, 1981, 17). In the Prologue she comments:

I discovered that with common sense, a bit of studying and a good deal of commitment, I could create for myself a new approach to health and beauty: an approach which would not only make me look better, but would enable me to handle the intense, multifaceted life I live with more clarity and balance, to say nothing of more energy and endurance. (Fonda, 1981, 10)

This issue of looks does not disappear but on the contrary is reiterated as a major benefit of working out. Fonda may still be a product, but she is also a producer, and she produces a better product than did the men, ranging from doctors to husbands and lovers, to whom she had previously confided her health and looks.

This move from product to producer is emblematic of her own professional evolution as a star, and ultimately enables her to surpass her father. Her accomplishment was officially recognised when she 'gave' him the film for which he received an Oscar. In her professional life, her success as an actress and then as the producer who provided her father with the long sought-after Oscar firmly established Jane as a Fonda in the tradition of her father, whose name, in spite of her gender, she continues to bear. It is Jane, not Peter, her brother, who formally continues the family line and tradition of independence and moral commitment, usurping the patrilineal privilege of the first son. Paradoxically, it is Henry Fonda (whose looks constituted his capital as a movie star) who offered Fonda her model of accomplishment. The issue of looks points to a moment of trouble within the Fonda family. As the psychoanalyst Eugénie Lemoine-Luccioni (1976) explains, it is the mother's 'looks' with which the child identifies, and this initial identification is disrupted by the father's look. In the Fonda paradigm, Jane must identify with the father's looks (his image) as the position from which she too might transform her looks into accomplishments. This 'trouble' paradoxically does not articulate itself in terms of 'gender' but in terms of 'star' and 'public' spectacle. Thus we see a form of gender bending in terms of a position that does not disrupt the heterosexual categorisation of masculine–feminine. However, by assuming control of her body, by making it over into an image that is her own, Fonda rejects a feminine heritage of passivity grounded in the helpless body. Helplessness signalled by the term 'ugly' as the inability to control the body – a body that is in excess of the self that controls it – is marked through reference to her mother. The biographer, Peter Carroll (1985, 224) comments:

Asked if she had inherited her physical endowment, Jane believes otherwise: 'I like to think a lot of my body is my own doing and my own blood and guts. It's my responsibility'.

I hesitate to push these issues but feel that there is a larger significance to the 'Fonda family romance', in Freud's terms. The dynastic history of the Fondas forms part of a culturally produced mega-text, deployed across different media. Their lives as contemporary Olympians provide narrative templates of mythic proportion that bear little relation to traditional forms of gossip. Jane's relationship to both her mother and father are part of the popular domain, a public negotiation of larger issues of familial conflict. The autobiographical section, including famous movie stills, of *Jane Fonda's Workout Book* is only one manifestation of a complicated network of narrative formations, which has been both produced by the Fondas but of which they are also products. Jane rewrites her regime of discipline and pleasure as a history of her body, an itinerary that moves her from the bad body of her mother Frances, who commits suicide, to the good 'wholly healthy' body, from the 'sinful body' to the 'holy body'. The bad body depended upon external mechanisms of control: drugs, doctors, cosmetics, and prosthetic undergarments. The good body produces itself through an internally regulated technology of control, manifested in the workout, but also in a diet of 'natural' 'counter-culture' foods. This process is one of self-realisation in which Jane progresses from what she terms 'the body abused' in her teenage years as a chronic dieter, bulimic, and so on, through her attempts to reconstitute her body for a sexualised male look, to a final moment in which she takes control of her body for herself. Through the workout and the discipline that it represents, Jane attempts to create a new matriarchal lineage. She dedicates *Jane Fonda's Workout Book* to her daughter Vanessa:

> I've decided to write this book ... because I want to share what I've had to learn the hard way with other women. I only wish someone had shared these things with me earlier in my life. That's why I've dedicated this book to my daughter. (Fonda, 1981, 10)

In this sense, Jane Fonda can be seen as renegotiating properly 'American' values within an evolving moral climate. Jane's political commitment has always been moral rather than practical, a commitment to the idea of 'justice' rather than to a specific political or economic agenda. In her activist days, she supported causes because they appealed to her moral convictions rather than because they corresponded to a specific world view. In *Ladies Home Journal* she is reported as saying:

> My gut-level attraction is to grass-roots organisations rather than democratic party politics. I don't want to lose my idealism. After seeing from the perspective of a politician's wife, I'm more convinced than ever that citizens have got to do it themselves – politicians won't do anything unless they're pressured. (Andersen, 1989, 117)

Fonda's need to establish a sense of tradition, a lineage, is symptomatic of her basic identification with 'Americaness' – with grass-roots organisations. The autobiographic passages in *Jane Fonda's Workout Book* underline this impulse of creating a history in which legitimacy is conferred matrilineally. The position of the matriarch is reconstituted as a positive force of control that, in an earlier subsection of part III, called 'Breaking the "Weaker Sex" Mold' (Fonda, 1981, 45), Jane traces back to a pioneer ancestor, Peggy Fonda, who rebuilt the family mill to feed George Washington's soldiers. She accompanies this story with an archival photograph of a woman seated on a plough drawn by horses, wearing a sunbonnet and overalls, which in fact is taken from a 1942 seed catalogue. The image, the origins of which are unspecified (who is this woman, when, why was the photo taken?), is rewritten through its function in the workout narrative as a historic image of feminine fortitude that seeks to invoke a 'universal' category of woman within the history of the United States (Fonda, 1981, 44).

In *Women Coming of Age*, Fonda repeats and emphasises this analogy. Midlife is 'the New Frontier' for women. 'To be a midlife woman in our society is, in many respects, to be a pioneer', states Fonda (Fonda, 1984, 19). By invoking history, she claims for the liberated woman as 'citizen', the legitimacy of an American past, a national heritage with which she encourages women to identify. She concludes *Women Coming of Age* by repeating the pioneer analogy:

> We are the pioneers – a first generation self-consciously, admittedly midlife women, charting a positive new trail for ourselves and our daughters through a previously misunderstood and ignored part of life. (Fonda, 1984, 418)

To come of age is also to embrace a past that legitimates the future: 'There was a time when heavy physical work was an accepted part of both men's and women's lives' (Fonda, 1981, 45). Women's past authentic femininity has been taken away from them by the Industrial Revolution which produced a 'cultural ideal' that demanded that 'a desirable woman' be 'delicate and decorative, like her aristocratic sisters' (Fonda, 1981, 45). The workout book in its production of a new femininity rejects the aristocratic as a 'false' ideal that must be replaced by returning to the democratic model of the 'pioneer woman who worked shoulder-to-shoulder with their men to push back the wilderness, build homesteads, plow the virgin prairies' (Fonda, 1981, 45).


THE POWER WIFE

In *Jane Fonda's New Workout and Weight-Loss Program*, establishing a history and a politics no longer has the same urgency because this history can now be taken for granted. The larger political issues of the first book, such as pollution and ecology, are removed in the fourth exercise book, published in 1986; however, the focus on exercise and nutrition is retained and amplified, maintaining the links between the new public femininity and a private femininity defined within the family. The first workout book itself was not a fixed moment in the process of producing femininities. If, in many ways, little more than a decade later, it already seems hopelessly outmoded, Fonda's function as a negotiator of political and sexual roles for American women continues. Her marriage to Turner offers the fairy-tale conclusion to a now transformed narrative of heterosexuality. Fonda offers a model through which women can reconstruct themselves as both objects and subjects and enables them to enjoy a degree of power and privilege in a culture in which heterosexuality is the norm. She pays a price: she must submit to a technology of the body, and to a ritual of product usage that will enable her autonomy to be effortlessly reinscribed as the object of masculine desire through the male look (here, the camera) within a heterosexual paradigm. The move away from feminist politics signals a necessary transition in Fonda's evolution, which eventually culminates in the dissolution of her marriage with the. left-wing politician Tom Hayden, as the transitional moment, and her marriage, finally, to media mogul, Ted Turner, as the correct fairy-tale ending.

Because within a heterosexual paradigm, feminine narcissism can be reread as the projection of male narcissism, Fonda's investment in the body now moves her to the position of the new power wife whose goal in life is to find her corporate prince. Now Fonda's goal is no longer 'control' and the cultivation of a self, but 'standing by her man, media mogul and Cable News Network founder Ted Turner' (Grant, 1993, 85), a happy fate guaranteed by her strenuously produced 'self'. This is finally the paradox of the workout 'culture of the self': Fonda's looks are her cultural capital. *McCall's* magazine comments:

> Fonda remains her own best advertisement: Most of us would be pleased to look at 34 the way she looks at 54, especially in Lycra'. (Ball, 1992, 96)

However, Fonda's 'beauty' marks her as tamed, 'a Kate conformable as other household Kates'. The pleasure that she takes in herself is legitimated by the male look, indicating her willingness to submit in the last instance to a patriarchal order regimented by a consumer economy.

The depoliticisation of the workout in her fourth book reflects this shift in which the conservative function of the workout narrative is underlined; however, a number of public events even more clearly illustrate this renegotiation of Fonda's political position. Most obvious was her public apology in 1988 to Vietnam veterans on prime-time television

during an interview by Barbara Walters for ABC's new magazine show, '20/20'. Less obvious were the economic reasons
behind this decision: demonstrations by veterans were imped-
ing the filming of *Stanley and Iris* (1989) (Andersen, 1990,
331). Her apology was symptomatic of a reordering of priorities in Fonda's life: in 1988, her workout industry would no
longer provide financial support to Campaign California. The
ties between 'doing Jane' and a public commitment to social
change were officially severed. However, it would be erroneous
to see this movement as a return to her earlier incarnation of
'Lady Jane', a renunciation of her position as 'Citizen Jane', to
use terms of her popular biographer Christopher Andersen
(1989, 1990). Rather, this move presents another reformulation of the role of the feminine 'citizen' – which in vernacular terms might best be described as the move from 'activist'
to 'power wife' (to borrow the terms of the popular press).

The 'power wife', represented in the political arena by
Hillary Rodham Clinton in the US 1992 election, takes a secondary place to that of her husband, but is clearly established
in her own right as a full citizen. Hillary Rodham Clinton's
position is guaranteed by her husband, but it is one that requires that she function within a public rather than a private
arena. If other 'First Ladies' served a public function, it was
always to represent the private concerns of family and culture,
within the public spectacle of self-governance. Though Hillary
Rodham Clinton's 'work' is still tied to traditionally private concerns of family and health care, these concerns have been pro-
fessionalised, officially marked as being of the public domain,
the concerns of public institutions rather than that of the
private institution of the family. The Clintons represent, then,
precisely a political position that coincides very closely to the
'new' tradition articulated within the fourth Fonda workout
book.

Fonda's own position as 'power wife' to Ted Turner represents a similar transformation within the public corporate
sector. Turner's and Fonda's marriage is described in the
popular press as 'a union of megastars' (Grant, 1993, 85),
'more a merger than a marriage' (Ball, 1992, 145). The choice
of Fonda over the more obvious array of 'Marla Marples',
young docile women whose capital is constituted by their un-

marked bodies and their receptivity – represents a departure from a romantic ideal that has informed the marriage plot since the publication of *Pamela* in 1748 (Radner, 1993). Fonda is rewarded not simply for her looks but also for her accomplishments. In other words, her marriage in her fifties signals that she has indeed transformed her looks into accomplishments, and rather than confronting a cultural capital diminished by age, Fonda as an older woman can look with satisfaction on her accumulation of wealth. *McCall's* comments,

> At 54, she's got what she wants: her dream man and the freedom to 'choose happiness'. (Ball, 1992, 94)

*McCall's* continues that Fonda:

> has decided that, in the 1990s, she'll focus on personal fulfilment. Which in this case means her new marriage. 'Right now', Fonda explains simply, 'I'm choosing happiness'. (Ball, 1992, 96)

It is precisely the notion of having the freedom to choose happiness, the US ideology of the individual, that Fonda now represents within feminine culture. For Fonda the pursuit of happiness is defined by 'what men think'.

> Well, men aren't rethinking beauty ... and to the extent that a woman is defined by what men think then it probably isn't being rethought. But one of the positive things about the fitness movement is that women tend to define their own body image. If they feel good about themselves, they're less apt to think, Unless I'm thin, I'm not lovable. (Quoted in Ball, 1992, 96)

The pursuit of happiness is regimented by the fact that her rights can only be maintained through the preservation of a body that she must continually reproduce. This regimentation, however, is not the result of a homogeneous coercive system but of a complex nexus of 'choices' that Fonda negotiates and presents to a world not yet 're-thought' by men:

I do think there's a large segment of women who aren't bound by those strictures ... They don't wear makeup, and they're much more independent of the culture that says you are how you look. They don't feel it necessary to push their feet into painful high-heeled shoes to make their legs look prettier – and I take my hat off to them. (Quoted in Ball, 1992, 97)

## PLASTIC SURGERY

The most important aspect of this negotiation was Fonda's well-documented capitulation to plastic surgery. She reportedly has had 'eyelid surgery' (blepharoplasty) and breast augmentation (Andersen, 1990, 325). It is rare that an article on her does not comment on this fact. Indeed she includes a section on plastic surgery in *Women Coming of Age*, reflecting a concern shared with high-fashion magazines, whose affluent readers might find cosmetic surgery more easily available to them. As Fonda herself puts it: cosmetic surgery is about 'buying yourself a few years' (Ball, 1992, 97). To return to Bordo's 1988 initial characterisation of the body – for Fonda, her body is a 'site of struggle', but it is also a terrain that can be recolonised endlessly for profit. Fonda's comments about her own identity show how her particular 'bricolage of the body' is part of a larger economic and political structure in which most women are not quite as lucky – or quite as adept at cultivating and exploiting their own bodies.

Yet it is this same body that Fonda herself chastised in the original workout book when she realised that a Vietnamese prostitute could raise her prices if she 'Americanised' her face and body through cosmetic surgery:

I was shocked into the realisation that I myself had played an unwitting role as a movie star and sex symbol in perpetrating the stereotypes that affected women all over the world. (Fonda, 1981, 20)

Certainly, no one forced Fonda 'at gunpoint' to undergo plastic surgery, in particular to risk the well-publicised dangers of breast implants. For Fonda this was a considered choice. 'What the hell is the big deal, as long as it's done carefully and with thought?' (quoted in Ball, 1992, 97) Of course, 'the big deal' is the promulgation of a certain feminine ideal within an economic and political sphere. Fonda's breasts are not merely signs of her 'pursuit of happiness' as an 'individual', but represent 'success' and 'cultural capital' for women as a social category. In terms of a humanistic ideal of individual happiness, one can argue as does Kathy Davis that:

> By taking agency as a relevant feature in how women experience cosmetic surgery, the decision can itself become a radical and courageous act. By deciding to undergo cosmetic surgery, they initiate a dramatic change, becoming agents in the transformation and remaking of their lives as well as their bodies. (Davis, 1991, 35)

Davis' position as a feminist scholar is reiterated almost word for word in *Cosmopolitan Magazine*, which comments that:

> It's not politically correct for anyone – let alone a female plastic surgeon – to suggest that changing your looks can profoundly affect the quality of your life, but, in truth, it definitely can. (Colen, 1994, 236)

*Cosmopolitan* continues:

> the vast majority of people who want a nose job are not alcoholics or manic-depressives or movie-of-the-week plastic surgery addicts. They're realistic women who think a smaller nose or flatter ears or slimmer thighs or bigger breasts will make them feel good about themselves and be noticed and approved of by others. (Colen, 1994, 239)

Thus, while agency might indeed constitute a relevant feature in the feminine experience of cosmetic surgery, this does not mean that plastic surgery ultimately has a radical or emancipatory function in terms of a social or public body. Though the woman chooses, and pays for, plastic surgery, she 'submits' her body to the discipline of the surgeon who wields the knife and regulates norms of social acceptability. She does so because she anticipates and for the most part receives a return on her investment: in other words the results are worth the rigours to which she submits her body. This of course reproduces existing social norms, but these norms are not simply 'gendered', they are also 'based on western markers of ideal beauty' (Balsamo, 1992, 213). Balsamo, feminist scholar, states dramatically:

> The female body comes to serve, in other words, as a site of inscription, a billboard for the dominant cultural meanings that the female body is to have in postmodernity. (Balsamo, 1992, 226)

She elaborates:

> Whether as a form of oppression or a resource of empowerment, it is clear to me that cosmetic surgery is a practice whereby women consciously act to make their bodies mean something to themselves and to others. (Balsamo, 1992, 226)

Plastic surgery is by its nature an ideologically contested act, and far from representing a departure from the initial Fonda practice of working out, plastic surgery reproduces the same paradox that informs the cultural articulation of the workout itself. The discourse produced by the workout may discourage women implicitly, or explicitly (see Fonda, 1984), from using plastic surgery, but it also establishes a 'culture of the self' that produces plastic surgery as the logical extension of its own practice. In so far as the workout functions in a world that has yet to 're-think' cultural standards of beauty, 'working out' will always be geared towards the reproduction of these standards. Otherwise it would not be a source of public empowerment and control. This is the paradox of the feminine culture of the body.


CONCLUSION

In Foucault's work, neither a model of penology (a coercive panopticon geared towards the production of docile bodies), nor of sexuality (the culture of the self), is adequate to the formulation of a theory of the feminine body. The feminine body is a terrain in which these two modes of cultural production both contradict and support each other, depending on the context. The Jane Fonda workout programme is a precise example of this duality. The discipline to which the feminine body is submitted is not maintained through the exercise of physical force or legal penalties; rather, the practitioner voluntarily submits her 'self' to a programme of discipline for which she receives a return in terms of status and even pleasure. On the other hand, the rigours of this discipline are a form of punishment visited on the body. The rigidity of the norms that this discipline reproduces speaks of a technology of social control that cannot be fully articulated as a culture of the self in which the subject submits voluntarily to specific practices in return for certain economic and social privileges. The transformations of the feminine body within the public arena, produced by a culture of the self formulated around such practices as 'doing Jane', testify to the difficulties of judging the terms and stakes of a discursive formation from within that formation.

Academic feminists might do well to pursue the ways in which our own 'practices' within the institutions of public education constitute a form of 'doing Jane', in which we have articulated not a new body but a new body of work – that empowers women but that also acquires legitimacy through its relationship to already accepted scholarship, an existing hierarchy of disciplines, and the demands of the marketplace. Fonda states in an article in *Mirabella*, a magazine directed towards mature women,

> Personally, I have always been financially independent. Just the comfort of knowing that I can take care of myself is powerful. The most important thing for women is economic independence; women being able to take their rightful position in the marketplace, on an equal basis with men. (Spitz, 1994, 74)

What does it mean to take one's 'rightful position in the marketplace'? In accepting the hierarchy of existing marketplaces are we accepting 'terms' that may in fact guarantee that we never receive an adequate return on our investment – that we never find our 'rightful position'? *Mirabella's* interview with Jane Fonda is summarily interrupted: 'Ted Turner is waiting' (Spitz, 1994, 74) the article concludes.

## Notes

1.  This article is a revised version of material that has earlier been published in Hilary Radner, *Shopping Around: Feminine Culture and the Pursuit of Pleasure*, Routledge, 1995, with the permission of the publisher.
2.  I would like to thank my colleague Kathleen Pyne for her on-going discussions of the issues raised in this chapter and for drawing my attention to this passage.
3.  There is a certain strand of feminism that privileges the feminine as generating an ethical ideal which men should learn to emulate. (See the work of Carol Gilligan, 1982, for an example of this position.)

## References

Andersen, C., 'Jane Fonda: I'm stronger than ever', *Ladies Home Journal* (October 1989), 112, 114–15, 117.
Andersen, C., *Citizen Jane: The turbulent life of Jane Fonda* (New York: Henry Holt & Co., 1990).
Ball, A. L., 'How does Jane do it?', *McCall's* (March 1992), 94, 96–7, 143–5.
Balsamo, A., '"On the Cutting Ege": Cosmetic surgery and the technological production of the gendered body', in *Camera Obscura: Journal of Feminism and Film Theory*, 28 (January 1992), 207–8.
Banner, L., *American Beauty* (New York: Knopf, 1983).
Bartky, S., 'Foucault, Femininity, and the Modernization of Patriarchal Power', in Diamond, I. and Quinby, L. (eds), *Feminism and Foucault: Reflections on resistance* (Boston: Northeastern University Press, 1988), 61–86.
Bordo, S., 'Anorexia Nervosa and the Crystallization of Culture', in Diamond, I. and Quinby, L. (eds), *Feminism and Foucault: Reflections on resistance* (Boston: Northeastern University Press, 1988), 87–118.
Bordo, S., 'The Body and the Reproduction of Femininity', in Jaggar, A. M. and Bordo, S. R. (eds), *Gender/Body/Knowledge* (New Brunswick, NJ: Rugers University Press, 1989), 13–33.
Carroll, P. N., *Famous in America: Jane Fonda, George Wallace, Phyllis Schlafly, John Glenn, the passion to succeed* (New York: E. P. Dutton, 1985).
Colen, H. S., 'Change your looks, change your life', *Cosmopolitan* (October 1992), 236–9.
Davis, K., 'Remaking the She-Devil: A critical look at feminist approaches to beauty', *Hypatia*, 6 (2) (1991), 21–43.
Doane, M. A., *The Desire to Desire* (Bloomington, IN: Indiana University Press, 1987).

Fonda, J., *Jane Fonda's Workout Book* (New York: Simon & Schuster, 1981).

Fonda, J., *Women Coming of Age* (New York: Simon & Schuster, 1984).

Fonda, J., *Jane Fonda's New Workout and Weight-Loss Program* (New York: Simon & Schuster, 1986).

Foucault, M., *Discipline and Punish: The birth of the prison*, trans. Alan Sheridan (New York: Vintage Books, 1979).

Foucault, M., *The History of Sexuality: Volume 1, An Introduction*, trans. Robert Hurley (New York: Pantheon, 1985).

Gilligan, C., *In a Different Voice: Psychological theory and women's development* (Cambridge, Mass: Harvard University Press, 1982).

Grant, R., 'Jane Fonda: Her toughest challenge is slowing down', *Shape* (February 1993), 85, 147, 152.

'Jane Fonda', *Redbook* (February 1988), 76–9.

Kaplan, E. A., 'Madonna Politics: Perversion, repression, or subversion? Or mask and/as mastery', in Schwichtenberg, C. (ed.), *The Madonna Connection: Representational politics, subcultural identities, and cultural theory* (Boulder, Col.: Westview Press, 1993), 149–66.

Lefevre, H., *Everyday Life in the Modern World (1950)*, trans. Sacha Rabinovitch (New Brunswick: Transaction Books, 1984).

Lemoine-Luccioni, E., *Partage des femmes* (Paris: Editions du Seuil, 1976).

McNay, L., *Foucault and Feminism* (Boston: Northeastern University Press, 1992).

Morse, M., 'Artemis Aging: Exercise and the female body on video', *Discourse*, 10(1) (1987–8), 20–54.

Radner, H., 'Pretty Is As Pretty Does: Free enterprise and the marriage plot', in Collins, J., Radner, H. and Collins, A. (eds), *Film Theory Goes to the Movies* (New York: Routledge, 1993), 56–76.

Reiss, T., *The Discourse of Modernism* (Ithaca, NY: Cornell University Press, 1985).

Schwartz, L. S., 'True Romance', *The New York Times Magazine* (October 23, 1994), 63.

Spitz, B., 'Jane Fonda', *Mirabella* (June 1994), 72, 74.

Willis, S., *A Primer for Daily Life* (New York: Routledge, 1991).

# 7 The Politics of Representation: Marketing Alcohol through Rap Music
Denise A. Herd

## INTRODUCTION

The new consumer society holds important implications for the politics of identity and social equity among ethnic and racial minorities. Where these struggles were formerly articulated primarily through conflicts over labour and production (particularly in the slave and post-reconstruction periods), increasingly they are mediated through the politics of consumption. In post-colonial society, oppressed groups not only fight for greater participation in the consumer economy, they also fight to defend themselves against some of its excesses, such as environmental waste from more affluent consumers, and the aggressive marketing of addictive products like alcohol and tobacco. As in previous eras, the conflicts over citizenship and participation are enacted in part through cultural representations. In the nineteenth century, images of savagery and bestiality justified social and military control over the labour and consumption behaviour of subaltern groups. In post-industrial society, the cultural forms of oppressed groups are appropriated by advertisers and infused with images and meanings that subvert resistance and increase domination and alienation. Within oppressed groups, the discourse regarding consumption issues is multi-faceted and ambiguous, reflecting the achievement of liberation through simultaneous themes of rebellion, disinhibition, pleasure seeking, restraint, abstinence, and participation. The following discussion examines these issues by exploring the role of rap music as an arena of cultural expression and resistance; its commodification by the alcohol industry; and the social responses to recent alcohol marketing practices by activists and community members.

## THE SOCIAL CONTEXT OF RAP MUSIC AND AFRICAN–AMERICAN YOUTH

> Rap is nothing new ... Rap's forbearers stretch back through disco, street funk, radio DJs, Bo Diddley, the bebop singers, Cab Calloway, Pigmeat Markam, the tap dancers and comics, The Last Poets, Gil Scott-Heron, Muhammad Ali, a cappella and doo-wop groups, ring games, skip-rope rhymes, prison and army songs, toasts ... all the way to the griots of Nigeria and the Gambia. (Toop, 1991, 19)

Contemporary rap music is the postmodern incarnation of a traditional African–American musical and rhetorical style. The cultural focus on improvisation, rhyming and performance has taken on new forms and meanings in the highly technological, post-literate climate of the 1980s and 1990s. Themes from video games, comic superheroes, sirens, and other sounds of urban chaos have all been incorporated into strident verbal monologues issued to the beat of rapid-fire dance music. Rap and the larger context of hip-hop culture (which include graffiti art and breakdancing) emerged among youth in the South Bronx neighbourhoods of New York in the early 1980s. These competitive forms of dance and verbal repartee replaced the fights and drugs associated with a particularly violent spree of gang warfare in the late 1970s. They offer a populist arena for artistic expression and leadership. In contrast to the social connections and financial backing needed to become a major commercial singer, rap musicians can take materials easily available in most inner city neighbourhoods – for example old records, turntables, speakers, their own voices, and everyday clothes – to create new music and messages that articulate their social and cultural experience (Toop, 1991).

Rap music is regarded as a major form of cultural resistance and social protest for black youth who are increasingly alienated and marginalised in cities suffering from decayed infrastructures, police oppression, and pervasive poverty. Black boys and young men are the special targets of increased police surveillance and attacks. For example, in 1988, through 'Operation Hammer', Daryl Gates, ex-Los Angeles Chief of Police, arrested '1500 black youths in South Central [Los Angeles] for merely "looking suspicious"' (Kelley, 1992, 793). The situation is exacerbated by the vacuum in leftist political leadership within the nation or black communities. The broad-based civil rights and social protests of the late 1960s and 1970s have been replaced by the rise of the conservative right and almost exclusively middle-class white social movements that take the form of self-help and personal transformation rather than political protests.

These social conditions have also taken a cultural toll on black youth. They no longer have access to the widespread public affirmations of racial pride that were a keystone of the 1960s' black power movements. Instead, their social worlds are increasingly penetrated by images that define wealth and conspicuous consumption as the markers of identity and personal worth. Designer clothing, foreign luxury cars, expensive electronic equipment, and car phones became major status symbols in the 1980s. At the same time, soaring unemployment rates and low wages made acquiring these luxury goods and indeed some basic amenities (health care, adequate housing and child care) nearly impossible for black teenagers and their families.

Within this oppressive setting, rap music emerges as a major form of cultural resistance. It allows for the expression of 'subjugated knowledges' using verbal, musical and iconic elements. In the words of Dyson (1991, 15):

> The rap concert creates space for cultural resistance and personal agency, losing the strictures of tyrannising surveillance and demoralising condemnation and substituting autonomous, often enabling, forms of self-expression and cultural creativity.

The strains of resistance take the form of both social protest and affirmations of self-pride and personal prowess. Message raps issue strident social commentaries on living conditions in ghettos, on racism and police assaults. Black pride, political awareness, and spirituality are asserted as the solutions to a racist and depraved society. Other rap music consists of personal boasts that assert the performer's uniqueness, creativity, and sexual abilities. Rap music, and hip-hop culture in general, thus serve as major vehicles for constructing and asserting multifaceted political and personal identities.

## DRUGS, RAP AND SOCIAL PROTEST

Historically, drug use was a significant theme in the political poetry that pre-dated rap music. Groups such as 'The Last Poets' and artists like Gil Scott-Heron composed and performed a number of poems or songs that opposed drug use and chronicled its debilitating effects on black communities. These works exposed the downward cycle of heroin addiction which include physical agony, social misery, and even death. The intended audience for these pieces was primarily young inner city blacks who were particularly vulnerable to the heroin trade operating in their communities. 'Jones Coming Down', by The Last Poets is a typical representation of this genre of political poetry:

> Day breaks
> Got the shakes
> nose runnin'
> Joint drippin'
> Body aches
> Jones comin' down
> Feelin' bad
> Funeral sad
> Another 24 hour drag
> Jim, I need me some SCAG
> Pawn my brother's do rag
> to cop me a transparent thin bag
> I'm strung out, strung out on a white witch.

(Nuriddin and El Hadi, 1992, 16)

Reflecting this legacy, protests against drug abuse are a prominent feature of the contemporary message rap. A number of rap groups and artists such as Donald D., The Genius, N.W.A. (Niggers with Attitude), Public Enemy, Grandmaster Mel Melle, and KRS 1 have attacked the use and selling of cocaine in black neighbourhoods. These artists have explored several major themes regarding drug-related problems in black communities. First, as did their predecessors, they warn potential users of the dangers of drugs. Donald D.'s Free Base Institute exhorts listeners to 'Stay away from [crack]. It makes you do crazy things' and will 'snatch your sister, your father, your mother, your brother, a whole lot of others' (Stanley and Morley, 1992, 94). Beyond portraying the harmful effects of using drugs, rap artists have also focused on the violence and greed associated with the drug trade. They depict drug dealing as a soulless enterprise that may be financially lucrative, but is selfish and homicidal. For example, in 'The Life of a Drug Dealer', by The Genius, the drug dealer brags that he's 'constantly counting up cash by the hour', but will do anything to keep control of his empire, regardless of how many victims are killed.

> Every day a homeboy dies, whether shot in the body or cyanide in ya Bacardi ... I'll shoot up funerals, firebomb wakes, vehicular homicides, whatever it takes. (Stanley and Morley, 1992, 139)

Other anti-drug raps focus on the politics of drug use and dealing in black communities. 'In the Dust' by Two Live Crew exposes the connections between racism, police brutality, the drug war and drug dealing. The text describes how blacks are stigmatised for 'pushin or pimpin"', and harassed and killed by the police; and points to the social causes of crime and drug use: 'The system is designed to lead us astray, So we turn to drugs and guns for pay' (Stanley and Morley, 1992, 367–8). Finally, another important theme in message rap is the economic exploitation of black communities through the drug trade that is orchestrated by wealthy white Americans and maintained through police cooperation. This focus is particularly significant because it expresses views that are central to the growing social movement against alcohol marketing practices in hip-hop culture and black communities. These issues are explored in an excerpt from 'Illegal Business' by KRS One:

> Cocaine business controls America
> Ganja business controls America

KRS One come to start some hysteria
Illegal business controls America
What can we get for sixty-three cents

A guy named Jack is selling crack
The community doesn't want him back
He sells at work
He sells in schools
He's not stupid, the cops are the fools

Cause everyone else
Seems to go to jail
But when it comes to Jack
The cops just fail
They can't arrest him
They cannot stop him
Cause even in jail
The bail unlocks him
So here is the deal
And here is the facts
If you ever wonder why
They can't stop crack
The police department
Is like a crew
It does whatever they want to do.

(quoted in Stanley and Morley, 1992, 41–2)

## ALCOHOL AND THE COMMODIFICATION OF RAP

The discourse on alcohol use is more complex than the pervasive anti-drug themes played out in many rap songs. Some rap artists celebrate drinking and drunkenness as part of a lifestyle of partying and wild behaviour. Other artists, in the tradition of message rappers, are protesting alcohol, using themes similar to those depicted in anti-drug raps.

In the pro-drinking rap, alcohol use is associated with disinhibition and rebellion. Getting drunk, cruising in cars, and picking up women are major themes that emerge in this genre. Old English 800, a cheap brand of malt liquor, has become especially popular with some rap artists. For example, Run-D.MC., a major group that pioneered the mainstream acceptance of rap, was famous for coming on stage with a 40 ounce bottle of Old English (Dawsey, 1991). '8 Ball' (8 Ball is a slang term for Old English malt liquor), a rap piece performed by NWA, is an ode to the role of malt liquor in the lifestyle of the black street youth.

Cold kicking
funky fresh Easy E
pull up a chair and I'm a tell this story
I don't drink brass monkey, like to be funky
Nickname Easy E you 8 ball junkie

Forty [forty ounce bottle] once in my lap
and it's cold as hell
Hook a right turn and let them go up
then I say to myself they can kiss my butt
Hip to get drunk got the 8 at my lips...

Cruising through the east side south of Compton
See a big butt and I say word
I took a look at her face and the girl was to the curb
But she was on my tip for the title I'm holding
Easy E's getting busy [having sex] got the 8 ball rolling...

Went to the store for some ole 8 ball
Acted real ill cause I was drunk
See a sucker punk had to go in my trunk
Reached inside cause it's like that
Came back out with a silver gack [gun]
Point it at the fool and it was all because
I had to show the boy what time it was...

Easy E's in effect and got the 8 ball rolling
Ole English 800 cause that's my brand
Take it in a bottle, 40, quart or a can
Drink it like a madman yes I do.

The above excerpt portrays an image of the 'outlaw' hero – reminiscent of the cowboy figure in the Old West – a young, hard drinking 'dude' who is fearless, 'hip', and sexual. In this scenario, alcohol use appears to be part of the cultural code for symbolising adulthood along with other qualities such as sexual prowess, boldness, and independence. This kind of rap expresses fantasies about being a man in urban settings that provide few other avenues for recognition or achievement. Although gangsters and cowboys have fired the imagination of young boys in many sectors of America, few other teenagers are living in situations where these images have become the only option for asserting adulthood and status. The absence of meaningful employment or opportunities for higher education has eclipsed the future for many black youth. Drinking thus becomes a part of the limited repertoire for constructing identities and dealing with the material and social oppression that is part of being young, black, and male in America.

Pro-drinking images have been propelled onto the national youth scene in full force through the use of rap artists to market high alcohol content malt liquors. Marketing alcohol through rap is part of a broader phenomenon in which

> Fast food, athletic wear, cars, clothing and even food storage advertisements [The Reynolds-rap campaign] have used rap music and Hip Hop aesthetics to sell commodities. (Rose, 1987)

The most prominent and controversial marketing campaign to date revolves around the use of rap singers to promote St Ides, a malt liquor that boasts the highest alcohol content of any mass produced beer (8.0 per cent by volume). Well known rap groups and individual performers such as EPMD, Geto Boys, Ice Cube and YoYo have aired a number of radio and television ads, some of which associate alcohol with explicitly sexual and violent themes. For example, a rap commercial by Ice Cube asserted that St Ides 'Gets your girl in the mood quicker' and 'Gets your Jimmy [penis] thicker'. Ice Cube's girlfriend YoYo performed a similar rap specifically for women stating that St Ides 'Puts you in the mood' and makes you so relaxed 'you'll be going for a six pack.' In another St Ides commercial, EMPD evoked images of personal power and violence: 'It's the E. and I'm smoking aka slayer, yes on one, Sharp as a blade, call me shogun.' In addition to being displayed in direct advertising, St Ides was prominently featured in John Singleton's *Boyz in the Hood*, a major film about black adolescents coming of age in South Central Los Angeles. Ice Cube, who starred in the film, is seen repeatedly toting and drinking 40 ounce bottles of the brew. After the movie's release, liquor store owners reported such brisk sales of St Ides that shelves of the malt liquor were completely emptied. The Los Angeles distributor of St Ides stated that he was forced to ration the stock since demand for the product rapidly outpaced normal supplies (Berstein, 1991).

The promotion of St Ides has unleashed a flood of community opposition from grassroots organisers and anti-alcohol advocacy groups that mobilised on the grounds that the ads promoted violence and sexuality and were targeting underage audiences (Bauder, 1991; Dawsey, 1991). The groundswell of community support was fuelled by networks of community groups that had successfully fought the distribution of 'Powermaster' (a malt liquor also designed for marketing in the black community) and who continue to engage in a number of activities protesting the 'targeting' practices (specific advertising directed at African–Americans) of the alcohol industry. Grassroots organisers have whitewashed billboards in urban neighbourhoods, organised marches and civil disobedience events and sought to enforce regulations regarding retail alcohol outlets. As a result, some of the more offensive advertisements have been removed from the airwaves (Marinucci, 1991), but St Ides is still heavily marketed towards black youth and sales of the beer continue to increase (see Marriott, 1993).

In the hip-hop community, the alcohol industry has come under fire from a famous hard-core message rapper, Chuck D. of Public Enemy. Chuck D. filed a $5 million lawsuit against Heilman Brewing Company, the parent company of McKenzie River for using his voice in a St Ides ad by Ice Cube (Harrington, 1991). Chuck D. also composed a searing anti-alcohol rap '1 Million Bottlebags' that appeared in his 1991 'Apocalypse 91' album. Aside from describing the harmful effects of alcohol, the song asserts that malt liquor is targeted to black neighbourhoods as a genocidal measure:

See the man they call Crazy Eddie
He give the liquor man ten to begin
To get his brains rearranged
Serve it to the home they're able
To do without a table
Beside what's inside ain't on the label
They drink it thinkin' it's good
But they don't sell that shit in the white neighbourhood
Exposin' the plan they get mad at me I understand...

Say I'm yellin is fact
Genocide kickin' in yo back
How many times have you seen
A black fight a black
After drinkin' down a bottle
Or a malt liquor six pack
Malt liquor bull
What it is bullshit Colt
45 another gun to the brain.

The themes of genocide have been picked up by activists and community organisers who contend that malt liquors marketed to the black community are lethal and more dangerous than products designed for whites. Community members are also protesting the easy availability of malt liquors to underage black youth. A recent television news show produced actual footage showing an eight-year-old black boy purchasing a 40 ounce bottle of St Ides in New York. Activists are confronting shopkeepers for these practices and pressing for stronger enforcement of laws governing the operation of liquor stores.

Another focus of the grassroots movement against alcohol in black communities is on the fate of burned out retail liquor outlets in South Central Los Angeles. A large number of these outlets were destroyed in the 1992 rebellion and there is a groundswell of black community sentiment that they should not be rebuilt (McMillan, 1992; Samad, 1992; Alexander, 1992). Petitioners collected more than 34,000 signatures of people opposed to re-issuing liquor licences when and if the stores are reconstructed (Los Angeles Sentinel, 1992).

Korean merchants who owned many of the liquor stores have staunchly opposed this movement on the grounds that it reflects anti-Korean sentiment and will deprive Koreans of business opportunities (Park, 1992). Relations between blacks and Koreans in this area have been tense for the past several years in the wake of several racist incidents, including one involving the shooting of a young black girl in the back by a Korean woman shopkeeper who was only sentenced to a brief period of probation. When Ice Cube, a major rap promoter of St Ides malt liquor, released a song protesting this and other anti-black Korean actions, Korean merchants retaliated by staging a major boycott of the malt liquor. The Heileman company soothed the angry merchants with financial incentives to restore the product to the shelves (*Seattle Post-Intelligencer*, 1991).

In spite of allegations that black communities oppose liquor stores because they are owned by Koreans, there is strong evidence that these communities have had long-standing grievances against the outlets prior to the current wave of Korean ownership. There have been consistent reports for at least thirteen years that black communities in California (not just Los Angeles) are opposed to the high density of outlets in poor black areas because in the minds of community members they are associated with high rates of criminal activity and drug abuse and do not meet community needs for other kinds of economic and commercial activities. These communities have issued moratoriums against new licences and have sought stricter regulations over the operation of existing establishments (Castillo, 1992; Johnson, 1992).

DISCUSSION

Alcohol is associated with complex and contradictory themes in hip-hop culture and in surrounding black communities. Drinking is being promoted as an accoutrement of identity, pleasure, sensuality, and personal power among major rap artists. Although some of the cultural functions attributed to alcohol in this milieu stem from themes indigenous to hip-hop culture such as the tradition of boasting about individual uniqueness, personal power and sexual exploits, the association of these characteristics with drinking has been greatly amplified through the power of the mass media and the commodification of rap to sell alcoholic beverages. At the same time, message rappers and activists have linked alcohol to genocide, racism, crime, poverty, and social distress in black communities. Malt liquor has been compared to liquid crack and lethal bullets, that are raining destruction onto black communities.

Both types of cultural images reflect broader themes in long-standing social movements in African–American communities. The anti-drug and alcohol stance of message raps and community activists is reminiscent of historical crusades in which blacks developed campaigns opposed to the use and sale of alcoholic beverages. Throughout the nineteenth century African–Americans were staunch supporters of temperance, developing their own full-blown movement during the *antebellum* period (Herd, 1985). The black temperance movement was an outgrowth of the abolitionist movement and had as its major goals emancipation and the achievement of economic and social parity. Alcohol use was socially, politically and symbolically linked with the slaveholding South. The symbolic and social connections between slavery and alcohol caused some black leaders to admonish the black population with statements that 'it was as well to be a slave to master as to alcohol', yet they freely acknowledged that drunkenness was no worse among blacks than among whites. Although the formal movement waned, abstinence norms continue to be promoted through religious organisations that are the backbone of black community organisation.

During the early twentieth century, a new image of alcohol emerged in the black population which shares some similarities with contemporary commercial views of alcohol as a symbol of power and sensuality. The rise of this image occurred in the wake of a dramatic shift in racial politics in the broader anti-alcohol movement, urbanisation of the black population and the increasing importance of blacks as small time producers and consumers of bootleg liquor (Herd, 1985). Despite the historical links between temperance and abolition, the post-reconstruction prohibition movement was avowedly xenophobic and was wedded to movements for white supremacy and black disfranchisement. The racist thrust of the movement drastically reduced its level of support among black leaders. At the same time, black migration to urban cities increased dramatically and gave birth to a flurry of artistic and cultural development. Conditions were ripe for the development of a new cultural focus on alcohol as blacks turned to bootlegging to increase their meagre earnings and white ethnics turned to these communities to market booze that was no longer acceptable to WASP Americans. In addition, during prohibition, pleasure-seeking whites flocked to urban black communities to enjoy drinking, jazz, and dancing in a number of 'exotic' nightspots run by white ethnics. These factors set the stage for the creation of black cultural images in which intoxication, sensuality and black 'primitivism' were dominant (Herd, 1991; Fredrickson, 1971).

The images of blacks in the early twentieth century are being revisited today in the representation of blacks in advertisements by rap groups. There is a similar focus on sexual prowess, disinhibition, and hedonism. Although rap music as a whole has a strong social protest orientation that includes vivid anti-drug and alcohol themes, the predominant image of rap in the commercial media associates drinking and blacks with sexual prowess, pleasure-seeking, and violence.

The prohibition years also pre-figured an era in which black consumption would be increasingly important. The struggles over race relations in the nineteenth century revolved around labour issues, or the use of black bodies for production (Herd, 1991). The discourse on racial politics during this period was animated by the desire to maintain a large, cheap, submissive labour force. However, a major thrust of racial domination in the post-industrial twentieth century is the use of black bodies as receptacles for consumption. This function becomes particularly important in the 1980s when markets for alcohol, tobacco, and drugs and other 'sin' products are rapidly shrinking in a drier, 'recovering' middle class white society.

The structure of oppression through consumption also defines the lines of social protest and resistance. Black rap artists attack the state authorities that encourage drug marketing in their communities. Community activists challenge regulatory bodies as well as the direct purveyors of products themselves – producers, distributors, and sellers of alcoholic beverages. These campaigns are perceived as defiant – for example as symptoms of race hatred from the perspective of Korean merchants – and as insubordinate in the same way that the bus boycott in Selma, Alabama (which launched the 1950s' and 1960s' American Civil Rights movement) was defined in almost criminal terms.

Now, as then, cultural images are an important dimension of the hegemony that subordinates black labour or consumption. During the nineteenth and early twentieth century images of the black man as a drunken brute were used as a rationale for prohibition (Herd, 1991). During the prohibition era, the rise of the image of blacks as sensual, exotic primitives signalled their continued subjugation as servants and entertainers for whites rather than as full citizens with equal rights. In the contemporary period, the promotion of drinking, sexuality and violence occur in the context of increasing racism and economic marginality of blacks. As in earlier decades, these kind of cultural images may help justify greater social control and decreasing social and economic opportunities for this population. However, a crucial difference in the promotion of images in the present day is the much greater extent and power of mass media. In an age of MTV, videos and VCRs, audio tapes, boom boxes, films, and radio, mass mediated images are more vivid and penetrating than ever. They may be powerful enough to override traditional agents of social and normative control in the black community in ways that were not possible during earlier decades. The rapid emptying of store shelves containing brand name malt liquor after airing of the film *Boyz in the Hood* or the swift climb of record singles celebrating drinking like 'Tap the Bottle' to a Top 40 hit are evidence of this possibility. In this heavily mass mediated era, the contest over black cultural representation is what animates conflicting discourses in black communities and liquor producers. Just as liquor producers dump unwanted and unhealthful goods in black communities, so do they freely dump instant and repetitive images that activists believe would be considered dangerous and immoral to promote in white communities.

Another critical development in the contemporary period of alcohol marketing is the focus on black youth. Compared to young whites, young blacks have consistently reported lower rates of alcohol use, drunkenness, and alcohol-related problems. High problem rates from alcohol are primarily located in black men over 30 (Herd, 1989). Black youth have been relatively protected from heavy consumption and problems due to cultural and religious factors – for example the strong influence of black Protestant churches (Harford and Lowman, 1989). The low drinking rates among young blacks have made them a prime target for industry marketing. The targeting of this group has raised the ante of social protest in the minds of many black activists. The regulation of industry and retail practices with regard to marketing to white young people is more heavily scrutinised, which limits some of the flagrant industry and retail practices observed with regard to promoting alcohol to black minor children and adolescents.

The heavy promotion of malt liquor is beginning to take its toll in hip-hop culture and in poorer black and Latino neighbourhoods. Daryl McDaniels, one of the members of the renown RUN-DMC rap group, was recently hospitalised for pancreatitis at age 28. He reportedly bought 16 bottles of 40 ounce malt liquor per day of which he drank eight singlehandedly (Marriott, 1993). Bushwick Bill of the Geto Boys was maimed in a drinking-related incident. While drunk and feeling remorseful for being abusive to his girlfriend and her infant child, 20-year-old Bushwick taunted the girlfriend and demanded that she shoot him. She shot him with the result that he lost his eye (DeCurtis, 1991). To the ire of activists, McKenzie River Corp. developed a series of ads using Bushwick to promote St Ides malt liquor with a glass eye (Russell, 1991). Black and Puerto Rican teenagers report that 40 ounce bottles of malt liquor are increasingly popular – they are the mainstay of 'hooky' parties where youth are truant from school and party and drink all day. Priced at only $1.25–$2.50 per bottle, the large size containers are a much cheaper alternative to cocaine, providing much more 'bang for the buck'. As a result, minority adolescents are showing up for alcoholism treatment at 16 and 17 years old (Marriott, 1993).

Black youth are being bombarded with alcohol ads at a time when they are experiencing unprecedented levels of deprivation, racism, and violence. Rap music as a cultural form has provided a means for these youth to help transform and transcend some of the limitations of their harsh environment. This

artistic form has enabled young blacks to channel their energies and creative abilities into a medium that synthesises the
traditional oral richness of African American culture with postmodern technology. It has become a vehicle of racial pride,
personal creativity, self-affirmation, and political and social
awareness. As rap music is commodified and used to purvey
potentially harmful consumer products like high alcohol
content malt liquor, its potential for social and personal transformation is greatly weakened. Instead of opposing cultural
and political oppression, rap becomes coopted into the system
of domination that profits from dumping useless and often
harmful goods, and the cultural images that package them,
into a community already overwhelmed with health and social
problems.

The conflicting cultural discourses about drinking among
black youth, community activists and alcohol producers reflect
a dynamic interplay of voices structured upon generational,
racial and to some extent, gender lines. The appeal of the racy
malt liquor ads to youth, particularly males, can be understood in the context of their rebellion and opposition to an
oppressive culture that is primarily societal (politicians, police,
teachers) but also intimate (for example desire for independence from parents and older relatives, particularly women).

The conflicts over racial portrayals are not new and are
rooted in the struggle over the social position and status of
blacks and whites. Primitivism in different forms has been historically invoked to justify blacks' subordinate position and
efforts for repression and control of their labour and spending power (Herd, 1991). In contrast, the black protest tradition has emphasised qualities associated with social betterment
and race improvement – for example abstinence, political
awareness, education, strong families, and collective responsibility (Herd, 1985). The emphasis on themes of violence, sex
and hedonism in contemporary alcohol ads reflects the desire
not only to sell a product but may also reify the ways in which
blacks are already perceived and which provides the rationale
for them to be further marginalised in an increasingly racist
society. Black activists' focus on genocide as an issue in alcohol
marketing is a response not only to fears about physical survival, but to concerns about maintaining cultural viability and
aspirations for socio-political equality. In this way, they may be

correctly discerning that as other avenues for cultural expression and socioeconomic participation diminish, black youth will look only to destructive gangster images and heavy drinking as a means for self-affirmation and racial identity.

## Note

An earlier version of this chapter was published in *Contemporary Drug Problems*, 20(4) (1993). Reprinted here by permission of Federal Legal Publications, Inc. Many thanks to Karolyn Tyson for help with research and transcribing rap lyrics and to Makani Themba and the Marin Institute for the Prevention of Alcohol and Other Drug Problems for providing resources and consultation on the role of rap music in alcohol beverage advertising.

## References

Alexander, H., 'Stop Exploitation', *Los Angeles Times* (July 12 1992).

Berstein, M., '"Boyz" Message is not about Drinking Beer', *The Plain Dealer*, Cleveland, Ohio (July 29 1991).

Bauder, D., 'Critics: Using rap heros of black teens for malt liquor ads unfair', *Democrat* (November 22 1991).

Castillo, S., 'Coalition Protest Plan to Loosen License Requirements in South Central L.A.', *Los Angeles Sentinel* (March 1992).

Dawsey, D., 'Beware of the March of Ides', *The Detroit News* (September 18 1991), 1-D, 3.

DeCurtis, A., 'Geto Boy Bushwick Bill Shot in Head', *Rolling Stone* (June 27 1991).

Dyson, M., 'Performance, Protest, and Prophecy in the Culture of Hip-hop', in Spencer, J. (ed.), *The Emergency of Black and the Emergence of Rap* (Durham: Duke University Press, 1991).

Fredrickson, G., *The Black Image in the White Mind* (New York: Harper & Row, 1971).

Harrington, R., 'Rapper Sues Malt Brewer', *The Washington Post* (August 28 1991).

Harford, T. and Lowman, C., 'Alcohol Use Among Black and White Teenagers', in *Research Monograph No. 18, Conference on the Epidemiology of Alcohol Use and Abuse Among Ethnic Minority Groups, September 1985* (Rockville: US Department of Health and Human Services, DHHS Publication, (ADM))89–1435, 1989).

Herd, D., 'We Cannot Stagger to Freedom: A history of blacks and alcohol in American politics', in Brill, L. and Winick, C., (eds), *The Yearbook of Substance Use and Abuse* (New York: Human Sciences Press, 1985).

Herd, D., 'The Epidemiology of Drinking Patterns and Alcohol-related Problems among U.S. blacks', in *Research Monograph No. 18, Conference on the Epidemiology of Alcohol Use and Abuse Among Ethnic Minority Groups, September 1985* (Rockville: US Department of Health and Human Services, DHHS Publication (ADM) 89–1435, 1989).

Herd, D., 'The Paradox of Temperance: Blacks and the alcohol question in 19th century America', in Barrows, S. and Room, R. (eds), *Drinking: Behavior and Belief in Modern History* (Berkeley: University of California Press, 1991).

Johnson, C., 'A Fight to Keep Liquor Stores Shut', *San Francisco, Chronicle* (July 1 1992), 1, 5.

Kelley, R., 'Straight from the Underground', *The Nation* (June 8 1992).

*Los Angeles Sentinel*, 'Coalition Signs up 34,000 to Oppose Liquor Stores' (August 20 1992).

Marinucci, C., 'Malt Liquor's Rapper Ads Changing Tone', *San Francisco Examiner* (December 15 1991), E1, 6.

Marriott, M., 'Cheap High Lures Youths to Malt Liquor 40s', *New York Times* (April 16 1993).

McMillan, P., 'Petition Drive Against Rebuilding Liquor Stores Gains Momentum', *Los Angeles Times* (July 27 1992), B1, B6.

Nuriddin, J. and El Hadi, S., *The Last Poets: Vibes from the Scribes* (Trenton, NJ: Africa World Press, 1992).

Park, T. B., 'Why Punish the Victims?', *Los Angeles Times* (July 15 1992).

Rose, T., 'Orality and Technology: Rap music and Afro–American cultural resistance', *Popular Music and Society* 13 (1987), 35–44.

Russell, S., 'Malt Liquor Ad by Rapper, 20 Draws Criticism', *San Francisco Chronicle* (November 2 1991).

Samad, A., 'Weaning a Community from a Drunken Stupor', *Herald Dispatch* (August 13 1992).

*Seattle Post-Intellingencer*, 'Brewery Forced to Stop Ads with Rapper Ice Cube', (November 1991).

Stanley, L. and Morley, J., *Rap: The Lyrics* (New York: Penguin, 1992).

Toop, D., *Rap Attack 2: African Rap to Global Hip Hop* (London: Pluto Press, 1991).

# 8 From the Margins to the Centre: Post-Industrial City Cultures

Justin O'Connor and Derek Wynne

## INTRODUCTION

'From the Margins to the Centre' refers to three related themes that have run closely together in the debates around postmodernity and the city in the 1980s. First, gentrification, a reversal of the movement out of the city centre by the affluent classes, results in a 'recentralisation' of previously 'marginal' areas of the city centre. Secondly, many activities deemed peripheral to the 'productive' or 'Fordist' city have now moved to centre stage and become a major concern for cities in the 1980s; that is, the concern with culture, consumption and image. Thirdly, previously 'marginal' groups have been made central to the city and have made the city centre central to themselves.

In this chapter we will look at these debates using Manchester as a case study. Our focus is on the claim that the transformation towards the 'postmodern city' is the operation of a designated class who, more than other social groups, are concerned with the promotion of a 'postmodern lifestyle'. This argument has been made most forcefully by Sharon Zukin. We focus on four aspects of the argument: first, the relationship between economic and cultural capital, stressing the 'relative autonomy' of the latter; secondly, the relationship between the global and the local in the restructuring of the city centre; thirdly, the relationship between 'landscape' and 'vernacular' in the city centre. Fourthly, we examine alternative notions of 'liminality' to throw open wider questions of the role of 'cultural intermediaries' in the process of cultural change of the postmodern city.

## LANDSCAPES AND THE COUNTER-CULTURE

Gentrification carries the sense of a 'return' to the centre by the middle classes, and more especially, by a new fraction within this 'middle class' who are seen to be 'on the rise' and hence often 'new'; it also involves a sense of displacement of lower social groups. We describe gentrification as the 'recentralisation' of areas that had lapsed into marginality. This implies a shift in power based on the economic, but also on cultural power (Smith and Williams, 1986).

Sharon Zukin's *Landscapes of Power* (1992a), building on her *Loft Living* (1982), represents a useful examination of the dynamics of gentrification. She contends that the gentrification of the centre is about the shift from production to consumption imposed by a cultural power, and that the crucial role in this shift is played not by developers, nor even by some general professional–managerial class, but by precisely those 'cultural entrepreneurs' who act as agents of this transformation.

For Zukin the restructuration of the new city centre is not just a 'creative destruction' (Harvey, 1986) of the built environment but a new perspective on the city, based on cultural power and mass cultural consumption, in a context where culture is no longer connected to place but driven by globalised flows of information, capital and cultural goods.

This cultural power transforms the fragmented vernacular of the old productive communities of the downtown area into an aesthetic landscape of cultural consumption. Disputing the simple equation of centrality and power, Zukin argues that besides representing political and economic centrality – the Central Business District (CBD) – city centres have also been centres of industrial production with a large working class population. Densely built and historically layered, downtown has been the 'urban jungle' pitting the cultural hegemony of economic and political power against an image of social diversity. It was a fragmented landscape, each section organised around different social and cultural worlds. As industry and wealthy residents moved out the centre declined, leading to 'its temporary abandonment as a landscape of power'.

It is this situation that allows for the economic and cultural project of gentrification. Working class areas have been undervalued compared to the adjacent CBD, but this value could not be realised until the vernacular was reabsorbed into a new landscape of economic, social and cultural power. This power is now reflected in consumption, and the reformation of the fragmented vernacular into a single landscape is an achievement of cultural labour.

This implies an aestheticisation of the buildings and the downtown associations. It is based on the cultural labour of a certain social group, not necessarily the main beneficiary of its own labour. Zukin calls it the 'critical infrastructure', which consists of specialists in the production and promotion but also in the consumption of cultural goods.

The transformation of the urban downtown is the focus of 'Loft Living'. The argument is well known, though its complexities are not often spelled out. SoHo was a downtown locality juxtaposed to a financial district intent on expansion in alliance with political forces that saw no future for manufacturing on Manhattan. The future lay with finance. However, its attempt at 1960s' style development was successfully resisted by the artist and ancillary community that had moved into the old nineteenth century lofts, attracted by the cheapness and space in New York, now the centre of the world art market. The victory, through an alliance with the growing communitarian and anti-development movement of the 1970s, led to the designation of SoHo as an artists' zone. But the end result was that manufacturing and 'down market' retail was pushed out, and the old vernacular became prime real estate as 'loft living' became a desirable commodity. Ultimately, many artists found it impossible to buy or rent, and any indigenous bohemian artist quality now became totally packaged, landscaped for wealthy residents.

The narrative in *Loft Living* is complex. Zukin wants to show how those dealing in cultural knowledge were responsible for the transformation of SoHo, creating a new value that could be recouped by development capital. Two forces were prominent. First, the historic buildings groups began to see the cast iron frontages as aesthetic objects that should be protected rather than torn down. This represented an aestheticisation of past use that devalued current industrial usage. Legitimate usage of these buildings was restricted to those who could appreciate this historical aesthetic. Secondly, the artists' community claimed for itself the central role in the revitalisation of a 'derelict' district. The economic importance of the artists to New York was stressed, but their cultural impact on the area was in fact primary. The 'loft' was a metonym for an artistic life-style which, drawing on the bohemian and countercultural elements of the 1960s, would bring back a new vibrancy to the downtown, now based on a 'life-style' no longer linked to a productive community. It was a life-style that could be consumed in the form of the newly fashionable lofts and a bohemian ambience of restaurants, bars, galleries and shops.

Once this had been done, however, the cultural specialists lost ground to those wielding economic power. The developers quickly appreciated the importance of cultural consumption in the revalorisation of undervalued downtown areas. After SoHo they became proactive, exploiting the fact that popularisation of the artistic–bohemian life-style was part of a much more widespread shift in cultural hierarchies. Expansion of higher education and the cultural radicalisms of the 1960s expanded knowledge of cultural goods enormously. The transgressions of the artist, the experimentation with new experiences, the desire to create the self as a work of art – all these became absorbed into a wider culture. This fed into the growing incorporation of art and culture into the design of consumer goods, and into the techniques of advertising and marketing.

In *Loft Living* the outcome is paradoxical, the victors ending up as losers. In *Landscapes of Power*, Zukin is much more explicit in linking the operations of the new cultural specialists both to the promotion of consumption and to the gentrification of the city:

> Production units function best in clusters of customers and suppliers. But consumption units are increasingly spread out, diffused, standardised and reproduced. Decentralisation reduces the power of consumption spaces: it requires conscious action to restore their specific meaning. Under these circumstances, mediating the dialectic of power and centrality depends on a critical infrastructure for cultural production and consumption. Here I am thinking of men and women who produce and consume, and also evaluate,

new market-based cultural products. Like artists, they both comment critically on, and constitute, a new kind of market culture. Their 'inside' view opens up new spaces for consumption. They enhance market values even when they desperately want to conserve values of place. (Zukin, 1992a, 201–2)

This is the tragic function of the counter-culture. Their concern with culture and the unique downtown space opens a new field of consumption which, exposed to the forces of abstraction and internationalisation, destroys the object of their desire.

## RELATIVE AUTONOMY

Zukin's work represents a severe indictment of culturally-based urban renewal, and of cultural specialists as mediators of the new consumption while also destructive of the values of place. It is precisely the promotion of cultural production and consumption – of, and in, the city – and the attraction of cultural specialists that cities in Britain and Western Europe have attempted to engage to open avenues to the 'post-Fordist' city. This is why it is important to evaluate how well Zukin's model applies, and as we shall see, its transposition to other areas is not without its problems.

In the United States the importance of cultural consumption in revalorisation was quickly recognised by developers. Standardisation and repetition led to a rapid elaboration of regeneration models that could be sold to city governments. By the late 1970s a number of large cities in North America, especially those with historic centres, began to invest in these regeneration models (Bianchini and Parkinson, 1993; Wynne, 1992). It soon became clear that whilst the 'artistic community' was often brought in to these local growth coalitions, it was the developer who held the upper hand.

The transformation of historical or waterfront areas into retail, leisure and residential developments was based around 'up-market' consumption coupled with a high cultural input. This could include cultural animation programmes, artists' residences, subsidised workshops and a public art that fitted well with a new 'postmodern' aesthetic. Such cultural input was encouraged by city governments employing 'percentage for art' programmes, and 'planning gain' initiatives. These areas had an 'up-market' ambience of speciality shopping and 'designer' restaurants and bars. They also aimed at establishing the sense of vibrancy that once attached to downtown areas, but a vibrancy now mediated by a bohemian image represented by the presence of artists and 'artisans'. The vibrancy was one of an aestheticised nineteenth century, where the image of the downtown was reappropriated via the image of the artist–bohemian in the guise of *flâneur*. The new–old urban spaces were of the original productive communities but designed for the middle class stroller who had the time and knowledge to absorb the vernacular as aesthetic.

It is this Ersatz urban realm which was initially characterised as 'postmodern', in a way that confused the debate. Both admirers and critics seemed to see this as an incarnation of the postmodern Zeitgeist, without inquiring as to how people used these places and to what extent, and on what basis, they were successful (Chambers, 1990; Cooke, 1988). It will be our argument that the transposition of this model of regeneration by developers is fraught with problems. If the imposition of a landscape of cultural power is to have any chance of success, even defined in narrowly economic terms, a critical infrastructure is indeed necessary. However, this critical infrastructure cannot just be created as required. Local specialists and insiders have a relative autonomy and a close knowledge of and relationship to place. A specific localisation involves a series of negotiations around the new emergent landscape which can be laden with meanings very different to the standardised 'postmodernity' of the development models.

## THE BRITISH CONTEXT

This model of urban regeneration, development around historical–cultural urban centres, was imported into Britain in the early 1980s. In this transposition the local context was crucial. First, the Thatcher government, having won a resounding second term in 1983, made 'inner cities' its target.

The riots in 1981 had underlined these inner cities as symbols of the 'British disease' (Robson, 1986). Secondly, these cities were mainly held by the opposition Labour Party. Central government was loath to give them credit for any possible success in urban programmes and blamed these councils for the socialist–bureaucratic failures of the 1960s and 1970s. Urban regeneration was to be a symbol of Thatcherite Britain's escape from the cycle of post-war failure.

Thirdly, the government wanted to use a free enterprise approach which demanded deregulation and a more flexible planning system. To this end a whole series of legislative changes were enacted restricting local government, freeing private capital's access to public land and development contracts, and creating new semi-autonomous bodies outside the control of local government (Thornley, 1992). Fourthly, this was done at a time of massive and catastrophic deindustrialisation. Apart from its social and economic consequences this was also a process of great cultural disruption, especially in the Northern industrial towns where identity, much more than in the south, was centred on manual and industrial labour. Urban regeneration was a conscious and explicit shift from manufacturing to service industries, symbolised by redrawing old historical industrial areas for leisure and consumption. Fifthly, many on the Left saw urban regeneration as a symbol of Thatcherism, and despised it for that. The debate around 'postmodernity', gentrification and the yuppie in 1980s' Britain cannot be divorced from this political context. This had direct impact upon the functioning of 'cultural landscaping' and the role of the 'critical infrastructure'.

Manchester is England's third largest city, although in terms of its historical role as ideological centre of the industrial revolution, it could be considered the second city, capital of the North. In 1988 a large swathe of land just south of the CBD and civic centre was given to Britain's first city centre Urban Development Corporation (UDC). The Central Manchester Development Corporation (CMDC), a semi-autonomous body (responsible to central government), was given a brief to cut through the socialist red tape and bring private money into city centre regeneration by using public funds as leverage. Its initial task was to draw up a plan for the area, and to then present the image of the new city to developers, private entrepreneurs and the people of Manchester.

The CMDC area already had a major industrial and science museum near the site of the world's first passenger railway station. Another whole area, Castlefield, was to become Britain's first urban industrial heritage park. Along with the museums went the promotion of waterway events on the canals and other animation programmes. The area also had a private residential development.

Between Castlefield and the centre a large area of disused land and parking lots was earmarked for Manchester's 'cultural quarter', and in nearby Whitworth street, some of the old nineteenth century warehouses would be converted for residential use. It is this area that was seen to be a prime site for the 'arts and culture'-led model of urban regeneration.

The cultural quarter was to be – in the words of one planning officer – 'Manchester's Montmartre'. It was clearly developer-driven. Manchester City Council had already transformed the disused central railway station into an exhibition hall and occasional concert venue. Next to this on CMDC ground was a huge, elaborately decorated Late Victorian goods warehouse. This was to be a 'Festival Shopping Centre' done by the company responsible for similar developments in North America (it is still empty). On the other side of the exhibition hall a concert hall was to be built on the site of a car park, uncovering the old canal arm around which offices and apartments would be constructed, along with the inevitable restaurants, bars and retail outlets. The apartments, in a refurbished warehouse, together with some of the office buildings have been finished for two years. The remaining projects began just after Christmas, 1993.

Whitworth – 'the village in the heart of the city' – which involved the refurbishment of a number of Victorian warehouses, helped increase the residential population of the city centre area from zero to 5000.

The cultural quarter and the residential areas were linked to the promotion of Manchester as a site of cultural consumption. The image of the city as a whole was tied up in this building-led process and enhanced land values would herald Manchester's economic regeneration. That the CMDC recognised the crucial role of image, of perspective, can be seen in the promotional literature that was concerned not just to outline the plans of the Corporation, but to present the Centre as an aesthetic object. The historical qualities of the Victorian city were brought out; detail and cropped-shot photography de-contextualised the buildings to present them to the aesthetic gaze. Warehouses, long-time symbols of northern industrial gloom re-emerged as Renaissance Palaces, Graeco–Roman Temples, brooding Gothic Piles.

For the CMDC it was the economic value of cultural consumption that was uppermost in both its political orientation and in its approach to the developers. The old landscape of industrial production was to be offered up for aesthetic consumption, but also as 'investment opportunities'. The cultural quarter with its 'flagship' concert hall would attract those with disposable incomes into the city after 6 p.m., thus fuelling spin-off leisure and retail developments. Similarly the area's cultural profile would attract 'prestige' offices occupied by business services and creative professions that both developers and sociologists believed to be intimately connected.

In order to enhance the cultural quarter Manchester's artist community was to be brought into consultation. The CMDC recognised the role of art in the image of cities, their brochure using Barcelona and the Pompidou centre as examples. There was talk of subsidised artists' workshops as a way of promoting the creative ambience which would both attract the 'culture crowd' and the creative professions. As such it represented an attempt by the CMDC to bring in and direct the critical infrastructure (cultural intermediaries), which in Zukin's terms, was crucial for the creation of a cultural landscape in SoHo.

The relationship between cultural intermediaries and capital is, as Zukin makes clear, a process whereby capital and public agencies learn about the value of culture. This is part of the story of Post-Fordism, flexible specialisation and the emergence of creative, designer-led industries from the mid-1970s onwards. The personnel and the organisation of the CMDC began to learn this model of cultural regeneration through seminars, fact-finding missions and consultancy reports. All this happened within the context of a Thatcher government explicitly hostile to 'intellectuals' – the 'chattering classes' as they were being dubbed (Frith and Savage, 1993). The counter-culture and the 'permissive society', symbols and causes of 'Britain's social and moral decline' were laid at the door of the liberal cultural establishment. The CMDC itself became a cultural intermediary justifying cultural value by its direct relationship to economic value. This was meant as an appeal to property developers, the local business elite, and the city council.

However, in Manchester the tie between cultural regeneration and economic arguments tended to undermine the cultural in two important areas. First, as Bourdieu (1984) makes clear, cultural capital, whilst related to economic capital, must also stress its distinction from it. Too close a connection undermines the claim of culture to be disinterested, to be more than economics.

Secondly, cultural intermediaries are precisely that – intermediaries. They are able to interpret, package, transmit and manipulate symbols and knowledge in a way that produces new value. As both producers and consumers they are able to claim an expertise, a close knowledge of the inner dynamics of the cultural field (Martin, 1991). As professions they grew up often ad hoc in the interstices of larger concerns providing them services that they did not even know they needed. There is a history of how these larger concerns sometimes have learned to benefit from the expertise, flexibility, creativity and 'counter-cultural values' of this new sector, and so on. But there is also another history of how large concerns fail to recognise this, with damaging consequences. The latter is a history familiar in Britain.

The initiation of culture-based urban renewal by a quasi-political body dominated by a 'free enterprise' ethos with an anti-cultural bias, had damaging effects. Development capital using tried and trusted models for the formation of a cultural landscape meant that the result had limited cultural resonance, especially amongst those whose labour would be crucial to the transformation – the cultural intermediaries. The CMDC and the developers operated in exclusively economic terms, not recognising the autonomy of the cultural field, excluding cultural specialists from the process to the detriment of cultural value. The 'state's substantive and symbolic legitimation of the cultural claim to urban space' was far from unconditional, and was indeed a product of negotiation and conflict.

GLOBAL AND LOCAL

City centres are periodically abandoned as landscapes of power. Manchester's landscape is paradigmatic of the way this occurred in the industrial cities of Britain. Industrial capital abandoned the centre after the Second World War (residents had left before) leaving large swathes of the central area to decay. These abandoned areas were reclaimed for the vernacular in an ambivalent fashion. In Manchester they became representations of northernness; industrial wasteland and old canal-rusted rails sunk in grassy cobbles. As sources of identity they were often an unwanted past, an unusable past – it is easy to forget this mix of attachment and redundancy. Northern wasteland has become a symbol of economic decline, which is why its regeneration, however viewed politically, worked on a vernacular that few were willing to defend. It coincided with a local cultural renegotiation of both northerness and the world of industrial work crucial to this identity (Shields, 1991). Very often presented as a devastating disorientation it was also taken as a possibility of change.

The new cultural landscape had different meanings, functions and beneficiaries as a specific spatialisation of the global, national and local. 'Re-imaging the city' was part of a general recognition by councils throughout the country that their 'smoke stack' image would work against them in the attraction of investment, especially in business services and 'high tech' industries. By the time CMDC was created, marketing consultancies were a common feature in local councils. The standard method of re-imaging was the offering of facilities that would attract professional – managerial 'executives' – golf courses, waterfront leisure developments, 'high' cultural venues and museums. This was a simple version of exploiting culture for urban growth (Meyerscough, 1988). Like the CMDC, Manchester City Council soon entered a learning curve away from the standard model of how to operate within the field of symbolic knowledge. It began to establish links with cultural intermediaries.

The networks between council (and to a lesser extent the CMDC) and cultural intermediaries proliferated and operations within the symbolic field became more sophisticated. It was recognised that the too obvious exploitation of cultural strategy to attract 'executives' was self-defeating. The consumption desires of these 'executives' had become standardised to such a degree that most cities could offer them in abundance. It was realised that to compete at a European and global level the city had to promote its cultural value in a more 'disinterested' fashion. Its cultural authenticity, and thus desirability, derived from its intrinsic and autonomous cultural production. The city as 'city of culture' had to present itself as a vernacular. The success of the city could only be built on Manchester's image with a distinctive historical and cultural tradition.

The gradual entry of relatively autonomous cultural intermediaries into the local government marked a convergence of interests in the cultural, economic and political fields. Whilst the abstraction and internationalisation of global finance undermines place in the elaboration of markets, local government has an interest in attenuating this. Developers find it relatively easy to disinvest as profitability declines. Local governments, stuck in place, must look to the longer term. It is not in the interest of the local state to allow the abstracted global market to act too disruptively on local cultural capital. This is of course a matter of politics, education and often brute financial power, and is a project by no means guaranteed, in terms of either conception or execution, as the landscape of many British cities can illustrate. Local government needs a local cultural infrastructure with a specific expertise which gives it a relative autonomy from the circuits of abstracted global finance. Its expertise involves a knowledge and feeling for place, which is, despite Zukin's pessimism, crucial for the successful localisation of capital in the form of cultural landscaping. Cultural intermediaries will be affected by the new networks and changing working practices. The dictates of this new cultural field put their autonomy and creativity at risk, but they also expand their scope of operations. Previously distant from local politics and economics (in the larger 'strategic' sense) they are increasingly proactive in lobbying public agencies for the importance of cultural investment – a fairly obvious stance from their point of view – but also for the need to defend their autonomy from short-term economic fluctuations.

The relationship between market and place is, as Zukin rightly points out, a crucial component of the landscaping of cities. Market dominance can lead to a decline in the value of places, especially if taken over directly by global finance. But the relationship between place and consumption in this context is much more complex. A sense of place can be negotiated precisely through the opening up of new spaces of cultural production and consumption. English cities have lacked centrality as a place to live and socialise but the model for creating them has been adopted not from North America but from Europe (Bianchini and Shwengel, 1991). The old vernacular has been replaced by replica of the 'European city', a space of socialisation, cultural and cultured consumption on a non-exclusionary basis. The original reality of this image may be open to question but an image of cafés, restaurants, spaces for strolling and sitting, of diverse social interaction, of galleries and concerts is associated with all its diverse applications. Cafés and croissants came to be the quintessential attribute of 'yuppie' consumption in the mid-1980s, but these sorts of images also provided ways in which various other identities were being negotiated.

The promotion of the 'European city' is part of a new globalised competition, and is an imposition of the specific habitus of cultural intermediaries and the expanding cultural sector to which they are tied. In a political context of economic and political domination from the centre, 'Europeanness' has been a means of redefining the relationship of northerness to Englishness in a way that bypassed London's cultural dominance. Thus Glasgow and Edinburgh stressed that they were European and not British cities. Location and space were used in negotiating identity. 'Provincial' culture has reached for autonomy in the 'Europe of the regions' and looked enviously to the great city states of Europe. The 'European city' was the image through which Manchester attempted to map itself onto a transnational 'cosmopolitan' space.

The European image of centrality had to be implanted on a space located in northern culture. This was the industrial city with a strong sense of working class identity, in which even the local establishment portrayed itself as 'down to earth', 'straight speaking', and concerned with work as opposed to the rentier elite of the South (Shields, 1991). Against the initial plans of the CMDC and the developers Manchester, along with other northern cities, decided to develop its cultural image on an authenticity derived from place, as opposed to what was seen as London's concern with money and hype. This reflects the traditional opposition to the 'unearned' incomes of the capital, now mediated not through 'hard graft' but through culture.

The new 'cosmopolitan' image is partly an outcome of the distinction strategies of the cultural intermediaries, but its political component should not be ignored. The 1980s saw a general revaluation of the qualities of the urban across a wide range of cultural fields. Not just a site of decay and abandonment it was increasingly celebrated as a vibrant realm in which a wide variety of people rubbed shoulders. The attempt to characterise this urban realm as that of the *flâneur,* floating signifiers and disembodied eddies of desire, by sociologists either friendly to or critical of some 'postmodern urban experience' has missed another crucial component of this re-evaluation. In an age of privatism, of the disappearance of the social (whether by Baudrillard or Thatcher) the urban realm was one of the few images of sociality remaining. The 'cosmopolitan city', the 'European city' were cities that would promote urbanity, a mixing and meeting of classes and groups and races in a way that would provide for an active citizenship.

It was for this reason that urban and cultural policy began to realign with the Left in the mid-1980s. This was less the work of the Labour party than that of the Greater London Council (GLC). At a time when the Thatcher government looked to the United States, the Labour-controlled GLC, across the water from Parliament, operating with an enormous budget and responsible for 6 million people, looked to Europe – especially to Italian cities (Bianchini, 1987, 1989). Again, the growing recognition of the importance of cultural politics is reflected here. The Gramscian politics of the Italian communist cities was taken as a model by the GLC, with the need to promote a sense of democratic citizenship around a post-proletarian, multi-cultural London. The use of culture was taken at its widest, and 'popular culture' given a new priority. The shift from pedagogy to entertainment in subsidised culture is not just down to commodification, but a demo-cratising impulse towards popular participation.

Such an approach had its problems, as 'the popular' fragmented into client groups. It also stressed cultural consumption

rather than production, with 'cultural industries' strategy left
to be developed by other local councils. But the fact that it
promoted popular cultural events, and that it opened up the
spaces of the city to these events, transformed the relationship
of large sections of cultural producers and consumers to these
spaces, and to the possibilities of a locally funded cultural
sphere. In terms of local cultural policies it was the single most
influential statement of the first half of the decade.

## LANDSCAPE AND VERNACULAR

In the final section of her article on postmodern urban landscapes, Zukin argues that space is both structured and structuring. It is structured in that is reflects macro-level economic
forces, but it is structuring in that it,

> structures people's perceptions, interactions, and sense of
> well being or despair, belonging or alienation ... Space also
> structures metaphorically. Because they are easily visualised,
> spatial changes can represent and structure orientations to
> society. Space stimulates both memory and desire; it indi-
> cates categories and relations between them. (Zukin, 1992a,
> 268)

In Zukin's model, urban renewal increases the importance
of consumption and incorporates place into the market, and
as a consequence the autonomy of the local is colonialised by
the global landscape. Zukin uses the word 'liminality' to describe 'the cultural mediation of these socio-spatial shifts'.

> Liminality in our sense depicts a 'no-man's-land' open to
> everyone's experience yet not easily understood without a
> guide. Defining the symbolic geography of a city or region,
> liminal spaces cross and combine the influence of major in-
> stitutions: public and private, culture and economy, market
> and place. As the social meaning of such spaces is renegoti-
> ated by structural change and individual action, liminal
> space becomes a metaphor for the extensive reordering by
> which markets, in our time, encroach upon place. (Zukin,
> 1992a, 269)

This is surely a singular logic in which macro and micro combine to insert the local landscape into the global organisation of consumption. It seems to ignore the structuring qualities of local space and the ways in which local action can intervene in such spatialisation. It also ignores the fluidity by which not only landscape but also vernacular interpenetrate in the city centre. A good example of this is that parts of Manchester's abandoned landscape have in fact been reconverted to a vernacular of cultural production and consumption. This is certainly the case with at least two areas of the city that we have examined.

Manchester's 'rave' scene emerged in a number of clubs located throughout the city centre and beyond. The Oldham Street area of the city centre has become an important meeting place for the style connoisseurs. A previously thriving working class area both for work and residence was neglected in the 1960s and 1970s as many workplaces closed and residents left. Today Manchester's 'youth cultural' scene has developed the area with shops, bars and clubs dedicated to promoting that 'scene'. Afflecks Palace, a previously disused three-story building, has been converted into low rental units where producers and consumers of this 'pop' culture can be found.

It could be argued that the new landscapes created by urban renewal, precisely because they attempted to invoke centrality, have invited new uses of the spaces that return them to the vernacular. This has already been argued to some extent in the case of shopping malls (Shields, 1992a). In Manchester, the cultural quarter and the residential 'village' were taken up into spaces of pleasure, spaces of cultural production and consumption not foreseen by the planners and property developers. One of Manchester's most animated areas is around the 'Gay village' which was not a part of CMDC's cultural landscape, just as the colonisation of one of the residential sites by gays was not foreseen by the in-house architect whose refurbishment aimed at a 'suburban' conservative taste scheme (Georgian door-knockers, antique lamps in brass frames and so on).

What has now become the Gay Village is a small area of the city centre located around the Whitworth Street corridor and the adjoining canal. Previously neglected, apart from policing activities associated with club and bookstore 'raids', the area has become a vital site for the celebration of alternative sexualities. The refurbishment of old warehouses into studios and one or two-bedroom apartments in the area has proved popular with many.

In Manchester the impact of the rave scene of the late 1980s completely redrew the cultural landscape of the city and the relationship of the local agencies to it. Looking to the cultural flows associated with Olympic bids and 'international' concert halls, Manchester was suddenly thrust into the very centre of the global information flow in the guise of 'Madchester'. Almost invisible to the developers and local politicians looking to one source of cultural capital, journalists, commentators and consumers headed for the city in search of another. They poured over its spaces as a new pop vernacular celebrating a new intersection of global and local, a local production out of a global cultural flow. Since the late 1980s the city has engaged these cultural producers in dialogue. Affleck's Palace, due to be torn down, was given a stay of execution at the last moment. Confrontational policing in the Gay Village (which has moved to the forefront of the club scene in recent years) gave way to community policing and liaison committees.

The dialectic of vernacular and landscape runs close. Cultural power may depend on landscapes presenting themselves as vernacular, just as vernaculars' can be taken up by landscape. Thus the 'Gay Village' is very ambivalent about gaining a respectability it has so long loved to shun.

## LIMINAL SPACES

We would argue that the initiation of the process whereby Manchester was to be culturally landscaped actually created new spaces within which cultural contestation and exploration could emerge. Whether we use the terms 'landscape' and 'vernacular' or not, they represent complex conjunctions of cultural production and consumption, local and global, market and place. These spaces can host hedonism and urbanity, civility and the frisson of anonymity; they can be the image of the social and the anti-social, the nomad and the villager. They are to be negotiated best by Berman's 'low modernism', the shout in the street (Berman, 1992).

Centrality may produce new spaces not just of power and exclusivity, but also as exposure, as stage, as theatre. Liminality is one of the attractions of centrality, not in the sense of a transition between production and consumption, but as the weakening of fixed roles. The recreation of the centre allows it to function as marginal space, as liminoid in Turner's sense (Turner, 1969; Shields, 1992b). This returns through another route to Zukin's fundamental contention as to the relation between marginality and habitus, and how they structure this centre. We conclude by throwing open this question by briefly examining the debates around 'cultural intermediaries' (Bourdieu, 1984) and cultural change, comparing Featherstone's use of this term to Zukin's 'critical infrastructure'.

Featherstone, drawing on Bourdieu and Elias (Elias, 1939), argues that rather than seeing postmodernism as a general implosion of social structures and hierarchies, it may be seen to be a result of shifting power relations between social groups. With reference to gentrified inner city areas and other key sites of 'postmodernisation', he argues that cultural intermediaries are the new petty-bourgeoisie – producers and distributors of a vastly expanded range of symbolic goods. They promote the consumption of cultural goods with an emphasis on stylisation, on the artistic life, and an openness to new experiences. They therefore have direct and indirect interests in the accumulation of cultural capital both on a personal basis, and in terms of that of their neighbourhood and the wider city (Featherstone, 1991, 108).

Zukin quotes an Italian designer: 'I knew that a new culture of consumerism was not the answer. Rather, I wanted to make the consumer aware that he is consuming' (Zukin, 1992a, 204). The function of their role is to guide us through 'mass produced and mass consumed culture'. The guides are also gatekeepers; as cultural intermediaries they establish their taste as the guide to taste. After destabilising existing cultural hierarchies their taste is presented as the taste of the social.

Featherstone, (following Turner, 1969), uses the concept of liminality to describe a suspension of social roles at a point of transition to other social roles. This concern grew in importance in the artistic and bohemian counter-cultures of the

nineteenth and early twentieth century, with the distinction
between the heroic life of art and ordinary life.

There are a number of problems associated with the emergence of the critical infrastructure out of old counter-
cultures. One is the tension between difference and imitation
central to fashion. As a style gets more popular, it loses its
distinctive power. Distinction is a zero-sum game. This is
clearly the tension felt in Zukin's critical infrastructure,
driven from one fad to the next in order to keep ahead in the
game of tasteful consumption. At the same time as the new
social group is concerned to destabilise fixed cultural hierarchies and promote a new attitude to life-style it has
difficulties in 'keeping the lid' on the process. Featherstone
sees this in terms of the prospects for re-monopolisation. Can
this new petty-bourgeoisie, after 'blowing open' the hierarchies and introducing liminality into the heart of the system,
manage to remain gatekeepers and guides in any meaningful
sense?

Featherstone becomes increasingly doubtful of this as his
book proceeds. He argues that techniques of destabilisation
have effects on groups above and below the new petty-
bourgeoisie. The result is a general tendency to fluidity of life-
style, to liminality. Featherstone identifies certain spaces as
privileged sites of liminality. Gentrification and the new petty-
bourgeoisie can be linked through informalisation and
relaxation of life experiences as part of a 'controlled de-
control of the emotions' in which rules, surveillance and
mechanisms of exclusion operate for those without the cultural competence to exercise this control. The mixture of
'security' and 'liminality' in shopping malls is an example.

We would argue that 'popular culture' becomes operative
in ways similar to the emergence of the 'Gay Village' and
'Madchester'. Commodification of culture, both high and
popular, together with a pervasive liminality destabilise cultural hierarchies and taste distinctions to a point where the
game of distinction itself collapses, which invites an 'articulation of alternatives'. Distinction as such may well be a description of a code applicable under 'scarcity' (Beck, 1992) and
have difficulty with the proliferation associated with popular
culture (Schulze, 1992). As a result, social identities may no
longer be 'read' from a neat fit between an individual's class

and consumption patterns; rather these exist as a combination of choices, articulated from a series of possible alternatives made available by this proliferation. Such alternatives may not only be discovered in the 'bricolage' of consumer goods, but also in modes of feeling, styles of understanding and 'life-style construction' as a whole (Martin, 1991, 82).

Zukin's idea of a critical infrastructure as intermediaries between vernacular and landscape, between place and market, between producer and consumer identities, ties the transformation of contemporary culture and the city to a unilinear and one-dimensional logic of capital. Even the 'relative autonomy' of cultural capital is collapsed in 'totally programmed spaces' (Thrift, 1993) by the imperatives of the global market. We have suggested that the changes associated with the 'postmodern city' are more complex. The creation of a new centrality out of the de-industrialised space of old industrial cities can produce a number of unforeseen consequences. These spaces can be the focus for a range of cultural re-negotiations – associated with the identity of place and the identities of those whose pleasures and anxieties interweave with the exclusions and monuments of global capital. Moreover, Zukin's attempt to close down and restrict the story of the counter-culture, based on her assessment of SoHo, is unwarranted. For those trying to theorise contemporary cultural change Zukin's can only be one story among many.

## Note

This chapter comes from research undertaken with support from the Economic and Social Research Council of Great Britain, grant ref. R00233075.

## References

Beck, U., *Risk Society: Towards a new modernity* (London: Sage, 1992).

Berman, M., 'Why Modernism Still Matters', in Lash, S. and Friedman, J. (eds), *Modernity and Identity* (Oxford: Blackwell, 1992).

Bianchini, F., 'Cultural Policies in London', New Formations, 1, *GLC* R.I.P. (1987).

Bianchini, F., 'Cultural Policy and Urban Social Movements: The response of the "New Left" in Rome (1976–85) and London (1981–86)', in Bramham, P. *et al.* (eds), *Leisure and Urban Processes* (London: Routledge, 1989).

Bianchini, F. and Parkinson, M. (eds), *Cultural Policy and Urban Regeneration* (Manchester: Manchester University Press, 1993).

Bianchini, F. and Schwengel, H., 'Re-imagining the City', in Corner, J. and Harvey, S. (eds), *Enterprise and Heritage* (London: Routledge, 1991).

Bourdieu, P., *Distinction* (London and New York: Routledge & Kegan Paul, 1984).

Chambers, I., *Border Dialogues* (London: Routledge, 1990).

Cooke, P., 'Modernity, Postmodernity and the City', in *Theory, Culture and Society*, 5 (1988), 2–3.

Elias, N., *The Civilising Process* (1939) (reprinted 1994) (Oxford: Blackwell).

Featherstone, M., *Consumer Culture and Postmodernism* (London: Sage, 1991).

Frith, S. and Savage, J., 'Pearls and Swine', *New Left Review*, 198 (1993).

Harvey, D., *The Urbanisation of Capital* (Oxford: Blackwell, 1985).

Martin, B., 'Qualitative Market Research in Britain: A Profession on the Frontiers of Postmodernity', in Kellner, H. L. and Heuberger, F. L. (eds), *Hidden Technocrats: The new class and the new capitalism* (New York: Transaction Press, 1991).

Myerscough, J., *The Economic Importance of the Arts in Britain* (London: Policy Studies Institute, 1988).

Robson, B., *Those Inner Cities* (Manchester: Manchester University Press, 1986).

Schulze, G., *Die Erlebnisgesellleschaft: Kultursoziologie der Gegenwart* (Frankfurt au Main and New York: Campus 1992). (To appear in English as *The Experience Society*, London: Sage, Verlag, 1995.)

Shields, R., *Places on the Margin* (London: Routledge, 1991).

Shields, R. (ed.), *Lifestyle Shopping* (London: Routledge, 1992a).

Shields, R., 'A Truant Proximity: Presence and absence in the space of modernity', *Environment and Planning D: Society and Space*, 10 (1992b).

Smith, N. and Williams, P. *The Gentrification of the City* (London: Allen & Unwin, 1986).

Thornley, A., *Urban Planning under Thatcherism* (London: Routledge, 1990).

Thrift, N., 'An Urban Impasse?', *Theory, Culture and Society*, 10 (1993).

Turner, V., *The Ritual Process: Structure and anti-structure* (London: Allen Lane, 1969).

Wynne, D. (ed.), *The Culture Industry* (Avebury: Aldershot, 1992).

Zukin, S., *Loft Living* (Baltimore: Johns Hopkins University, 1982).

Zukin, S., *Landscapes of Power: From Detroit to Disneyland* (Berkeley: University of California Press, 1992a).

Zukin, S., 'Postmodern Urban Landscapes: Mapping culture and power', in Lash, S. and Friedman J. L. (eds), *Modernity and Identity* (Oxford: Blackwell, 1992b).

# 9 'Gaming is Play, It Should Remain Fun!': The Gaming Complex, Pleasure and Addiction

Sytze Kingma

*Professional entertainment is the dominant agency for defining what entertainment is.* (Dyer, 1977)

## THE GAMING COMPLEX

Consumer culture is a culture of pleasure, both in terms of activities and as a motivating and legitimising concept. This is realised by way of a sandwich formula, a double process. Fun value is added to exchange value, for instance in the case of fun shopping. On the other hand pleasures have been commercialised, ranging from personal hobbies and festivities to sports, games and the arts. Consumer culture is enriched by the immense diversity in and the stylisation of articles and services, and by the new respectability of formerly disregarded or even legally contested enthusiasms, notably in the fields of 'sex and drugs and rock'n roll'. Production-related values like thrift and saving seem to be ridiculed by a consumer ethic that promotes spending and self-fulfilment through leisure (see Schulze, Chapter 3 in this volume). The prime condition for this consumer culture is, of course, money, valued as an instrumental asset and also because of the fantasies and excitements involved in the acts of selecting and spending.

These features of consumer culture combine in gambling, a direct way of converting money into pleasurable experience. Gambling games have won legitimacy in, and have become part of, consumer culture; in their turn the games have been adapted to the mores of consumption. Commercial gaming markets, including lotteries, casinos and slot machines, have

173

mushroomed, not only in the Netherlands, the country I will focus on, but the world over.

Gaming is now widely accepted, but addiction appears to be an unforeseen concomitant of the expanding gaming market. Whereas the ideology of consumption highlights the glamorous, the exciting and the happy-go-lucky aspects, addiction emphasises the negative sides, that is stress, debt, filth, disease and crime. With the legalisation and liberalisation of gaming, controversies over addiction have superseded the earlier moral controversies.

The juxtaposition of pleasure and addiction is a social construction: what it stems from, how it is put into practice and how it transforms gambling markets are social and discursive processes.

The core context of the analysis in this chapter is the 'gaming complex', a network of semi-autonomous consuming, producing and regulating practices. I stress the gaming complex because the recent transformation of gaming, apprehended as the integration of gaming in consumer culture, is not limited to the invention of new games or to new characteristics of individual games. Rather, the changing gaming complex involves the signification of gaming, market composition, public, the time–spatial availability, the techniques of production and mass marketing, and the bureaucratic institutions and procedures of regulation, varying from research, judicial supervision and policing to health care. Gaming has, to paraphrase Hannerz (1992), evolved from a relatively simple into an increasingly complex culture.

With the example of Las Vegas in mind, an account is given of the recent expansion of gaming in the Netherlands. Subsequently, the 'creative production' of the gaming scene is considered, after which the concept of addiction will be discussed. Finally some spatial consequences of addiction control are put forward with respect to the Dutch regulation of slot machines.

## COMMERCIAL GAMING

The development of the Dutch commercial gaming market roughly took place in two successive and overlapping phases.

In the 1960s and 1970s, in the context of an affluent and permissive welfare state, growth was mainly realised through the gradual expansion of lotteries. The involvement in these games, which have a 'long odds' profile, can be characterised as 'passive' and 'soft'. The gambler has few options to choose from, can hardly influence the game matrix and the stakes are infrequent and low. These games are also 'instrumental', as they are mainly, though not exclusively, motivated by money. Morally, lotteries are linked to public causes, such as taxation, charity, welfare and sports. Between 1955 and 1991 the total revenues grew from around 10 million to nearly 400 million guilders.

The second wave took shape during the 1980s, in the context of a crisis in the welfare state and with new hopes set on market forces. This time expansion was mainly realised through casino games (roulette, black jack), slot machines and bingo for charity. In contrast to lotteries, these games can be characterised as 'short odds', 'hard' and 'active'. Active gaming carries strong expressive connotations such as playfulness, excitement, style, sociability, honour and identity. These games are primarily linked to commercial interests and in some cases fully operated by private enterprises, as is the case with amusement arcades and slot machines. Between 1980 and 1991 in this segment of the gaming market the total revenues grew from an estimated 300 million to nearly 2 billion guilders.

The given oppositions in game profiles, for instance passive–active and instrumental–expressive, are not solely determined by game type. Besides the various ways in which consumers give meaning to gambling games, the profiles are affected by distribution networks, marketing techniques and control measures. This has become especially relevant since from around 1990 onwards the lottery market modelled their products on principles of activity, expressivity and availability. More operators were allowed on the market, competition increased as did advertising, on-line terminals installed at selling points quickened the interaction between operator and players, the frequency of draws intensified up to one a day and television shows provided draws with a playful ambience through which lottery players could feel part of a virtual gaming community. The 'instant lottery', introduced in 1993, is a case in point. This hybrid game mingles individual characteristics of many traditional games. It blurred most significantly the boundaries of passive–active and instrumental–expressive gaming. At that time gaming addiction had become a big issue fostering market restraint.

What I am concerned with at this point is the shift in the dominant mode of signification. Gambling is decreasingly judged and practised in the instrumental rationale of 'easy money' and more in the expressive rationale of playful pleasure and lifestyle. This instrumental–expressive opposition is constitutive for many, if not all, fields in consumption. The media (information versus entertainment), eating (nutrition versus taste), and sports (fitness versus sociability, fun and good looks) provide striking examples. Perceptive analyses of tensions and changes within this opposition can be found in Corbin's (1988) reconstruction of the 'desire for the coast' that our seaside resorts presuppose, and in Falk's (1994) analysis of 'patent medicines' of which Coca-Cola is one descendant. In both cases, as in gambling, an initial promise of curative 'use value' was superseded by the 'experiential' aspects of consumption.

Life-style concerns are considered especially relevant to the middle classes (Bourdieu, 1984), which are also supposed to provide an important basis for the expansion of gaming. This does not simply mean that commercial gaming is dependent upon a middle class public. It means first that gambling games, under the standards of pleasure, have won legitimacy for a mass audience, undermining (middle class) second thoughts about gambling. Secondly, the middle class orientation is manifest in the new target groups for market expansion. Most types of gambling have high status traditions as well as low status variants. Both guises of gambling have been adapted to supposedly middle class tastes. Attempts at exploring the 'middle class gap' in gambling can be recognised in the popularisation of elitist games, notably casino games, and in the social ascendancy of working class games such as betting, slot machines and bingo. There is a pressure on gaming markets to be less exclusive, dissociating from status groups and also from old age, gender and ethnic distinctions.

Of course for the new target groups money retains its relevance as a major signifier. After all, money is the quintessence of gambling. But money is less related to the necessities of life, relief, and survival, motives that have been ascribed to the poor and the working class; or the exact opposite, namely 'conspicuous waste' of which Veblen (1899) notoriously accused the rich. Rather, money refers to the fantasies of a 'profane paradise': sports cars, holidays in the tropics, luxurious estates, breathtaking human (sex)ideal models, exotic cocktails, expensive and fashionable clothing, yachts and jewellery.

These fantasies and life-style ideals are, in advertisements for instance, associated with games in which big money can be won in an instant, in particular with casino games and lotteries. However, even in these games, and to a greater extent in other gambling games, the rationale of winning is less spectacular. It is related to the euphoria of winning generated in the momentary act on the gambling spot. Then the valuation of money is confined to the time–spatial enclave of the gaming encounter. All this is about is simply 'having a good time'.

This confinement, coupled with a vicarious appreciation of gambling, is stressed by various theorists of modernity. According to Thomas (1901), gaming is one expression of how modern man keeps up the pleasure–pain sensations of an instinctive 'conflict principle'. Simmel (1910) conceived of gambling as an 'adventure', a momentary release from the lassitude of modern life. Huizinga (1938) formally defined playful gambling in terms of highly segregated rituals pursued for their own sake and very different from 'ordinary life'. Elias and Dunning (1969) understand gambling to represent a 'quest for excitement' in otherwise unexciting societies. And as stipulated by Goffman (1969), who stresses 'character contests' and identity formation in gaming, it is not the transaction of the gamble but the action of gaming that is important.

In the perspective of everyday life, what is meaningful seems to be the *possibility* of wish-fulfilment ingrained in the fantasies of gamesters rather than the realisation of such fantasies, a mechanism which Campbell (1987) historically traced and theorised as 'imaginative hedonism'. What is consequential for other life interests and for the future is not so much the amount of money you win, but rather the amount of money you can afford to lose. This loss is the price paid for having a good time.

The significance of a lucky strike is again reduced by an emphasis on the theatrical performances, the self-presentations at, and the architectural entourage of, gambling scenes. In this respect gambling has been pulled into the domain of 'Lifestyle Shopping' (Shields, 1992). An 'aura of extravagance' is nowadays considered to be a basic mental state of the archetypical postmodern gambling scene of the Las Vegas Strip (Spanier, 1992). Here, the profane paradise – ENTER PARADISE, a sign on the Strip says – can be tasted by masses of people as a temporal fake reality. In the words of a Las Vegas casino top manager, cited by Spanier (1992, 251): 'We are not in the gambling market any more. We are selling entertainment, an environment to have fun in. What people are really doing is buying time.'

Vicarious or mimetic identification consists, furthermore, of watching the performance of surrounding individuals, the rituals of players as well as personnel, by socialising, and by making sidesteps into additional non-gaming entertainment: food, drinks, music, cinema and theatre at the gambling locale. In the case of the Netherlands, this is most likely to take place at the invariably nearby urban pleasure scene. For this identification a small and quick shot at gambling serves as an excuse rather than as the prime motive for involvement.

A decriminalisation, a commercialisation and a positive (re)definition of gambling as innocent entertainment is stressed by a controversy about vocabulary. Respectable operators and regulators denominate their industry by 'games of chance', 'entertainment', 'customers', 'guests' and 'consumers', rather than 'gambling' and 'gamblers', as these last words carry connotations of excessive and irresponsible gambling for money. Therefore, they prefer the word 'gaming' over 'gambling'. In the field of gambling studies, gambling is increasingly studied in terms of leisure and play, rather than in terms of (ir)rational calculation, moral deviancy or psychic pathology. In the realm of science attention has shifted away from the games towards opinions and spending behaviour of a generalised public, and towards the operation and regulation of gaming (Downes *et al.*, 1976; Abt *et al.*, 1984; Eadington and Cornelius, 1991).

## CREATIVE PRODUCTION

The 'euphemisation' of gambling – the redefinition of gambling as innocent entertainment, through the tempering of gaming norms, the confinement and the stylisation of gambling is controversial, susceptible to contradictory interpretation and strategic manipulation. On the one extreme, it is interpreted as a disguise of the devil, a facade built by the gaming industry to legitimise the expansion of their industry, or even a sophisticated strategy to seduce and trap unwary consumers and government officials. On the other extreme, it is the real thing, driven by authentic motives and concerns over the pleasures and the well-being of consumers. This complaisance is generally fuelled by business ethics and long-term market interests.

One reason for this range of possible associations and strategies is the relative autonomy of the various disciplines involved. For instance, in their well-known study of the Las Vegas Strip, Venturi, Scott Brown and Izenour were able to identify the postmodern symbolism and urban sprawl of the Strip irrespective of a concern over what this was (also) all about. They explain:

> Just as an analysis of the structure of a Gothic cathedral need not include a debate on the morality of medieval religion, so Las Vegas's values are not questioned here. (1977, 6)

The same could be said about safety measures, marketing, financing or health care.

Of particular importance is the diversity of gaming reality. With the rise of legal and commercial gaming, illegalisms in and of gaming persisted and have to be confronted over and over again. Likewise, the different motives for gambling, including divertissement and style as well as the instrumental ones, exist side by side and keep their relevance between and within gaming forms. For example bingo-players, in order to create and continue a pleasurable involvement in gaming, employ strategies of 'negating instrumentality': (the consequences of) loss or profit in bingo should not be taken too seriously (Kingma, 1991).

In general, a creative reception of consumer articles and services is crucial for understanding consumer behaviour (Willis, 1990; McCracken, 1990; Featherstone, 1991). However, the same holds for the producers of pleasure markets as it does for the operators and regulators of the gaming industry. They encode ideal consumer behaviour in gaming facilities through time–spatial arrangements, gaming rules, price setting, advice – notably 'budget gambling', restrictions on access and premises behaviour, codes and procedures for competition, advertising and supervision. This is a process of 'creative production' to be taken seriously. While I would subscribe to arguments like Willis' that consumers always 'exploit a gap between how things are supposed to be consumed and how they really are or might be used' (Willis, 1990, 133), for the present debate I would hold that the range and direction of this creativity is to a considerable extent prescribed and controlled by a collusion of state and market forces.

In shaping gaming facilities, state and market interests collide, but they also converge. Both engage just as much as the players in a process of negating instrumentality, first and foremost because in commercial gaming the odds are always against the player in the long run. Reflexivity and self-restraint in players are anticipated, subtly stimulated, prescribed and, if necessary, realised through repressive measures and (re)socialisation programmes. This becomes particularly clear in the case of gaming addiction.

ADDICTION

The seductive qualities of gambling, the devastating consequences of excessive gambling, and even a compulsive involvement in gambling, have long been recognised. The various accounts given in explanation of gambling excess, however, are ranging widely and contradictory. Significantly, in all cases they are extensions of the rationales given for moderate gambling. (Over)-indulgence is seen as stemming from greed and deprivation as well as prodigality and affluence, from moral deviancy and symbolic resistance as well as psychic pathology, from rational financial strategy as well as defective reasoning, from indifference and boredom as well as enthusiasm and risk taking, or from narcissistic escapism and estrangement as well as social desirability, honour and prestige. From this perspective, the contexts in which specific interpretations of gaming excess figure and gain dominance are taken to be decisive. Whereas pleasure has become the major concept in moderate gaming, with the rise of commercialised gaming addiction has become the dominant concept in gaming excess.

The process of addiction in gaming is well documented, in particular on the level of cognitive rationalisation (Lesieur, 1984; Lesieur and Custer, 1984; Dickerson, 1984; Meyer and Bachman, 1993). The process can be captured as a violation of the law of negating instrumentality in gambling . Addicts play down the losing instant or overstress the winning instant. Via vicious circles addicts are caught up in a process of escalating commitment to gambling. They try to cover losses by gambling, they incur debts, commit fraud, steal. Ultimately, they can become desperate and even consider suicide. This process is reinforced by 'tolerance' (an increasingly high level of need for the experience) 'operant conditioning' (the occasional win and the prestige effect) and 'illusions of control' or 'superstition' (a system or a clue to winning). Socially and economically, addicts get isolated in gaming worlds, neglecting work and family life. The obsessive gambler loses a sense of autonomy, and therefore a sense of pleasure too. As Dostoevsky remarks, in one of the first and hardly excelled accounts of obsessive gambling, in *The Gambler*: 'I have to win ... I don't gamble for fun.' Among addicts one can find the fiercest opponents of gambling.

Addiction as the dominant concept for evaluating gaming excess can partly be explained by the commercial mode of gaming. We are now enabled and seduced to stake money continuously or to develop a life-style, and a life-long routine in gaming. Because gaming scenes constitute a real (fantasy) world of their own, gamesters can easily be trapped, especially if, for whatever reasons, they are in need of a comforting and gratifying haven.

But the new relevance of gaming addiction cannot only be explained by the gaming scene. The vast majority of players simply do not become addicted. What is more, addiction denotes a generalised syndrome, not a specifically gaming-related one. Addiction is related to many pursuits (alcohol, tobacco, marihuana, heroine, medicine, food, work, car driving, sports, shopping, love, etc.). Gaming addiction underscores that the phenomenon of addiction not only applies to stimulating or depressing substances, but also to experiences (Peele, 1985).

To become manifest, addiction needs a suitable, that is a meaningful and consequential, object. Without the grave financial consequences you can hardly imagine gaming addiction to be controversial. The other precondition, however, is formed by an addiction-prone subject. From this logic, the addiction syndrome should be understood and studied in terms of the subject–object dialectic, which comes out as a problem of life-style integration; a problem of resourceful and meaningful linking of the various compartments in life.

What I basically argue here is that together with the expansion and omnipresence of gaming, moderate gaming has increasingly become dependent upon a provident and self-regulative stance taken by gamesters, and that it is precisely the concept of addiction that is socially effective in demarcating this. To elaborate on this proposition, it is instructive to point out that the identification of addiction involves the ordering of behaviour within a three-dimensional space of interpretation, voiced by two different brands of theorising (see Figure 9.1).

In the first two-dimensional approach the concept of addiction hints at, and in the end dissolves into, a broad category of 'gambling problems'. The problems include obsession, stress, low self-esteem, rule-breaking, agitation and crime. This somewhat clinical brand of theorising, mostly based on accounts by gamblers under treatment, evolved from the psychoanalytic approach to gambling excess (Freud's essay on Dostoevsky, 1928; Bergler, 1957). This approach has gradually been extended to a broader disease model which in its turn was extended by the psychological control model of 'problem gaming' (Lesieur, 1984; Dickerson, 1984; Rosecrance, 1988). Within this perspective, gambling is considered to be an accepted leisure form, of which excessive use and destructive consequences should be confronted, including parasitic relationships between gamblers and their environment

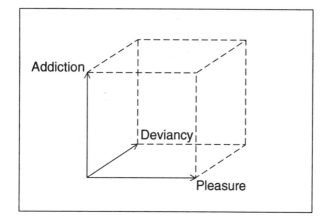

*Figure* 9.1 The three-dimensional space of life-style integration in gaming; these dimensions are independent, continuous and inclusive

(Figure 9.1 with pleasure left out of consideration). Compulsiveness is regarded to be one of the major causes of the unpleasant personal and social consequences of immoderate gaming. And this addiction is seen as a reversible two-way process, whether induced by treatment or otherwise. Treatment should determine the extent to which trouble actually relates to gaming and addiction. Resocialisation generally aims at coping strategies, counselling and the rationalisation of emotions and behaviour. A successful handling of problem gaming can, to some extent, legitimate an addictive involvement. Clearly, within the rationale of problem gaming, not all addicts break the rules and not all rule-breakers are addicts. Even if gamblers could be objectively classified as addicts they, or others, do not have to acknowledge that. Addicts first have to 'come out'.

Secondly, from the standpoint of subculture theory, the concept of addiction hints at, and in the end disappears in, the quicksand of pleasure. This perspective is generally put forward in studies that deal with gamblers and addicts in 'natural' settings (Thomas, 1901; Becker, 1963; Waldorf and Reinarman, 1975; Herman, 1976; Oldman, 1978). Almost all cultural pursuits are considered to be susceptible to (being labelled as) addiction. This time the degree of commitment and the respectability of pleasure is held significant (Figure 9.1 with deviancy left out). It is argued that pleasure is manifest in various ways, depending on the way it is managed within life-styles. This can range from a carefully hidden indulgence, via socially acceptable habits, up to the marginal careers in subcultures, where the catering for 'addictions' – by legal or illegal means – is a matter of subsistence (that is work). The new respectability of gambling can, to some extent, legitimate an addictive involvement. In short, not all pleasure involves addiction and not all addicts experience pleasure. And even if gaming behaviour could objectively be classified as addictive, social acceptability and consequentiality are decisive in order to acknowledge that.

To make a difference between normal and abnormal gaming within the pleasure–addiction–deviancy space (Figure 9.1), the addiction dimension needs to be subsumed under the dimension of pleasure, if it is to be accepted, or the dimension of deviancy, if it is to be dismissed. This puzzle is somehow dealt with by all those involved in the gaming complex. In theory and in practice it is hard to distinguish addicts from ordinary gamblers as well as gamblers facing non-addiction-based troubles. To operators, legislators and police, addicts remain ordinary consumers, as long as they adhere to their standards of gaming behaviour. In many cases immoderate punters resist allegations that they feel compelled to gamble. In other cases problem gamblers willingly adopt the vocabulary of addiction from professionals and informed lay helpers. In anticipation of qualified aid they conform to scientific viewpoints. This indicates a process of 'proto-professionalisation' (de Swaan, 1990), supportive to many fields of expert knowledge.

Through these and other classificatory practices (at times highly creative and harmless – a criminal pleading for reduction of punishment because of gaming addiction; Nintendo advertising its computer game PAC-ATTACK as *highly addictive!*; the bingo player claiming addiction for lack of a more persuasive argument; the distinguished lady who, afraid of addiction, doesn't dare to touch a single French roulette jeton) – addiction is put to work as a 'disciplinary concept', exorcising gaming excess and at the same instant enabling fancy moderate gaming. Some major consequences will now be outlined with respect to Dutch slot machine regulations.

## SLOT MACHINE SPACE

In alliance with moral and legislative gaming norms, surveillance, policing and health care, the time–spatial modes of 'disciplinary power' (Foucault, 1979) are basic strategies in gaming operation and regulation. Slot machines offer a case in point. In the Netherlands, addiction and problem gaming are closely associated with slot machines (Kingma, 1993). The slot machine market also is dispersed and spatially varied.

In 1986 a revision of the Gaming Act made slot machines a legal free enterprise industry. Legislators stated that illegal or condoned practices should be ended, and that, under conditions of registration and safety measures, a sound commercial operation of slot machines should be possible. The law anticipated and sought to bring about a pleasurable involvement in gaming, most explicitly through a maximum loss of an average of 50 guilders per hour, and through the confinement of slot machines to surroundings of consumptive pleasure. Apart from the highly specialised legal casinos (10 by 1993), and some 300 amusement arcades, slot machines were allowed in a wide range of tens of thousands of small–scale venues, in places such as restaurants, pubs, cafes, coffee shops (some also dealing in soft drugs), cafeterias, pool centres, sports canteens, youth and community centres. A concern about pleasure remained implicit in the consideration that slot machines were expected *not* to be addictive. Gambling machines were also supposed *not* to attract a youthful public.

The expansion and rearrangement of the slot machine market that followed the 1986 Act had a number of unintended consequences. Most significantly, it led to a concern about gaming addiction. This concern, raised by regulators, Gamblers Anonymous and the state-controlled addiction bureau, did not stand on its own. It was reinforced by the rise in (petty) crime and the law and order campaigns following this. The concern and vigilance over slot machines was further reinforced through the association between slot machines and a suspect public, particularly young people. The slot machines' trade was made even more suspicious by a concern over malicious operation and indifference.

In reaction to these controversies, from around 1990 onwards one local government after the other ordered preventive and corrective measures. The new local gaming policies appeared in two basic shapes, depending on whether or not, and to what extent, slot machines were permitted in the small-scale venues of restaurants, lunchrooms, cafes, pubs, coffee shops and cafeterias.

The controversy over this spatial category, which I will probe into a little further, highlights two major strategies of time–spatial discipline. Four ideal types of locales can be distinguished (Figure 9.2). The distinctions are roughly based on the degree of segregation between and within slot machine venues (segregation with respect to public and with respect to speciality, that is, alternative articles and services), and the degree of supervision over and within locales (supervision by owners with respect to immoderate gaming and youth involvement in slot machines).

To exemplify the interplay of segregation and supervision I will outline slot machine control in the 'mixed spaces', the controversial category, and in the specialised amusement arcades.

With the recent upgrading of many Dutch arcades, discipline aims at refining and rationalising gaming behaviour. This is done by improving the servicing and controlling capacity of personnel. Gambling behaviour is continously monitored. Video camera-assisted, the cashier oversees the entire arcade from a panoptic view. In addition, personnel casually mingle with gamesters in order to provide instant service, to lend an ear, and to be able to intervene immediately if someone steps out of line. Pin-ball and video machines are strictly separated from slot machines, and non-gaming-related behaviour, especially dealing in drugs or stolen goods and social gathering or eating, is prevented. This enhances the level of slot machine segregation from within the arcade. The arcade also provides a disciplining atmosphere. Together with a luxurious (re)decoration, through light, colouring, cleaning, artificial plants and air-conditioning, this is achieved by a moderation of sound levels produced by

| Time/space SEGREGATION | Time/space SUPERVISION | |
| --- | --- | --- |
| | High | Low |
| High | Casino<br>Amusement arcade<br>Betting shop<br><br>*(Specialty space)* | Illegal gambling venues<br>Home gambling<br>Tele gambling<br><br>*(Hidden space)* |
| Low | Restaurant<br>Cafe<br>Pub    (High threshold)<br>-------------------<br>(Low threshold)<br><br>Pool centre<br>Coffee shop<br>Cafeteria<br><br>*(Mixed space)* | Welfare centre<br>(Sports) canteen<br>Social club<br><br>*(Informal space)* |

*Figure* 9.2   Ideal types regarding time–space control

the apparatuses, by providing modest background music and by the banning of loitering. A sign posted at the entrance communicates the basics of this idealised gaming behaviour embodied in the arcade:

- Minimum age 18. Proof can be requested.
- The operator is entitled to expel gamblers.

- Two persons per machine maximum.
- Alcoholic drinks not allowed.
- Seats for players only.
- No feet on the machine.
- Our arcade is clean, keep it clean.
- This arcade is video-monitored, for our safety and yours.

In conclusion one is reminded:

GAMING IS PLAY: IT SHOULD REMAIN FUN!

In this way arcade discipline mimics the 'total' or 'closed space' of the legal Dutch casinos, where time–space boundaries are selectively permeable and closely and continuously watched.

These modes of 'constructed' discipline, which accentuate the segregation of gaming in daily life, stand in opposition to what I call 'contextual' discipline. Contextual discipline is implicit, less specialised and less reflexive. It is effected by non-gaming responsibilities and activities. Mixed spaces depend to a greater extent, and informal spaces to a far greater extent, upon modes of contextual discipline than the arcades do. Serious doubts about the effectiveness of contextual control questioned mixed spaces as proper spaces for slot machine operation. Within the category of mixed spaces again, distinctions were sharpened by the notion of 'high threshold' and 'low threshold' venues (Figure 9.2).

On the including side of the threshold divide, slot machines are permitted, or reduced in number, in locales that cater for alcoholic beverages – not to be sold to minors, in particular cafes, pubs and restaurants. Here contextual discipline is primarily set by characteristics of space. The clientele is motivated to extend their stay through drinking, eating and socialising. Slot machines are supposed to bring in only 'additional revenues' to the owner and to offer 'additional entertainment' to customers. The owner is expected to supervise the entire place including, in line with the responsibilities regarding alcohol abuse, the one or two slot machines.

Within the most controversial instance, on the excluding side of the threshold divide, slot machines have been excluded, or limited to one slot machine only, in cafeterias and similar establishments. Here contextual discipline primarily depends on characteristics of time. These businesses rely on high-speed money returns through petty transactions with vast quantities of consumers. Such fast-food features imply a limited segregation in public and a limited duration of stay. Slot machines are supposed to be a means of 'killing time' while waiting for a snack order. The controlling capacity of the owner is restricted behind the counter, in front of which the consumption space is designed and used as a kind of momentary 'parking lot' for street life. Slot machines are seductively positioned here, within the public sight and easily accessible to anybody, including young people.

In some cities slot machines have been completely removed from all mixed spaces. In others, slot machine operation continued in the high-threshold venues or even in the low-threshold ones. This continuation, however, was part of a deliberate policy directing measures of enhanced control. These policies generally entail covenants, and are therefore consensual, between local government, slot machine entrepreneurs and the owners of locales.

The measures of enhanced control taken are in line with the constructed discipline of amusement arcades. Owners have to impose a strict age limit, warn players of the risks involved in gaming, inform them about treatment opportunities, and identify and ban excessive gamblers. Operators are expected, moreover, to check upon each other to correct 'free riders' who can easily undermine the system of control and jeopardise the market. In one or two cities a 'gaming watch' has even been introduced. Through these measures the entire slot machine market is organised as a rationalised total space akin to arcade control.

## THE NEW AUTONOMY OF GAMING

The outlined processes and structures signalling the integration of gaming within consumer culture can be captured by the unifying concept of autonomy (Kingma, 1995). The gaming complex increasingly functions according to a dynamic of its own, irrespective of the environing society.

This concept of autonomy figures prominently in the works of Bourdieu, in particular with respect to the interaction between status groups and cultural fields. 'Autonomy' refers to the distancing from instrumental motives and from status histories in gaming, and to the concepts of pleasure and addiction. As a corrective on gaming excess, additional control safe-guards the gaming complex from over-use. On the other hand 'autonomy' also refers to the modalities of supervision which enable the gaming complex to work and play on relatively independent and predictable grounds.

The autonomy of gaming has developed, as stipulated, together with new modes of gaming control. This brings to light one of the major paradoxes of commercial gaming and indeed consumer culture. The paradox resides in the process of consumer sovereignty and market freedom becoming effective under conditions of self-regulation by consumers and entrepreneurs.

This paradox of control entails a difficult theoretical issue (Wouters, 1986). In order to explain the new issue of reflexivity and self-regulation in gaming, several inherent contradictions should be taken into account. First, market freedom in gaming has not implied a resignation of state control. Rather, state control has evolved from prohibition-centred policies into sophisticated and indirect modes of regulation (Dixon, 1991). Second, autonomy in gaming is realised through a change of gaming practice itself. In particular the tempering or the 'euphemisation' of gaming is relevant. Third, self-regulation in gaming relates not only to the state, but equally to the market. Market forces surely compelled the state to give in to gaming. And the sheer abundance of opportunities forces people to make deliberate, self-conscious and gaming conscious choices (Bataille, 1988; Schulze, 1992). Fourth, self-regulation in gaming is relative in respect of the emotional, social and economic dispositions of consumers. This is obvious in the restriction of gambling to adult life and in the countervailing practices of addiction control. More generally, the greater the gap between the options offered by the gaming complex on the one side and the circumstances of life offered on the other, the greater the strain on gamblers becomes. This is particularly relevant in view of the powerful and seductive simulacra, such as the world of gaming, built by consumer culture. These 'virtual worlds' can 'really' be experienced as alternatives to life-interests on which participation depends. The amplification of experiences and possible consequences, and not the play with chances, makes the gaming complex part of 'Risk Society' (Douglas, 1985; Beck, 1992).

With this a final paradox in consumer culture is encountered, since the same neo-liberal politics that applaud market forces and have liberated the gaming market most fervently express a concern over law and order. But the one clearly relates to the other. In the case of gaming, addiction policies did not in the first place spring from a concern over the well-being of gamesters. This concern intermingled with market interests and with concern over public order. Consequently, addiction policies mainly address the supply side of the market leaving the life-world of consumers aside.

## Note

For feedback on the initial paper on which this chapter is based I thank, besides the editors, Eeva Jokinen, Sue Fisher, Els Kok, Rob Shields, and Professor Lodewijk Brunt together with my associates at Amsterdam University: Rieke Leenders, Richard Staring, Thaddeus Müller, Norbert van Bemmel, Dieteke van der Ree, Gerben Kroese, Heleen Ronden and Gert Vogel. This chapter is based upon research endowed by the Netherlands Foundation for Scientific Research (NWO).

## References

Abt *et al.*, 'Gambling: The misunderstood sport – a problem in social definition', *Leisure Sciences*, 6 (1984), 205–220.
Bataille, G., *The Accursed Share* (New York: Zone Books, 1988).
Beck, U., *Risk Society: Towards a new modernity* (London: SGE, 1992).
Becker, H. S., *Outsiders* (New York: The Free Press, 1963).
Bergler, E., *The Psychology of Gambling* (New York: Hill & Wang, 1957).
Bourdieu, P., *Distinction* (London and New York: Routledge & Kegan Paul, 1984).
Campbell, C., *The Romantic Ethic and the Spirit of Modern Consumerism* (New York and Oxford: Basil Blackwell, 1987).
Corbin, A., *Le Territoire du vide: L'Occident et le désire du rivage (1750–1840)* (Paris: Aubier, 1988).
Dickerson, M., *Compulsive Gamblers* (London: Longman, 1984).
Dixon, D., *From Prohibition to Regulation* (Oxford: Clarendon Press, 1991).
Dostoevsky, F., *The Gambler* (Chicago: University of Chicago Press, 1972 [1866]).

Douglas, M., *Risk Acceptability According to the Social Sciences* (London and New York: Routledge & Kegan Paul, 1985).

Downes, D. M., *et al.*, *Gambling, Work and Leisure* (London: Routledge & Kegan Paul, 1976).

Dyer, R., 'Entertainment and Utopia', in During S., (ed.), *The Cultural Studies Reader* (London and New York: Routledge, 1993 [1977]).

Eadington, W. R. and Cornelius, J. A. (eds), *Gambling and Public Policy* (Reno: University of Nevada, 1991).

Elias, N. and E. Dunning, 'Quest for Excitement in Leisure', *Society and Leisure*, 2 (1969), pp. 50–85.

Falk, P., *The Consuming Body* (London: Sage/TCS, 1994).

Featherstone, M., *Consumer Culture and Postmodernism* (London: Sage, 1991).

Foucault, M., *Discipline and Punish: The birth of the prison* (Harmondsworth: Penguin, 1975; New York: Vintage Books, 1979).

Freud, S., 'Dostoevsky and Parricide', in Halliday, J. and Fuller, P. (eds) (1928) *The Psychology of Gambling* (London: Harper & Row, 1974).

Goffman, E., 'Where the Action is', in Goffman, E., *Interaction Ritual* (London: Allen Lane, 1969).

Hannerz, U., *Cultural Complexity* (New York: Columbia University Press, 1992).

Herman, R. D., *Gamblers and Gambling* (Lexington, Mass. and Toronto: Lexington Books, 1976).

Huizinga, J., *Homo Ludens* (New York: Beacon, 1950 [1938]).

Kingma, S., 'De legitimiteit van het kienen en bingo of de smaak van de noodzaak', in *Fragmenten van vermaak* (Amsterdam and Atlanta: Editions Rodopi, 1991), pp. 123–51.

Kingma, S., *Risico-analyse kansspelen* (Tilburg: Ministerie van WVC/ Universiteit Brabant, 1993).

Kingma, S., 'The Political Culture of Gaming', in McMillen, J. (ed.), *Gambling Cultures* (London, Sydney and New York: Routledge, 1995).

Lesieur, H. R., *The Chase: Career of the compulsive gambler* (Cambridge, Mass.: Schenkman, 1984).

Lesieur, H. R. and Custer, R. L., 'Pathological Gambling: Roots, phases and treatment', *Annals of the American Academy of Political and Social Sciences* (1984), pp. 146–56.

McCracken, G., *Culture and Consumption* (Bloomington and Indianapolis: Indiana University Press, 1990).

Meyer, G. and Bachman, M., *Glücksspiel* (Berlin: Springer-Verlag, 1993).

Oldman, D., 'Compulsive Gamblers', *The Sociological Review*, 26 (1978), pp. 349–71.

Peele, S., *The Meaning of Addiction* (Lexington: Lexington Books, 1985).

Rosecrance, J., *Gambling without Guilt* (Pacific Grove, California: Brooks/ Cole Publishing Company, 1988).

Schulze, G., *Die Erlebnisgesellschaft: Kultursoziologie der Gegenwart* (Frankfurt am Main and New York: Campus Verlag, 1992). (To appear in English as *The Experience Society*, London: Sage, 1995.)

Shields, R. (ed.), *Lifestyle Shopping* (London and New York: Routledge, 1992).

Simmel, G., *On Individuality and Social Forms* (Chicago: Chicago University Press, 1971 [1910]).

Spanier, D., *Inside Las Vegas* (London: Secker & Warburg, 1992).

Swaan, A. de, *The Management of Normality* (London and New York: Routledge, 1990).

Thomas, W. I., 'The Gaming Instinct', *The American Journal of Sociology*, 6 (1901), pp. 750–63.

Veblen, Th., *The Theory of the Leisure Class* (New York: Macmillan, 1899; London: Unwin Books, 1970).

Venturi, R., Brown, D. S. and Izenour, S., *Learning from Las Vegas* (Cambridge, Mass., London and New York: MIT Press, 1977 [1972]).

Waldorf, D. and Reinarman, C., 'Addicts – Everything but human beings', *Urban Life*, 4 (1975), pp. 30–53.

Willis, P., *Common Culture* (Milton Keynes: Open University Press, 1990).

Wouters, C., 'Formalization and Informalization: Changing tension balances in civilizing processes', *Theory, Culture and Society*, 3(2) (1986), pp. 1–19.

# Part III
# Regulating Needs and Pleasures

# 10 The 'Consumer' in Political Discourse: Consumer Policy in the Nordic Welfare States

Kaj Ilmonen and Eivind Stø

Consumer policy is a relatively new field of political discourse in the Nordic countries. It is hard to date its birth, as all kinds of societal discourses have long prehistories when they are not conscious of themselves as discourses. They are, as Foucault says, discursive practices that are the necessary condition for the establishment of a science or social policy (Foucault, 1972). In describing discursive practices, Foucault uses an umbrella concept of 'knowing' which includes several elements: (a) the objects that are considered to deserve special attention, (b) the cognitive space that serves as the framework within which a subject relates itself to these objects, (c) the field of coordination and subordination of presentations that define concepts and prescribe their use, and (d) the possibilities of application that these presentations serve (Foucault, 1972, 202–3). These elements may or may not form a scientific–political discourse. In this chapter, we will focus on consumer policy, rather than scientific discourse, following the path – 'discursive practice–knowing–policy (science)' – that Foucault recommends.

Once the discursive field has established itself and achieved a relatively stable societal shape, it starts to produce its own objects of interest and its own playground. These objects are the main focus of our chapter. We will be asking: What are the most fundamental objects of emerging consumer policy? How are they related to each other? What attributes are attached to them? How have they changed since the 1960s? As research material we use the relevant official committee reports and recommendations of consumer legislation in three Nordic countries, Finland, Norway and Sweden.

## PHASES OF NORDIC CONSUMER POLICY

The birth of social discourse is a complex and largely unpredictable process where every phase builds upon the preceding one. A new phase can thus be understood as an interpretation of the phase that preceded it, but it also offers arguments concerning future constellations, thereby serving as the legitimation of the next phase. What are seen as problems, as perspectives and approaches, as relevant categorisations, orders and differences, or as the most important qualities – all these serve as preparation for the next phase. In this sense, every implementation phase is interconnected both discursively and socially (Foucault, 1972, 232).

What is true of social discourse in general is also true of consumer policy, which has undergone several phases loosely linked with socioeconomic development in the Nordic countries. The phases in consumer political discourse follow broader changes in societal policy, but not exactly. Much depends on the development of the markets, on the relationship of producers and consumers, and especially on how all this has been interpreted in the general debate.

Consumer problems have existed for as long as consumer goods have been sold on the market. However, they did not cause any collective reaction before the nineteenth century. The first consumer cooperatives were founded in England in Rochdale as early as 1844; and just after the turn of the century, consumer cooperative unions were established in Sweden (1899), Finland (1904) and Norway (1906). During the following 50–60 years consumer cooperatives came to play an important role in Nordic labour and consumer policy. Furthermore, the Nordic countries got their first governmental and non-governmental consumer organisations rather early.

Notwithstanding, consumer policy and consumer organisations were largely created in the years subsequent to the Second World War. Their distinctive character has been established and developed in four phases since 1935 (Stö, 1984; 1989; 1991). In

Norway and Sweden the phases occurred synchronously. The same phases can be found in Finland as well, but they do not coincide with those in Finland's Scandinavian neighbours.

In the first phase, 1935–45, consumer policy and consumer interests were defined rather narrowly. Consumer problems were linked solely with questions concerning home economics. In 1936, the Norwegian Advisory Service for Home Economics was established, with twenty local offices around the country. In Sweden, the Home Economics Research Institute was founded in 1944, and Finland followed suit in 1947. As the names of these institutions reveal, they were mainly concerned with consumer problems in the kitchen. The goal of consumer information was to strengthen the rational behaviour of consumers at home. Most of the information from consumer institutions to consumers referred to housekeeping and the home, especially cookery. Consumers were expected to learn to prepare food and take care of clothes. Consumer institutions were only marginally concerned with consumer protection or questions related to the marketing of goods and services.

A slight shift in consumer matters took place between 1945 and 1960, when national consumer institutions were established: the Norwegian Consumer Council in 1953, the Swedish National Consumer Council in 1957 and, lastly, the Finnish Consumer Council in 1965. The Nordic women's organisations played an important part in this process. The need for consumer information through consumer organisations was first recognised by various women's organisations, linked with the labour and farmer movements and consumer cooperatives. All the new consumer institutions were established by governments and financed by Parliament. On the other hand, they were relatively independent from governments politically. In all three countries representatives of women, households, and labour organisations were members of the board of the Consumer Council. These Councils were, however, not independent of producers; commerce and industry had representatives on the same boards.

Another important event in this second phase of Nordic consumer policy was the abolition of remaining regulations on imports and exports and the formal freeing, between 1955 and 1960, of the market for consumer goods from wartime restrictions. This also influenced consumer information. The scope changed from home economy to market economy. In addition, the new consumer institutions became increasingly concerned with market practices; they launched their consumer magazines in this period. The Nordic countries also established declaration committees for consumer goods, designed to reach voluntary agreement with producers regarding the labelling of consumer goods.

During the third period, 1968–78, various changes in consumer policy took place in the Nordic countries. Some of these changes were parallel in all of them, which reflects specifically Nordic thinking in consumer affairs. 'Consumer policy' in the modern sense of the term was then formed in the Nordic countries. Much important general consumer legislation was passed in the Nordic parliaments in these years. The right to seek redress was ensured by a general Sales of Goods Act (Bjarköy, 1993), and consumers were protected against unfair and misleading advertising by the Market Control Act (Graver, 1986; Bernitz, 1984). In addition, various other consumer laws were adopted in some of the Nordic countries. There were differences between the national laws, but by and large consumers enjoyed the same level of protection in all the Nordic countries.

When adopting new laws new consumer protection institutions were also established in the Nordic countries. The Marketing Control Act in the early 1970s set up a separate institution – the Consumer Ombudsman – to enforce the law. Consumer complaint boards were introduced to ensure consumers the right to seek redress. These consumer laws and institutions are a clear illustration of a transition in Nordic consumer policy. Although consumer information was still important, consumer protection was becoming the key political goal by the end of 1970s.

The fourth phase in consumer policy, 1980–93, is complex in two ways. First of all, there are big differences between the countries; secondly, we may note various tendencies within one and the same country. Although deregulation is the main trend in Nordic consumer policy in this period, new consumer laws were passed in all three countries. There was new legislation dealing with product safety and product liability on the one hand and consumer economy and consumer credit on the other. Thirdly, consumer protection was not stressed as heavily as earlier. Instead, we see a return to emphasis on consumer information. In this respect Nordic countries have come closer to the EU pattern of consumer policy.

## KEY SOCIAL DISCOURSES AND FORMATIONS RELATED TO CONSUMER POLICY

In what follows we will focus on the last two phases. These made up the period when consumer policy as a social discourse became established in the Nordic countries. Of course, many social and discursive formations are relevant in understanding the birth of consumer–political 'knowledge'. The trends in consumption patterns after the Second World War provide the social background to this process. Furthermore, in the Nordic setting the following discursive formations would appear to be the most important:

(a)  discussion about 'affluent society' and its criticism;
(b)  discussion concerning consumers *vis-à-vis* producers and markets; and
(c)  the extension of citizenship rights in the Nordic context, that is discussion about 'social citizenship'.

It is hard to say which of the three discourses has been the most important in constituting consumer policy. It is certain, however, that the rapid increase in private consumption after the Second World War and related social issues has been one of the preconditions of consumer policy in the Nordic countries.

These changes in consumption patterns are complex. Suffice to say that they were much the same as elsewhere in OECD countries. The Nordic societies became real consumer or market capitalist societies from the 1960s onwards. Indicators of this transformation were (a) the rapid consumerisation of the population, (b) change in consumption patterns, (c) the emergence of new qualities in consumer goods and (d) the transformation of distribution systems (Ilmonen, 1986, 1987; Laurila and Kallinen, 1985).

The extension of the field of private consumption and the qualitative changes within it produced new consumer problems alongside the old ones (shortage of money, product forgery, and so on). People's economic and social dependence on consumption grew concurrently with the weakening of their ability to master cognitively and emotionally the growing flow of goods on markets and the increasing nuances of new products (Ilmonen, 1987). In addition, the economic and spatial concentration of retail sales put people as consumers in a completely new situation. It became necessary to order this new condition, both cognitively and legally.

The rapid increase in private consumption in the late 1960s was a natural basis for discourses comparing market economy with socialist economies. In the debate it was claimed that market economies were more effective than any socialist economy. The latter were seen as suffering from all kinds of material shortages whereas market economies were undergoing rapid economic growth. Living standards in the latter had risen considerably, and they were becoming affluent societies.

It did not take long for the vision of affluent society to attract its critics. They were quick to point out that the affluence was unequally distributed. Even the most affluent societies like the United States had their own poor populations. That was not, however, considered the worst problem. More important was the nature of commodities and people's growing dependence on them. The new criticism of commodities concerned the intrinsic irrationalities of market economies. One of the best known representatives of this line of criticism in the Nordic countries, Vance Packard, claimed that it is not in the interests of enterprises in market economies to produce the best possible and durable products because this would soon lead to a glut on the market. In other words, the best solutions are not chosen even if they are economically possible. On the contrary, a considerable amount of planned obsolescence resides in commodities. They are, consequently, not so much 'goods' as 'harms' for consumers, who basically cannot trust them (Packard, 1967, 57–70).

In the Nordic countries, this argument was not adopted in full, although researchers from different fields of consumption started to talk about planned obsolescence and deterioration of commodities. However, what did catch on was the Frankfurt School's concept of 'manipulated consumers' (Adorno and Horkheimer, 1979), which drew attention to increased marketing efforts in market economies. It was based on the assumption that consumers are helpless objects in the hands of Packard's 'hidden persuaders', (Helenius, 1974, 63–111).

This critical moral sentiment started at the beginning of the 1970s, when it was noticed that the other side of the coin of higher living standards was a growing waste problem. It was argued that the mass consumption society made inefficient use of its natural resources by producing useless and qualitatively weak goods. Moreover, it was pointed out that even the purchased products were underutilised and misused; they were thrown away while still physically usable (Packard, 1967, 47–56; Helenius, 1974, 49–59). This was said to lead to an increasing deterioration of living conditions in market economies.

Much of the criticism of affluent society was exaggerated and many of its themes died out slowly in the 1970s in the Nordic countries, but not without leaving an imprint on the fabric of society. There emerged a sizable machinery of committees that produced discourses (texts and legislation) on marketing in general and advertising in particular (see, for instance, SOU, 1972).

The concentration and centralisation of the economy in the hands of a few enterprises in strategic branches of the consumption industry and retail trade took place in several waves in the Nordic countries. One of these was in the 1960s, when home markets were rapidly released for free competition after the regulation of the war economy. In addition, the merger rate accelerated throughout the 1960s. This gave rise to worries in the media and, consequently, among politicians in Nordic countries at the end of the decade. Various studies were undertaken and committee reports published at the beginning of 1970s in Finland, Sweden and Norway (Böök and Ilmonen, 1989).

This economic concentration and centralisation gave rise to two concerns that are of interest here. The first was the increasingly unequal distribution of power in society. According to the ethos of the times, the concentration of power was defined mainly in economic terms. It was maintained that such economic concentration meant that societal power passed into the hands of the economic elite. This was seen as an offence against the democratic principles that governed political decision making in the Nordic countries. In contrast, what was desired was the extension of citizen's rights by economic rights – in other words, the democratisation of economic life (see, for example, Israel, 1969).

A second issue was the power relationship between producers and consumers. Economic concentration and centralisation were seen as disturbing the market mechanism and, in this sense, as posing a real threat to 'consumer sovereignty'. Liberal critics maintained that centralisation tendencies would limit alternatives in consumer choice. This argument was based on the idea that firms in oligopolistic markets will focus exclusively on solvent demands – which, in turn, will increase concentration tendencies in the domestic economy. More radical critics of concentration and centralisation added that these trends would lead to monopoly pricing and the reduction of consumer influence. The observed imbalance in power relations in the commodity market in the late 1960s caused another type of worry as well. It was claimed that consumers had little say in decisions about product development, that they got inadequate information about products, and that they had poor chances in the fight for their rights in markets. In sum, consumers did not have the influence on markets that neoclassical economic theory claimed they had (Helenius, 1974, 21–84; Ilmonen and Suomela, 1987, 14–22).

Attention was also paid to the difficulties involved in the concept of 'consumer'. Liberal theorists were eager to stress that all consumers were in the same position. Critics of this view maintained that, on the contrary, there were great differences among consumers. Relevant knowledge and time resources were seen as unequally distributed among consumer groups. Above all, however, there was deep concern about the unequal allocation of material preconditions for consumption. There were considerable income disparities despite the social–political measures to reduce them in all Nordic countries. This was considered to disadvantage especially low-income groups (Israel, 1969, 22–4; Ilmonen and Suomela, 1987, 17–19). Thus, not only were consumers the weakest link in the market chain, there was an even weaker group within this weakest link.

Another problem was the growing dependence on consumer status. It has gone hand in hand with the universalisation of wage labour, which has created social security problems unknown in earlier times. These problems were taken seriously in the West even before the Second World War. The social security system was extended partly under the pressure from the labour movement. Social security rights were added to citizens' rights in the Nordic context even before the Second World War. However, we can talk of the systemic development of social citizenship only after the war (citizens' rights to unemployment, disability and retirement income, and to health services). Once again Finland brought up the rear, but once started, development progressed rapidly. The second half of the 1950s saw new legislation concerning employment, retirement, health care and disability, and so on (Riihinen, 1992, 279).

The situation in social citizenship rights in all Nordic countries changed radically with the emergence of the tripartite corporatist system. Almost every round in incomes policy agreements added some new elements to social rights or improved them. This went on until the 1973 oil crisis which interrupted the long period of economic growth, but the trend was resumed in the second half of the 1970s and lasted until the late 1980s.

There have also been differences among the Nordic countries. The so-called 'Nordic model' has never been homogeneous. For example, Denmark's economic policy has been the most liberal, while Sweden and Norway have operated a social democratic or Keynesian model, and Finland can be placed somewhere between the two versions (Esping-Andersen, 1990). Nonetheless, the development of social rights in all Nordic countries created for people a sense of social security as citizens and ensured their ability to function as consumers also in cases when they lost their jobs or ceased to be active members of the workforce.

CONSUMER POLICY: A SUBSYSTEM OF EVERYDAY LIFE

Partly parallel to and partly based on the discourses presented above, the discussion about consumption and its consequences gathered momentum in the early 1960s in all Nordic countries. The significance of consumption had grown, from the point of view of both the national economy and individual consumers. This directed public attention to the position of consumers. The fundamental elements of this newly defined discourse consisted of: (a) own bodies and interest organisations that produced and reproduced it, (b) more or less well defined objects and boundaries, and (c) its own language and texts. In the Nordic countries, emerging consumer policy fulfilled in this sense all the criteria Henri Lefebvre has set for 'the subsystem of everyday life' (Lefebvre, 1971) – an idea very close to the Foucauldian idea of 'social discourse'.

Although almost everyone was convinced that something would have to be done for the benefit of consumers, here again new controversies emerged. In general, the representation of commerce and business wanted these measures to be on a voluntary basis; in contrast, consumer organisations and leftist parties preferred a state-based machinery protecting consumer interests. Their underlying argument was that people were unable to organise themselves purely on the basis of consumption. Therefore, what was needed was a state body that would watch over consumer interests.

There were already some state organs, namely Consumer Councils, handling certain consumption-related matters, mainly price questions and consumer information. They aimed at helping consumers cope rationally with markets. It was no accident that these bodies were in the beginning located among state organs dealing with social policy (Forbrukerrådet, 1978, 9–10). By focusing on price questions and consumer information, the Nordic Consumer Councils took over some tasks from existing voluntary associations that had been active in consumer affairs; otherwise they had 'a very low profile' in the beginning (Forbrukerrådet, 1978, 22). Later, in the 1960s, these councils attempted to awaken greater public concern for such matters. They began to consider themselves interest organisations of consumers and started to organise this field. Thanks to their efforts, the three social discourses mentioned in the previous section were transformed into a more coherent political discourse.

This new field was renamed 'consumer policy'. This referred to 'measures carried out by the state alone or together with voluntary associations' aimed at 'improving the citizens' position in the consumption of goods' and increasing consumer influence in relation to private economy (Forbrukerrådet, 1978, 23). These tasks were connected to the promotion of general social welfare, but this was still considered an autonomous field of societal policy rather than part of social or economic policy. Its special function was 'the surveillance and promotion of consumer interests in the purchase and use of goods' (Komiteanmietintö, 1972, 76, 124).

Because consumer policy was now seen as a distinct field, it was considered important for it to have institutions of its own. They were organised differently in each Nordic country. In Sweden, governmental control was ensured by amalgamation of all consumer institutions in a National Board of Consumer Policy (Konsumentverket). In Finland, consumer affairs (Elinkeinohallitus/Kuluttaja-asiain osasto) were financially subordinated to the Ministry of Industry and Commerce, but were permitted organisational autonomy. The Finnish Consumer Council became a consumer organisation based on member organisations and individual consumers. The Norwegian solution was a compromise between the Finnish and Swedish models: an independent consumer organisation without individual members. It is worth noting that representatives from industry, wholesalers and retailers were not invited to take part in the new consumers' organisations and institutions. Consumers and business have different and often opposite interests in the market, and the compromise between consumers and producers–retailers, it was argued, should not be made within the consumers' organisations, but in the market.

After the passing of new consumer protection laws in the 1970s, the significance and strength of consumer organisations grew in all Nordic countries. One indication of this was the founding of Consumer Ombudsman institutions, official bodies implementing and supervising the application of consumer laws. Committee reports and consumer political bodies identified as the main target of this policy 'the consumer and his/her interests'. By 'consumers', they meant individuals as agents in commodity markets and users of public services. Consumer policy was thus seen as a complementary element of social policy, as the latter had been charged solely with the production of welfare services. In this sense, clearly, consumer policy was kept apart from people's roles as citizens and wage workers, but at the same time it was regarded as complementary to social rights (Komiteanmietintö, 1972, 126–7; Forbrukerrådet, 1978, 23).

Consumer interests, in turn, were understood in the same way as citizenship rights were seen in welfare theory (cf. Roche, 1992; Culpitt, 1992): as four kinds of rights. These were the right to consumption resources, to participation in decision making in production, to consumer choice, and to consumer protection (Komiteanmietintö, 1972, 134–6; Kivivuori *et al.*, 1978, 13–16). That consumer interests were understood in this way answers the question of which bodies should be charged with promoting these rights. They include voluntary organisations, but because these suffer from a lack of resources, responsibility is delegated mainly to the state. Official consumer policy, as it was called, had to promote consumer interests directly with respect to the markets.

How broad consumer policy should be was for a long time an open question, but after the determination of how consumer policy was to be enacted this problem was partly solved. The most important means of realising consumer policy became consumer information, consumer research, consumer protection and consumer advocacy. The first three aspects of consumer policy are perhaps readily understood, but the last needs some further clarification. It includes activities ranging from statements made by the state and governmental bodies to the preparation of consumer legislation (Komiteanmietintö, 1972, 137–8). The aim was for consumer bodies to be equally influential as interest organisations were in economic life (Forbrukerrådet, 1978, 24). In order to exert influence in consumer affairs, official consumer bodies had to produce their own texts – which they did with devotion. From the 1960s onwards there emerged many texts: juridical and related texts, consumer information (consumer bulletins, leaflets, posters, and so on) and reports on consumer research.

## THE PRODUCTION OF 'THE CONSUMER' IN POLITICAL DISCOURSE

There seem to be four aspects of the consumer which are of particular relevance in the formation of consumer policy. These are the relation of the consumer to: (a) him- or herself,

(b) each other, (c) producers and the state, and (d) the ecological environment. We will restrict our discussion to points (b) and (c) because, as our previous studies show, these are the most contested areas of Nordic consumer policy. This makes these dimensions the most prone to change with developments in general social policy.

In the first and second period of Nordic consumer policy, from 1935 to 1957, consumer policy was developed within the paradigm of consumer-controlled production (Rask-Jensen, 1986). Official consumer documents did not emphasise the conflict between consumers and market, nor did they stress basic consumer problems related to market activity. Although these documents did not see consumers as sovereign in the market, it was a common understanding that they would benefit from the market economy. The main consumer problem related to the market was lack of information about goods and services. This problem could be solved through consumer magazines, product labelling, product testing and consumer education in schools. Educated, informed consumers were regarded as the best guarantee of rational consumer behaviour.

In the next period, from 1957 to 1977, the relationship between consumers and the market was seen as more problematic, for three reasons: (a) consumers were not as rational and informed as economic theories had assumed, (b) there was lack of competition in the market due to strong monopolies, and (c) consumers had difficulties in influencing the supply and quality of consumer goods. For these reasons, in both Norwegian and Swedish official consumer documents governmental officials argued against classical economic theories (SOU, 1971, 37; Stortingsmelding, [1977–8]). A Swedish commission discussed the need for a new consumer policy in 1971 as follows:

'The household does not hold a very strong position in the economic interplay. The scope for rationalisation is limited as the household is a small scale enterprise. It is one of the duties of consumer policy to counter this weakness arising from the small scale production of the household, another to guard the interests of the household in the interplay between the different factors. (SOU, 1971, 28)

In this consumer political discourse, the market is not only the friend of the consumer, it is at the same time a potential enemy. Consumers, although they function as 'small scale enterprise[s]', are seen as weak actors on the market who need protection against sellers and producers. This change in discourse in the late 1960s resulted in new consumer legislation and new consumer institutions during the next decade.

The 1970s saw consumer protection and consumer policy placed on the agenda. This created a new paradigm in consumer policy, 'producer-controlled consumption' (Rask-Jensen, 1986). Producers were now seen as the strongest actor on the market. They decide both the production and demand of consumer goods and services through advertising and product promotion. Thus, there was a need not only to protect consumers but also to increase their influence on the market mechanism. In the Nordic countries, Marketing Control Acts were passed, and a new body, the Consumer Ombudsman, was established to enforce this legislation. Consumers were protected against offensive marketing by the new Door Sales Act, and the right to seek redress was strengthened by radical changes in the Purchase Acts in all the Nordic countries (Graver, 1986; Bjarköy, 1993).

The discourse about relations among consumers contains many different elements. First of all there is the question: Is it possible to distinguish consumers from other actors in the market? Do all consumers have the same interests? In the Nordic consumer discourse, the answer to the first question is 'yes', to the second 'no'.

First, consumers could be divided into many different groups and along different dimensions. It was seen to be possible to distinguish between producer–consumers (consumers who earn the money) and mere consumers ('pure' money spenders) (Aas, 1966). Another common way to distinguish consumer groups from each other was to use variables such as age, sex, income, occupation and education. The differences between consumers and consumer groups were emphasised in the consumer political discourse of the 1970s. Consumer policy was to focus on questions relevant to consumers with special problems in the market. This approach is clear in the Swedish document *Konsumentpolitik* of 1971 (SOU, 1971, 37, 27):

This can well apply in particular regarding those groups who have to subsist on very limited means: low income groups, disabled people and so on.

The same framework was developed in Norway, where the concept of the weak consumer was introduced (Stortings-melding, 1977–8). Some consumers are weak, in terms of re-sources, knowledge, information and skills in the market. The task of consumer policy was to protect the interests of weak consumers. For example, children had to be protected against flammable textiles, but the same standard was not required for clothes of adult consumers. In the Norwegian Marketing Control Act consumers were also protected against sex dis-crimination in advertising (Sverdrup and Stø, 1992). Although couched as a gender-neutral provision, in practice this article was aimed to protect women against sexist advertising. The idea of the weak consumer was also reflected in the way the Norwegian Consumer Council was organised. Many of the members appointed to the Consumer Council came from or-ganisations representing such weak consumer groups as the elderly, women, the single, youth, and disabled people (Stø, 1984, 1989).

However, according to the Nordic consumer political dis-course, consumers have not only different interests in the market. It was also maintained that there existed common consumer interests. Consumers had them against producers, sellers and advertisers. It was, however, difficult to formulate this principle in official documents, and especially to explain it. This was done by official consumer advocates in the 1971 Swedish document *Konsumentpolitik* as follows:

It is a well-known fact that in many significant respects, in matters of diet for example, these pretensions can be alto-gether too modest. As in other public sectors the needs here must be formulated in terms of norms, based on the community's ambitions regarding the well-being of the individual. (SOU, 1971)

This statement also reflects the Nordic paternalism of the 1970s, which continued, to a certain degree, to characterise the consumer discourse until the next phase in consumer policy.

## THE FATE OF NORDIC CONSUMER POLICY

The most recent period of consumer policy started in the early 1980s that marked the beginning of the process of deregulation and decentralisation in consumer policy. The need for regulating the market and protecting the consumer has been countered by an international movement towards deregulation. This movement became a political force as early as the late 1970s, especially in North America and Western Europe. It is also reflected in the official documents of consumer policy in the Nordic countries. This period has seen a renewal of emphasis upon the market mechanism on the part of policy makers. Since the collapse of Communist rule in the former Eastern bloc, it has been commonly maintained that markets are the most effective way to make an economic system work (see SOU, 1985, 32, 185).

One apparent conclusion from this view is that all rules and state institutions that aim to regulate markets should be reduced to a minimum. Because the welfare state and its institutions have been among the most important elements in the Nordic setting that have protected people from the distortions created by markets, advocates of market liberalism launched an open attack against it in the 1980s. Their message was mostly political in nature. They claimed that the welfare state meant, at least partly, ineffective use of national resources, that it had a demoralising effect, and that it impeded the free functioning of labour markets. By the end of the decade, all of the Nordic nations had entered a deep economic recession and experienced fiscal problems. This provided market liberals with a good reason to advocate the tearing down the structures of the welfare state and the related state elements. This was also mirrored in consumer policy.

New winds in politics were reflected in official documents on consumer policy although, as mentioned earlier, the chosen policy progressed slowly, as can be seen from the passing of some special consumer political legislation (for example, the product safety law, the consumer credit law and the improvement in the legal standing of house buyers.) (Finnish Consumer Council, 1983, 47). It was still admitted that 'households are generally speaking in a worse off position in relation to enterprises' (SOU, 1985, 32, 66) and that there existed 'weak' consumer groups that deserved special attention. These facts were, however, not interpreted as having been caused by failures of the market mechanism, but by the fact that households were unorganised, irrational and under the pressure of heavy marketing (SOU, 1985, 66–7; Finnish Consumer Council, 1983, 4). Therefore, it was not necessary to protect them so much as to 'strengthen their possibilities to effectively use their resources', because they still were seen as 'small-scale firms' (SOU, 1985, 72). In other words, the problems of households are not external to them, but located within them, in their non-rational way of functioning.

The political conclusions of the new consumer political discourse proved unexpectedly complex. Tendencies varied within each Nordic country. The large differences were counterbalanced by some similarities. First, in the consumer political strategy consumer information was given priority over consumer protection. This suited the new aim of improving the resources of households and of increasing the efficiency of their use of these resources (Finnish Consumer Council, 1983, 10–20; SOU, 1985, 32, 74). Secondly, it was suggested that consumer political institutions in the Nordic countries should be reorganised and pared down radically. There was also the recommendation that the Consumer Ombudsman institution, which had been created to supervise the adaptation of consumer protection laws, be separated from the rest of consumer political administration. This was done in Finland, but not in Norway and Sweden. In these two countries, however, there are currently plans to weaken the position of other consumer institutions.

One alternative to these reorganisations was suggested: support for local and voluntary solutions (SOU, 1985, 32, 74, 107–8). The only problem foreseen in this strategy was that there were no voluntary organisations or movements primarily concerned with consumer matters. Nor was it clear how these could be created at the grass roots level. The only alternative available to those making recommendations for a new policy was to lean on existing mass movements like trade unions and consumer cooperative movements, but there were also some doubts as to how well these would articulate consumer interests (SOU, 1985, 194–5).

To sum up, the latest phase has seen three general trends in the discourse on Nordic consumer policy. These are the stress (a) on market mechanism and competition, (b) on local and voluntary consumer organisations, and (c) on consumer information. In consumer policy this change has meant a return towards the paradigm of consumer-controlled production. But due to the strength of the Nordic model of the welfare state, consumer protection laws have remained in force. Therefore, the emerging paradigm is a mixture of old and new, what in Rask-Jensen's terms could be called 'an interdependence between production and consumption' (1986, 396).

According to the new view, consumer needs are not automatically reflected in the shopping process. Producers are able to influence consumer choice, but in the long run they will have to meet basic consumer needs. In a sense, there emerges a balance in the market. Consumers and producers keep each other in check. This is possible only to the extent that consumers are adequately informed. That is a necessary, albeit insufficient prerequisite for a balance between producers and consumers, because consumers are still seen as the weaker partner in this relationship. Therefore, consumer protection is also needed. However, this should not be too comprehensive, lest the free functioning of the market mechanism be disturbed. The Nordic countries will thus have to abandon some of their most far-reaching laws and directives concerning, for example, product safety.

These changes in the Nordic consumer political model can easily be interpreted as an anticipation of and adaption to the current consumer policy of the European Union. According to EU consumer policy programmes, other resolutions and consumer directives, such as the right to choose and to be informed, are given higher priority than the right to be heard and the right to safety (Stø, 1990; 1991, 15–17). Consumer influence within the EU is thought to be ensured through the market mechanism and through independent consumer organisations. Consumer protection, in turn, is to be handled by certain official organisations of the EU.

The process described raises the question of whether it is still meaningful to speak of the Nordic model of consumer policy (Federspiel, 1993). There is no clear answer to this. It seems evident that there will be some changes in Nordic consumer policy. In 1993–4 Swedish consumer policy was evaluated by a committee set up by the government, and in its final report some dramatic changes were proposed (SOU, 1994, 14). But since then, elections have been held in Sweden, and the new social-democratic government has withdrawn the proposals made by the former centre-right government. In Norway, a governmental committee started (October 1994) an evaluation of Norwegian consumer policy, and a report was expected to be made to the Ministry of Consumer Affairs in June 1995. The final result of this process depends on the recently completed negotiations between the EU on the one hand, and Finland, Norway and Sweden on the other. These countries signed the EEA agreement in 1993, and Finland and Sweden are now members of the EU. Since 1987–8, the Nordic governments have for long looked to Brussels when making important political decisions, even in the field of consumer policy, and the gap between Nordic and European consumer policy has been narrowed.

The contradiction between market and protection has to a certain degree been replaced by a positive interdependence between market economy and consumer policy in official consumer documents. This change in the consumer paradigm does not mean a return to the 1950s, however. The balance between market and state has been established at a new level, compared with the consumer policy of the first decade after the Second World War.

## References

Aas, B., *Forbrukeren i det moderne samfunnet* (Oslo and Bergen: Universitetsforlaget, 1966).

Adorno, T. and Horkheimer, M., *Dialectic of Enlightenment* (Thetford: Verso, 1979).

Bernitz, U., 'Guidlines Issued by the Consumer Board: The Swedish experience', *Journal of Consumer Policy*, 7 (1984), 161–5.

Bjarköy, T. F., 'Consumers Rights Access to Justice', in Stø, E. (ed.), *Consumer Policy in the Nordic and Baltic Countries* (Copenhagen: Nordic Council of Ministries, 1993).

Böök, S-A. and Ilmonen, K., 'Problems of Contemporary Cooperatives: Consumer cooperatives in Sweden and Finland 1960–80', *Economic and Industrial Democracy*, 10 (1989), 499–515.

Culpitt, I., *Welfare and Citizenship* (London: Sage, 1992).

216 *Nordic Consumer Policy*

Esping-Andersen, G., *The Three Worlds of Welfare Capitalism* (Cambridge: Polity, 1990).

Federspiel, B., 'Consumer Policy and Consumer Organisation', in Stø, E. (ed.), *Consumer Policy in the Baltic and Nordic Countries* (Copenhagen: Nordic Council of Ministries, 1993).

Finnish Consumer Council, *Consumer Political Programme* (Helsinki, 1983).

Forbrukerrådet, *Forbrukerrådet 25 år* (Oslo, 1978).

Foucault, M., *The Archaeology of Knowledge* (London: Tavistock, 1972).

Graver, K., 'A Study of the Consumer Ombudsman Institution in Norway with Some References to the Other Nordic Countries, I, Background and Descriptions', *Journal of Consumer Policy*, 9 (1986), 1–23.

Helenius, R., *Konsumera allt och alla* (Stockholm: Raben & Sjögren, 1974).

Ilmonen, K., *The Enigma of Membership* (Helsinki: KK-Kooperativa Institutet, 1986).

Ilmonen, K., 'From Consumer Problems to Consumer Anomie', *Journal of Consumer Policy*, 10 (1987), 25–37.

Ilmonen, K. and Suomela, K., 'Poliittinen kuva kuluttajapolitiikasta', in Suomela, K. and Ilmonen, K. (eds), *Kuluttakoon ken voi!* (Helsinki: Tammi, 1987).

Israel, J., *Välfärdsamhället–och därefter* (Stockholm: Aldusserien, 1969).

Kivivuori, A., af Schulten, C.G., Sevonand, L. and Tala, J., *Kuluttajansuoja* (Helsinki: Tammi, 1978).

Komiteanmietintö, *Kuluttajapolitiikan suunnittelukomitean mietintö* (Helsinki, A 26, 1972).

Laurila, E. and Kallinen, T., *Consumption in Finnish Economy in the Years 1900–75* (Helsinki: The Research Institute of the Finnish Economy B 42, 1985).

Lefebvre, H., *Everyday Life in the Modern World* (New York and London: Harper Torchbooks, 1971; New Brunswick: Transaction Books, 1984).

Packard, V., *The Waste Makers* (Aylesbury: Pelican Books, 1967).

Rask-Jensen, H., 'The Relevance of Alternative Paradigms as Guidelines for Consumer Policy and Organised Consumer Action', *Journal of Consumer Policy*, 9 (1986), 389–406.

Riihinen, O., 'Sosiaalipolitiikka ja legitimiteetti', in Riihinen, O. (ed.), *Sosiaalipolitiikka 2017* (Helsinki: WSOY, 1992).

Roche, M., *Rethinking Citizenship* (Cambridge: Polity Press, 1992).

SOU, *Konsumentpolitik–riktlinjer och organisation* (1971) 37.

SOU, *Reklam II* (Stockholm: Liber, 1972).

SOU, *Hushållning för framtid*, Betänkande av konsumentpolitiska kommitten (Stockholm: Liber, 1985), 32.

SOU, *Konsumentpolitik i en ny tid* (Stockholm: Civildepartementet, 1994), 14.

Stø, E., 'Forbrukerinnflytelse og forbrukerorganisering', in Grønmo, S. (ed.), *Forbruker, marked og samfunn* (Oslo: Universitetsforlaget, 1984).

Stø, E., 'Norsk forbrukerpolitikk fra kjøkken til marked og samfunn', in Bergan, E. *et al.* (eds), *Forbruksforskning i går – i dag og i morgen* (Lysaker: SIFO femti år, 1989).

Stø, E., *Forbrukerpolitikk under press*, Report no. 4 (Lysaker: SIFO, 1990).

Stø, E., *Forbrukernes Europa?* – *en studie av forbruker-konsekvenser av en nordisk harmonisering til EFs forbrukerpolitik* (Copenhagen: Nordic Council of Ministers, Nord:31, 1991).

Stortingsmelding, 44, *Om forbrukerpolitikken* (Oslo, 1977–8).

Sverdrup, S. and Stø, E., 'Regulation of Sex Discrimination in Advertising: An empirical inquiry into the Norwegian case', *Journal of Consumer Policy,* 14 (1992), 371–91.

# 11 Designing the Good Life: Nutrition and Social Democracy in Norway

Thor Øivind Jensen and
Unni Kjærnes

## WELFARE STATE PATERNALISM AND THE CONSUMER SOCIETY

The knowledge of experts is commonly used to help citizens approach a scientifically determined good life. Such help can be paternalistic and take several forms. The broadest and most complicated relation between the daily life of the citizen and expert activity takes place in consumption activities. Consumer rights, which closely resemble those of the general citizen, are defined (Kennedy, 1962) as rights to protection, information, choice and channels for feedback. Foodstuffs are especially important in the everyday lives of consumers. Nutrition policy, therefore, has a strong potential impact on daily life, habits and private values. At the same time, food as a commodity is important to industry and other production interests.

In this chapter,[1] we will discuss early and contemporary variants of paternalism based on the social democratic mix of scientific optimism and socialist ideology. The Nordic welfare states were built under the strong influence of social-democratic political ideology, an ideology that links expertise with state regulation of markets and individuals. We shall discuss two kinds of expert involvement in consumer policy. In the first, experts attempt to influence consumer behaviour on the basis of their more 'informed' position. In the other, experts play a central role in market regulation. An understanding of both of these aspects will require an analysis of differences between the early developmental period and the later, more mature, institutionalised welfare state system.

The Norwegian 'Joint programme' to which all political parties after the Second World War were committed was a kind of social contract to promote harmony and cooperation. It manifested strong agreement on the principle that basic welfare rights were the state's responsibility. Seen from the point of view of citizens, the 'joint programme' implied that the individual could rely more on public services for child care, education, and help in critical situations. The rapid extension of state involvement introduced a 'social-democratic' paternalism which became embedded in many aspects of daily life. The client of the welfare services became subordinated to a system characterised by professionalisation, specialisation, and bureaucratisation (Dahl, 1983). The role of this state 'system' in relation to the individual was rather strong, when compared with classic liberalism, but this was seldom a matter of political or academic debate. In the 1980s, however, the tight bonds between the state and professions came to be criticised in terms of neo-liberal and individualistic distrust of bureaucracy and state.

While issues of production have been an explicit focus of contestation and organisation for over a century – involving political parties, laws and regulations, huge interest organisations and a cultural basis for understanding interests, conflicts and bargaining – in comparison, consumer interests have been quite neglected. The role of the consumer, which has been relatively disregarded in Scandinavian political culture, has only recently come to be seen as very important for well-being and happiness. The high consumption levels typical of affluent countries mean that more decisions affecting daily life are taken by, or in cooperation with, formalised public or private supplier institutions. There is now a contrast between established political culture and daily-life roles and interests. Political culture, both in Parliament and in the corporate–pluralist channels, lend most of its support to supply-side interests (owners and workers in production). The relatively weak, state organised and paternalistic consumer movement in the otherwise highly participatory Nordic countries underlines the fact that consumer interests are not a major factor in the political culture (Jensen, 1993b). Dependence on the public apparatus of the welfare state represents an area of the expert regulation of daily life, relatively unimpeded by the counterbalance of consumer influence (Dahl, 1983).

## SCIENCE AND STATE POWER: THE IDEA OF HYGIENE

In the 1930s when the Nordic welfare state system emerged, market disturbances, hunger and war characteristic of liberal market-based industrialism, created conditions for strong government. Belief in the power of science and 'scientific' answers to most problems in politics, economy and private life was common (Seip, 1989). Wide-ranging planning based on these beliefs seemed natural. The distinctive political movements of this period – communism, fascism and social-democracy – shared basic assumptions on the role of expertise and the individual and departed radically from liberal ideology. In particular, they shared a belief in strong state involvement, both in markets and in private life. Further, they each espoused a 'scientifically based' policy and the use of experts and planning in a new and large-scale state apparatus. To some extent, they also had a joint vision of a 'welfare' society with social security and strong state obligations regarding essential needs, together with ideas for linking organisations (for example, labour unions) and experts to the state through corporative arrangements. Of course, there are important differences, especially between fascism and the two others, but the parallels illustrate important aspects of the political culture.

On the communist left, science was heavily emphasised. This movement argued for a scientifically-based construction both of a new society and a 'socialist human being'. Modern science emphasised that people were influenced by social forces, which fitted well with classical Marxism. Changes in the social and physical environment, it was argued, could raise the masses to new levels of achievements in health, education, production, art, culture, family life and ethics. Social-democrats made a similar link between science and politics. They adopted arguments from the communists on topics like health, nutrition, the importance of education and the strategy of influencing individuals through collective organisations. However, as their aim was reform rather than revolution, they had stronger interest in finding practical ways to handle and organise a society that gradually could bring 'welfare to all'. The social-democratic goal of regulating dynamic markets according to social goals requires a specific expertise different from that of the 'total central control' approach of communism and fascism. Norwegian economists from the late 1930s played a major role in making Keynesian ideas operational, eventually resulting in a macroeconomic planning system (and two Nobel prizes). Scientific work and policy plans attempted to bridge the gap between private life and macroeconomics. The aims of nutrition, housing and full employment became parameters in the macroeconomic models used in governmental planning (Sandmo, 1991).

Several issues of public debate legitimised political involvement in private life: especially in education, housing, upbringing of children, alcohol, food, sexuality and family life. One issue linking politics and private life had particular importance, that of hygiene. Hygiene encompassed sickness prevention and health promotion. In this century, bacteriology and cleanliness have become important for linking individual health to social conditions and state responsibility. The idea of keeping contagions out of the body was itself contagious: easily understandable and catching, as well as sensible and ethical. Helped by the radical group 'Towards Dawn' – an elite group of communist academics and scientists which included a number of members who went on to become leading politicians and public administrators – and others, the idea of hygiene was extended.[2] The political (and paternalistic) concern for the quality of the population was important. For socialists, the causes and remedies for bad health were turned into social and political problems. Even morality in families became a political matter (Jones, 1986; Schmidt and Kristensen, 1986). This was evident in the way that social hygiene and sexual hygiene were taken as indicative of a clean and orderly life which, in turn, would prevent diseases, such as syphilis, psychiatric disorders and alcoholism. Hygiene became a symbol of how knowledge made it sensible and natural to bring politics and science into the private sphere. This political aspect of hygiene was followed by intense activities directed towards individuals and organisations. The masses were to be educated to obtain a better life. Hygiene was approached from several angles: health and mental hygiene and also birth control for a working class with restricted resources. The last element also included women's liberation and their ability to exert control over their own lives. This had some very positive implications for the health and welfare of most people, but also clearly points to paternalism and elitism.


NUTRITION POLICY

In the 1930s, nutrition had for some time been a central theme within hygiene. The goal was to influence people towards 'rational' dietary practices. This 'rationality' was based on scientific knowledge: economy, nutrition and 'scientific household routines'. The image of the 'modern housewife' was closely linked to hygiene (Schmidt and Kristensen, 1986). Also underlining the importance of living conditions, these rational household ideals were adopted by leftists. In addition to welfare and education, a third perspective of market regulation should also be added. Since the First World War, views on state intervention in markets changed; regulatory measures gradually developed. This is mostly due to the farmers, who have traditionally been a strong and influential political force in Norway (Jacobsen, 1968). When dairy farming, Norway's most important agricultural production, faced increasing problems of surplus and falling prices in the 1920s, they increased pressure for support and protection from the state. Farmers stressed their important task in ensuring national food supplies, linking their interests to national independence and nation-building. To emphasise how volatile the situation was, one government was forced out of office over an issue regarding margarine.

Conflict over social security and poor relief was aggravated in the inter-war period. The controversy over this issue in the early 1930s was instrumental for bringing nutrition policy onto the political agenda (Kjærnes, 1993). During the depression in the 1920s and early 1930s, food and nutrition arguments were linked to poor relief provided to the unemployed. Protests and indignation increased when 'The Menu of the Ministry of Justice' was presented. This menu consisted mainly of foods of low cultural and sensory esteem.[3] The Ministry was advised by nutritional experts, who had developed dietary schemes meant to satisfy nutritional needs at a minimum level. Restrictions were expressed in other ways as well. Relief had normally been delivered in cash, but now relief in kind or as food coupons became common. In this way, the authorities could control consumption and help local food producers. Relief in kind was flatly refused on the political Left and in the labour movement. This must be seen as an antipaternalistic reaction. Relief in kind was regarded as an unacceptable restriction of the individual's freedom of choice.

The Association of Socialist Physicians under its leader Karl Evang was instrumental for refomulating the opposition into a question of nutrition. Evang and associates had performed studies of dietary habits and nutrition among unemployed and low-income families (Evang and Hansen, 1937). The correlation between income and nutritional intake was underlined. 'Protective' foods – a concept of 'nutrition' within the hygiene tradition, but neglected by ministry officials, comprising a diet of whole milk, fruits and vegetables – were too expensive for low-income families. The study became a serious critique of the relief programme and its scientific basis. The critique was immediately regarded as part of working class politics, and it obtained considerable attention in public debate (Nordby, 1989). The Leftist perspective won the battle, while the minimum approach implied in the Food list from the Ministry of Justice, lost most of its legitimacy.

Soon after this incident nutrition was accepted by the Social-Democratic Labour Party as a new issue that needed attention. They had taken over government in 1935, and Evang was asked to write a nutrition policy programme. Nutrition was presented and documented as an extensive social problem, linked mainly to economic resources in the families, and a lack of knowledge and motivation.

The solutions proposed were different kinds of state actions. Improved social security systems and support to the unemployed were relevant, but mostly the aspect of production came into focus. This shift of attention had several causes. Nutritional standards had been developed parallel to standards on other aspects of living conditions, such as housing. These standards, were incorporated into macro-economic planning. Dietary recommendations pointed towards a steep increase in milk consumption (and production) (Sandmo, 1991). This was a radical attitude when the market problem was seen to be one of surplus due to low purchasing power.

The emphasis on production issues can also be explained by the political situation in the 1930s. The Social-Democratic Labour Party sought political support from agricultural labourers and small farmers. The Labour government had come into power in 1935 through support from the Agrarian Party. Measures to raise welfare, while simultaneously supporting a crisis-ridden industry, were received with enthusiasm. Nutrition became 'a good cause' and an instrument in directing consumption according to the needs of production interests. The government put priority on state support for production of foods that were both needed for health reasons in the working class and supported agriculture. Urban and rural interests were linked together along with health science and welfare, all within the framework of national independence and Keynesian macroeconomics.

Belief in state involvement, economic planning, and harmony and cooperation between different interests all pointed towards a corporative system of implementation, based on representation, organisation and negotiation. A National Nutrition Council, with Evang at its head, was established in 1946 with representatives from different branches of the food industry, different ministries and experts. Its main task was to make plans for food supply regarding nutritional needs (Lien, 1990).

Educational tasks had not been forgotten. They were the responsibility of the school system, public health institutions and home economists, not the nutrition policy bodies. Nutrition information and its reference to scientific advice had a strong paternalistic flavour. Concern for national food producers was emphasised. Drinking milk promoted both health and agriculture.

In the 1950s and 1960s nutrition again created scientific and political conflict. This conflict and the resulting compromise clearly reveal the intrinsic ambiguity of Norwegian nutrition policy – with its emphasis on science and expertise, alliance with agriculture, lack of consumer representation and paternalistic tradition. Then, cardiovascular mortality rates for Norwegian men had risen by 40 per cent and had become the main cause of death among middle-aged men (Jensen, 1994). Coronary disease was linked to the fat intake, the main sources being dairy products and margarine. This time the new insights and the political challenge came from Conservative scientists and were mostly denied by health authorities. The new findings changed perceptions of nutrition: the total fat intake was now to be reduced considerably; milk, margarine, cheese and butter went from good to bad (Lien, 1990). Questioning, as it did, the existing alliances between health and agriculture, this was not easily accepted. Dairy producers reacted with anger. Among the sceptics was also Karl Evang. The fat hypothesis challenged central aspects of his welfare policy ideology.

It took more than ten years of debate and quests for a reformulated policy before the issue was put on the formal policy agenda. New policy goals were formulated in 1975 in a Report to parliament. The suggestions were not in line with the new knowledge. Nutrition again became an issue of agricultural policy, dealing with global food production and national self-sufficiency. The Report attempted to integrate the demands of conflicting interests through planning and coordination. The outcome was contradictory on several points. A main issue was dairy production and the impending fat surplus. The fat intake was to be reduced, but the ultimate goal was negotiated. The original expert advice of 30 per cent fat in the total diet (down about 10 per cent: a significant change) was moderated to 35 per cent of calories. This example shows that experts may even negotiate their recommendations in the face of interest conflicts. Intricate calculations were used to show that the dietary target could be obtained by reducing the consumption of imported fats. The total message was rather diffuse, but had a content like 'Eat less fat, but more butter' (Kjærnes, 1993).

Nutrition policy was confronted with problems even in pursuing these moderate goals of fat reduction through the corporative, negotiating system. Introduction of low-fat milk may serve as a case: starting in the 1960s, the National Nutrition

Council and consumer bodies demanded milk with less fat. The demand soon became a political issue. Low-fat milk was implemented after fifteen years and in several phases. The whole agricultural sector resisted. In the end, the dairy industry itself took an initiative, probably because the lack of a low-fat alternative threatened gross milk consumption. With nutrition and consumer interests only watching, there was a confrontation between the agriculture-based industry and the fat-hardening industry (including margarine) over how to handle the expected butter surplus. The dairy industry had its way and produced a new type of margarine–butter mix, which was eventually very successful on the market. For some variants they also tried to conceal the butter content from public knowledge (Jensen, 1994). Margarine composition at this time was regarded as less risky for health than butter, and this was a fact known to the public. The outcome was ambiguous. The final availability of low-fat milk was important, but the active marketing of butter in margarine was a problem. Consumers tried to behave in a healthy way by demanding low-fat products, but were obstructed by public food policy.

This points towards a nutrition policy and a food market controlled by agricultural interests. On the other hand, postwar consumption has dramatically improved nutritionally despite policy elements that suggest otherwise. The shift started in the 1960s and accelerated after 1985. A reduction in fat intake from 39 per cent to 34 per cent of caloric intake is an important result, indicating a better composition of the diet (Kjærnes, 1993). One explanation may be high public interest and knowledge regarding nutrition. A survey as early as the mid-1960s showed that most of the population knew the health problems associated with dietary fat. In formal policy, little happened in the 1970s; negotiating strategies only obscured the nutritional issues. In the 1980s, however, nutritional questions were brought back to the agenda. Policy contradictions were criticised, public debate increased and information campaigns focused more on nutritional improvements. Greater liberalism in food markets, ideological claims for individual freedom, greater health consciousness among consumers, increasing scepticism towards expertise, and a nutritional policy in transition now seems to have put food issues back onto the public agenda.

## CONSUMERS CAUGHT BETWEEN SCIENCE AND PRODUCER INTERESTS

We have discussed market regulation and expert influence as two sources of paternalism in the social-democratic tradition. Two phases can be identified. In the first, strong beliefs in expertise and planning went together with the ambition of influencing daily life. The means of achieving these goals involved connecting experts and planning, on the one hand, and political mobilisation and organisation, on the other. The second involves the institutionalisation of an established system around the new solutions. Centralised negotiations and expert advice derive their power from bureaucratic routines whose legitimacy was created in the early years. Political mobilisation of public interests declined as significant factors in the second phase.

Both macro planning and market regulation entail the danger of producer power coming to influence or even dominate policy making. The relevant 'client' may shift from the well-being of citizens to the interests of well-organised producer groups who are closer to the system. In studies of public policy the tendency for relatively weak interests to be captured or coopted is well documented. In the initial phase, when nutritional values were built into policies and planning, the health of citizens and producer interests were mutual, or at least not contradictory. In these circumstances, macroeconomic planning and the negotiating structure of agricultural policy may have seemed wise and logical. The need to protect health values against strong economic interests was less obvious. The risk of cooptation existed, but the consequences were not dramatic. The process of formal institutionalisation will in itself remove bureaucrats and experts away from political processes among clients and citizens.

One pessimistic conclusion, then, may be that successful health-oriented central planning requires compromising the interests of citizens with those of producers. Indeed, significant positive results are obtained when producers and consumers have parallel interests, which can be modified by political mobilisation. In the first phase, such mobilisation, combined with cultural and scientific developments, helped to make market regulation operational. Producers were not able simply to force their demands into policy.

Early social-democracy not only had high ambitions concerning regulation and replacement of market mechanisms; these ambitions also extended to people's private lives. Today, the paternalism of radical socialists in the 1930s may seem frightening; there was a thin wall between private and public space and few areas were immune to public action. However, the idea of scientific rule over private life was probably sensible in the 1930s. The evils of the free market and weak state were evident. Socialist planning was tightly linked to reforms, better living conditions, health and education (Hirdman, 1990). Elitist educational advice, popular information and designs for a good life were not hidden in governmental institutions. They were an open part of public debate and organised political work inside a socialist ideology. Strong belief in science, planning and state involvement was common and social-democracy was probably in its least authoritarian phase.

After the formation period, the huge modern welfare state system emerged. When a policy is left to professional experts inside formal bureaucracies, the links to popular movements fades. The health message will be diluted inside the responsible, negotiating, compromise culture that is the environment of the staff in their daily work. If health conflicts with other values, the public will probably only know the negotiated result. A professional bureaucracy may also direct focus away from popular organisation, mobilisation, information and discussion into more manipulative top-down methods. The very short-lived Norwegian proposal of establishing a 'Lifestyle Directorate' can be seen in this light along with the emphasis on educational science, psychology and professional marketing used in modern health promotion. The idea was to combine public bodies working with alcohol, narcotics, tobacco and nutrition into one Directorate. The proposal was withdrawn at the same time as it hit the headlines.

If one measure of paternalism is the number of people that, 'with the best of intentions', are occupied with monitoring and influencing daily life, then paternalism is stronger now than ever. Paternalism is difficult to counteract if the foundations of formal consumer or client rights are weak. It is typical of the welfare state that formal rights are weak as a resource for clients to use (Marshall, 1981). The lack of a role for the individually active and politically organised consumer is a feature of the second phase of institutionalisation.

## WHEN IS PATERNALISTIC POLICY BETTER THAN NOTHING?

The conclusion from the Norwegian experience of nutrition policy is that in the modern welfare state the role of scientific expertise is ambivalent. Modernity places high value on scientific rationality and the universalist idea of the 'public interest'. These ideals have been recognised throughout the political spectrum. Scientific rationality and public interest have been the common ground for accepting welfare state paternalism even in consumer policy, in spite of the simultaneous disrespect for consumer sovereignty.

However, in the production-centred society, expert knowledge is filtered through particular interests, in particular those of the producers. It has in some occasions been twisted to adjust to those interests and served to camouflage them as the public good. This has created a problem of trust that jeopardises the legitimacy of the welfare state as a whole.

In the new consumer society the violation of consumer sovereignty in the name of scientific rationality and public interest is no longer taken for granted. On both the political left and right, distrust in established bureaucracy and political parties, the desire to choose one's own life-style and a critical attitude towards institutionalised public services have become driving forces for political change (Held, 1987). It is easy to see contemporary neo-liberalism and its emphasis on individual freedom as the voice of an educated and affluent middle class. Even in the face of the fading legitimacy of modernity's core values, regulation, structural reforms and collectively organised politics may serve the interests of the ordinary consumer (Jensen, 1993b). However, paternalism is now difficult to defend, and we must therefore face the question: 'Under what conditions is institutionalised policy better than no policy at all?'

We have discussed the weak independent position of consumers in the social-democratic political culture, where they are often regarded as a subcategory of working class interests. Women's roles as consumers are important. Severely under-represented in the formal, full-time work force, they are typically in charge of running households and are especially dependent on the (weak) consumer role. More general cultural factors have also made women the main victims of the paternalism described in this chapter. The ambition of structuring daily life is especially directed towards women in their role as housewives. Some authors (Touraine, 1974; Melucci, 1990; Keane, 1988), have sought the answer to these problems in a new emphasis on the 'actor' and a free 'civic culture', seen from a different angle than that of classical liberalism, or its various contemporary manifestations in the 'new right'.

The establishment of early liberal political institutions took place in a period of uneducated masses. Few citizens had the necessary resources and experience for political work. Elitism had to be built into political life in most forms. In rich countries the situation is now very different. Education levels are high; indeed, evidence shows that the population was, for many years, much better informed than formal nutrition policy would have led them to be. Consumption patterns show evidence of a healthy judgement from the consumers. Tendencies to use less milk fat even had to be counteracted by special price reductions and advertising campaigns. Consumption of the bad-tasting cod-liver oil shows a pattern that fits well into changes in knowledge on its importance for health (Jensen, 1994). Even broader changes in food consumption (less fat, more vegetables) seem rather reasonable. Now, expectations of participation are high and resources of many relevant kinds are widespread. Free time, transportation possibilities, organising experiences and tools for communication and printing are everywhere. A natural solution would be more participation and freedom among citizens, and therefore a more important and independent civic culture with stronger claims on a less paternalistic state system.

Changing assumptions in many sciences, along with general cultural changes will further weaken those in the social sciences and politics who advocate top-down planning on the assumption of predictable behaviour. Based on new knowledge and shifting situations the policy content may shift dramatically. Salt was necessary to keep food fresh, now it is a health problem. Butter and other animal fats were an efficient source of calories but came to be regarded as a major health problem. Coffee, once regarded as dangerous, is now accepted, but may again turn into a health hazard. In such a dynamic area, is it wise to use institutionalised policies? Structures, bureaucracies, professions and negotiated solutions are very slow to change, they defend the original values that they were built around. Issues of consumer policy are moving in the direction of dynamic and unpredictable social processes outside the strong formal institutions and towards civic culture with all its ad hoc organisations, citizens' initiatives, self-help groups, semi-organisations and complicated patterns of trust and distrust.

Market regulation arrangements are also developing in new directions. The old national licensing regulation agency is no longer the model. An important European trend is acceptance of market freedom and international harmonisation. This is then balanced out by giving the consumers formal individual rights to protection and giving general guidelines in declarations on values like safety, information and participation (Jensen, 1993a).

Our discussion of expert involvement in the food and health sphere suggests one hypothesis regarding how and when such involvement is acceptable. If expertise is removed from civic culture and isolated in bureaucratic and professional institutions, its influence easily becomes undemocratic and its aim of serving the citizen shrouded. If experts have to negotiate goals and remain loyal to their position in the corporatist–pluralist culture, their expert ability and legitimacy of action is compromised. People are then manipulated according to an unclear balance of values negotiated by the equally unclear elite or 'new class' of politicians, bureaucrats and experts, which have each other as clients. On the other hand, if experts have their legitimation based in living civic culture and political mobilisation, and their organisational setting gives them a firm platform independent from other parts of public policy, their acceptability is higher and the risk of manipulation against the interests of ordinary people is smaller. These issues are especially important for the consumer role due to the contrast between its very weak position in social-democratic culture and its importance for modern daily life. A strong consumer role built on pluralistic activity patterns, making claims and alliances with experts within a suitable ideological framework, would be logical and link modern consumer culture to the political system.

## Notes

1. We wish to thank Ralf Helenius, John Holmwood, Dietrich Rueschemeyer and Pekka Sulkunen for valuable comments on this chapter.
2. One of its most important figures was Karl Evang (1902–81). Evang was a doctor who engaged very successfully in public debate and agitation for improvements in working class health. He eventually became head of the Health Directorate in 1938, a post he held until 1972. He was active in the formation of the World Health Organisation (see Nordby, 1989).
3. The menu consisted of potatoes, grain (but little wheat), salted herring and pork, some margarine, sugar and skimmed milk. When distributed in kind, the foods were often of poor quality (see Kjærnes, 1993).

## References

Dahl, T. S., 'Forholdet mellom individuelle motiver og kollektive interesser i sosialpolitikken', *Nordisk Sosialt Arbeid*, 3 (1983) 3–14.

Evang, K. and Hansen, O. G., *Norsk kosthold i små hjem* (Oslo: Tiden, 1937).

Held, D., *Models of Democracy* (London: Free Press, 1987).

Hirdman, Y. *Att lägga livet till rätta – studier i svensk folkhemspolitik* (Stockholm: Carlsson Bokförlag, 1990).

Jacobsen, K. D., 'Public Administration under Pressure: The role of the experts in the modernization of traditional agricultrue' *Scandinavian Political Studies*, 10 (1968).

Jensen, T. Ø., *Safety in Services* (Bergen and Paris: Centre for Social Science and OECD, 1993a).

Jensen, T. Ø., 'Nutrition: A dilemma in the politics of food', in Kjærnes, U. *et al.* (eds), *Regulating Markets – Regulating People. On food and nutrition policy* (Oslo: Novus Forlag, 1993b).

Jensen, T. Ø., 'The Political History of Norwegian Nutrition Policy', in Burnett, J. and Oddy, D. J. (eds), *The Origins and Development of Food Policies in Europe* (Leicester: Leicester University Press, 1994).

Jones, G., *Social Hygiene in Twentieth Century Britain* (London: Croom Helm, 1986).

Keane, J., *Civil Society. New European perspectives* (New York: Verso, 1988).

Kennedy, J. F., 'Special Message on Protecting the Consumer Interest' 15 March (Washington, DC, Government Printing Office, 1962).

Kjærnes, U., 'A Sacred Cow. The case of milk in Norwegian nutrition policy', in Kjærnes, U. *et al.* (eds), *Regulating Markets – Regulating People. On food and nutrition policy* (Oslo: Novus Forlag, 1993).

Lien, M., *The Norwegian Nutrition and Food Supply Policy: Accomplishments and limitations of a structural approach, SIFO Report,* 4 (Oslo: National Institute for Consumer Research, 1990).

Marshall, T. H., *The Right to Welfare* (London: Heinemann Educational 1981).

Melucci, A., 'Paradoxes of Postindustrial Democracy: Everyday life and social movements', paper presented at XII Sociology Congress (Madrid, 1990).

Nordby, T., *Karl Evang. En biografi* (Oslo: Aschehoug, 1989).

Sandmo, A., *Ragnar Frisch and the Optimal Diet,* LOS-Notat 91/32 (Bergen: LOS-senteret, 1991).

Schmidt, L. H. and Kristensen, J. E., *Lys, luft og renlighed. Den moderne social-hygiejnes fødsel* (Copenhagen: Akademisk Forlag, 1986).

Seip, A. L., 'The Influence of Science on Social Policy in Norway in the 1930s', presented at the conference *Welfare State in Transition* (Bergen: University of Bergen, 1989).

Touraine, A., 'Towards a Sociology of Action. The *raison d'être* of a sociology of action', in Giddens, A. (ed.), *Positivism and Sociology* (London: Heinemann, 1974).

# 12 The Construction of Environmental Risks: Eco-Labelling in the European Union

Peter Simmons

## ENVIRONMENT, SCIENCE AND POLICY IN THE RISK SOCIETY[1]

The long-run social and technological changes that have shaped consumer society have been accompanied, in the late twentieth century, by an increasing public awareness of and concern with the anthropogenic risks that accompany these developments. Traditional societies were faced with natural hazards such as famine, disease or drought, hazards visited by the hand of providence. Modernity promised an end to the rule of nature through the application of scientific knowledge and technique. But with one of history's inescapable ironies, the advance of modernisation has brought with it the proliferation of socially-produced risks. As the twentieth century has advanced these risks have become increasingly pervasive until, in their global implications, they far surpass the still-unconquered scourges of the past in their catastrophic potential. Today, as market relationships are insinuated into every sphere of our lives and the principle of consumer choice is declared to be sovereign, we are faced with a growing recognition that the market creates and circulates 'bads' as well as 'goods', and that the risks that threaten our well-being, and even our existence, are a product of human choices. With that recognition comes the anxiety that the consumer society's horn of plenty might ultimately prove to be the last trump.

There is a growing body of scholarship that draws attention to the sociological significance of risk and risk management in high modernity (see, for example, Short, 1984; Giddens,

1990; Luhmann, 1993). Risk has become constitutive of the social fabric of contemporary societies to the extent that we may speak of the emergence of a 'risk society' (Beck, 1992). Issues concerning the definition and distribution of risk – whether environmental risk, health risk or social risk – have become central arenas of struggle between diverse collective actors (Abel, 1985; Lau, 1992). It is very difficult, however, to represent these new agonistic relations in terms of a clear structure of conflict or to institutionalise them successfully, making coherent collective action increasingly difficult for all the parties involved (Lau, 1992). These controversies also change the relationship between scientific knowledge and public policy:

> the more scientific findings and arguments are used as strategic resources the more the idea of a technical and instrumental use of objective and definite scientific results becomes obsolete or even proves to be a social fiction. (Lau, 1992, 243)

The widespread public environmental concern that has emerged since the late 1960s can be seen as a manifestation of the inchoate anxiety arising from the culturally pervasive consciousness of risk (Erikson, 1990; Giddens, 1990). As arenas of collective action, environmental issues are characterised by shifting fields of conflict that constantly form and reform, and within which scientific knowledge is mobilised increasingly to strategic ends. The specific issues, technologies and products around which these anxieties and conflicts coalesce may be quite adventitious, shaped as much by social factors as by the existence of 'objective' risks; for example, by the opportunity structure created by institutional arenas such as public inquiries, by arena characteristics that render some issues inherently more 'winnable' for environmental NGOs, or by the occurrence of specific incidents that provide a focus for public concerns and collective action (Grove-White, 1993). Similarly, constructions of what are embraced by notions of 'environmental' or 'green' are also variable, both within and between national cultures. This culturally founded variability contrasts starkly with the realist discourses of environmental risk characteristic of science and policy institutions.

The social and cultural dimensions of environmental issues introduce ambiguities and tensions which frequently go un-recognised or unacknowledged by policy makers due to the realist framework within which they operate. The European Union's eco-labelling scheme, which is the focus of this chapter, is a case in point. Divergent problem constructions have given rise to tensions which have already surfaced in con-troversy and which threaten to undermine the credibility of the scheme. In this chapter, I examine the underlying tensions between differing constructions of environmental issues which have been brought to light by conflicts over the EU scheme, and their implications for eco-labelling as a response to the deepening environmental concern that has emerged in con-temporary consumer societies, with particular reference to the development of the scheme in the United Kingdom.

In brief, the argument put forward is that the eco-labelling mechanism is, and will continue to be, vulnerable to challenge because of the contestable nature of its embedded assump-tions: assumptions about the primacy of the market, about the nature of science, about the nature of environmental prob-lems and about the nature of environmental concern. I suggest that, whereas established institutional processes assume a realist stance both on the criteria for labelling prod-ucts as ecologically sound or unsound and on the basis of public environmental concern, problem definitions, scientific practices and public concern are all, in various ways, socially constituted. The point of this argument is not to deny the exis-tence of environmental risks but rather to draw attention to the fundamental uncertainties in our knowledge of these risks and in the social practices and relations with which they are bound up. The problems encountered by the EU eco-labelling scheme represent a challenge to the knowledge and practices which structure the search for environmental solutions, and to the socially produced 'closure' of the inherent indetermina-cies within technocratic discourses (for example, around notions of ecologically sound or unsound products). The cul-tural and moral dimensions of environmental problems and of environmental concern can erupt into the policy arena through controversies which often delineate deeper social ten-sions. In the remainder of this chapter, following a brief description of the EU eco-labelling scheme, I focus on one case where such tensions have emerged around the issue of animal testing of products, and examine its implications for environmental consumer policy.

## THE EU ECO-LABELLING SCHEME

June 1993 saw the official launch of the EU eco-labelling scheme. Eco-labelling aims to reduce the environmental risks and impacts associated with the operation of consumer markets. The EU scheme is based on a process for evaluating the environmental impact of a particular category of products using a technique known as life-cycle analysis (LCA). LCA is a form of technology assessment (TA) which assesses the environmental resource demands and environmental burden associated with each phase of a product's life cycle, 'from cradle to grave' as it is often expressed. On the basis of the LCA, environmental criteria are developed which are then used as the benchmark for deciding whether an individual product merits an eco-label. Designated national bodies select groups of products that are perceived to have a significant environmental impact, commission an LCA to establish the nature of those impacts throughout the product life-cycle and, subject to agreement at EU level, develop threshold criteria as the basis for awarding the eco-label to 'greener' products. Participation in the scheme by manufacturers is voluntary but the award of an eco-label is intended to inform consumers, on the basis of a disinterested scientific evaluation, that a product has relatively less environmental impact than similar unlabelled products. When first proposed the EU eco-labelling scheme was welcomed by many environmental and consumer groups as a means for enabling consumers to make informed choices about the environmental implications of their purchases. However, the attempt to get it off the ground has been fraught with political and technical difficulties and has been the subject of public controversy.

The EU eco-labelling scheme attempts to create a mechanism by means of which the environmental concern of consumers, guided by a scientific definition of ecologically sound and unsound consumer products, may be translated into market signals. The scheme's stated objectives are:

[(a)] to promote the design, production, marketing and use of products which have a reduced environmental impact during their entire life cycle; and [(b)] to provide consumers with better information on the environmental impact of products. (EEC, 1992, 2)

The second of these objectives was all the more pressing due to the flood of false and ill-founded environmental claims made by manufacturers and retailers in response to the upsurge of consumer concern in the late 1980s. The proliferation of misleading advertising and product labelling which claimed or implied that products were in some way 'environmentally friendly' was a major concern for many consumer and environmental groups at that time. Quite apart from the confusion created by spurious or inappropriate environmental claims, such labelling also fuelled public scepticism about the bona fides of business. In Britain the problem led to regular complaints to the Advertising Standards Authority and to calls for an extension of the relevant consumer protection law, the Trade Descriptions Act, to cover environmental claims. UK Friends of the Earth reacted by instituting a 'Green Con' award, which highlighted claims that the group felt to be particularly disingenuous or misleading. Another response was a growing lobby for an official environmental labelling scheme. The British government began consultations on a national scheme in 1989 and established a National Advisory Group on Eco-Labelling (NAGEL) to develop recommendations (NAGEL, 1991). Work on a national scheme was subsequently suspended in the light of parallel EU developments. The United Kingdom has been a leading supporter of the EU scheme and has taken an active role in laying down the groundwork for its development (House of Commons, 1991, 1993). Its enthusiasm for a pan-European scheme can be traced to political concerns that the increasing number of national eco-labelling programmes, each with different procedures and labelling criteria, would become a barrier to trade in the Single European Market.

The aims of the scheme fall in line with broader EU policy commitments: to improve environmental protection through stimulating the development of cleaner technologies; and to increase market transparency (which includes protecting consumers from misleading claims) in order to encourage the market for such goods. Thus it is an attempt to create an instrument both for technology policy and for consumer policy. The scheme also conforms with a growing political commitment to using non-interventionist market mechanisms that is evident in both UK and EU environmental policy (DoE, 1990; CEC, 1992a).

For implementation to be possible, however, and to command widespread credibility, the EU eco-labelling scheme is crucially dependent upon establishing a number of boundary conditions, which itself involves aligning a diverse array of actors, in order to achieve agreement on:

- The boundaries of individual product groups (For example, is the dishwasher category to include only those electrical appliances sold as dishwashers or, as was argued in Canada, are 'low-tech,' and low impact, alternatives such as washing-up mops and bowls to be included too?);
- The boundaries of the scheme's 'environmental' remit (Is it to concentrate on factors such as resource use, emissions and wastes, or should it include other concerns such as impacts on animals or indigenous peoples?); and
- The boundaries and procedures for the life-cycle assessment of product groups (How far back upstream in the production process should the assessment of impacts go? Should it stop with the main raw materials or include all materials? Should it extend as far back as the primary production processes such as mining from which raw materials derive?).

Once these parameters have been established, specific criteria of 'greenness' for the various product groups must be agreed that will have credibility with environmentalists, consumers and industry.

Crucially, the scheme depends upon the support both of industry, which controls much of the data upon which life-cycle assessment depends and without whose voluntary participation there will be no products to label, and of environmentally concerned citizens in their capacity as consumers, without whom there can be no market and therefore no incentive for industry to make changes in its products. It is in the attempt to align the various actors and establish stable boundary conditions that the underlying tensions have emerged, tensions that highlight not only interest-based differences but also the social assumptions and epistemological commitments embedded within the scheme. While many individuals associated with the scheme privately acknowledge its compromises and ambiguities, the way in which it operates reflects a construction of environmental problems that defines them purely in terms of physical processes. This is exemplified in the way in which eco-labelling frames social responses to these problems in terms of technological solutions that reify notions of the 'green' product as solution. Increasingly, however, the technocratic assumption that environmental problems can be understood solely in terms of the dominant reductionist forms of scientific knowledge and resolved by the application of a technological fix is being challenged by social scientific analysis which points to the social indeterminacy which is inherent to such problems (see, for example, Beck, 1992; Wynne, 1992a). This can be illustrated by reference to two aspects of the eco-labelling process: life-cycle assessment and the setting of environmental criteria for awarding the eco-label.

## LIFE-CYCLE ASSESSMENT: THE SOFT BOUNDARIES TO HARD SCIENCE

The scientific assessment of the environmental impact of products over their life cycle is a fundamental constituent of the philosophy and practice of the eco-labelling scheme. The scientific credentials that LCA brings to the scheme are vital to its credibility. However, the actors engaged in the eco-labelling arena recognise the fragility of the scientific basis of LCA. Appeals to a scientific warrant that figure in the legitimating rhetoric of the scheme are, not surprisingly therefore, a little cautious. The Chairman of the UK Ecolabelling Board (UKEB) has observed that

> ecological labelling ... is *a comparatively new science* which is constantly evolving, [and concludes that] *even the science* we are using *is not an exact one.* (Nelson, 1993, emphasis added)

Nevertheless, science plays a defining role in the eco-labelling process, one that merits closer examination.

Although the Eco-labelling Regulation (EEC, 1992) does not specify the methods by which it should be implemented, the EU scheme aims for criteria based on a quantitative scientific assessment of a product's environmental impacts throughout its life-cycle. This has raised an immediate difficulty because there is, as yet, no agreed standard methodology for conducting LCAs nor, indeed, for defining a 'life-cycle': whether, for example, it should include the resource depletion associated with primary extraction processes such as mining that precede the actual production process, or whether account should be taken of the social and cultural impact of such processes, for example on indigenous people. Although definitions vary somewhat, a quantitative LCA can be said to consist of a number of distinct stages (Guinée *et al.*, 1993). Once the preliminary step of defining the goal and consequent scope of the LCA study has been made, in this case to develop criteria for the award of an eco-label, there are three stages prior to deciding upon specific criteria:

1.  The *inventory* or *ecobalance* of all the inputs and outputs to the environment during the life-cycle of a product;
2.  The *classification* or *impact assessment*, from which is produced an environmental profile of the product; and
3.  The *valuation* of the different elements of the environmental profiles, which provides the basis for determining criteria for the particular product group.

Although the lack of a common methodology is acknowledged by practitioners to be a problem, the inventory phase is often presented as being the least controversial stage of the process. At a conference promoting LCA, held in November 1992, one prominent member of the Society of Environmental Toxicology and Chemistry (SETAC), the industry-dominated body that has established itself as the main international forum for developing a standard LCA methodology, passed over the inventory phase as 'basically a traditional chemical engineering exercise' (de Oude, 1992). At the same conference, a representative of France's main LCA consultants, ECOBILAN, asserted that the methodology for the inventory phase has evolved over twenty years (from energy analysis to ecobalances or inventories), and is well established. (Bensahel, 1992)

Yet one scientist involved in implementing LCA for ecolabelling, interviewed in 1993, observed that although most practitioners now claimed to be adopting the SETAC methodology, in practice they all tend to interpret it differently. This view was endorsed by a recent review of LCA methodology conducted by a team of leading Dutch scientists, which concluded that 'the inventory is not yet clear cut' (Guinée *et al.*, 1993). Their study compared a number of recent studies of milk packaging and discovered marked differences in assumptions and conclusions. Although they use these findings to support their argument for a common methodological framework, the authors acknowledged that certain problems are unlikely to be resolved by a single solution but that, nevertheless, 'they may strongly influence the results of a particular study' (Guinée *et al.*, 1993, 12). Guinée *et al.* also note that the growing number of projects that aim to develop the methodology and improve the data for LCA are themselves using different methodologies.

So, although it is presented as an objective scientific approach to evaluating the environmental impact of a product, variations in LCA practice entail judgements about method and application that very often reflect both the professional scientific cultures of its practitioners and the institutional structures within which they are embedded. These variations in practice will be resolved, if at all, by a process of influence and negotiation over the *bounding* and *defining* of 'life-cycle'. Thus attempts to treat these questions purely as technical issues have already become a focus for environmentalist criticism, with one well-established British environmental group which had given early support to the use of LCA complaining that it had been unable to gain access to SETAC, the main international forum for developing LCA methodology. Similarly, moves towards negotiating a wider consensus on LCA have not been particularly successful in Britain. An attempt to establish an LCA forum that brought together business and environmentalist interests, sponsored by the Confederation of British Industry under the slogan 'Consensus Equals

Credibility', failed to get beyond its inaugural meeting due to mutual distrust. A number of companies withdrew their support from a venture that would involve some of their most vocal critics, and some of the environmentalists present felt that their names were being used to legitimise an industry-dominated venture. This is not to suggest, however, that differences over the science of eco-labelling are merely interest-based or reducible simply to political manoeuvring. To take one example, the question of how extensive an LCA study should be has already highlighted differences in national science and policy cultures.

UKEB's approach, in keeping with British policy culture in general, is acknowledged to be 'pragmatic'. Consultants are commissioned to conduct a limited, 'streamlined' LCA to develop eco-labelling criteria which focus on those aspects and stages of the product's life cycle in which it is deemed to have the most significant environmental impact. For example, in the case of washing machines UKEB's consultants, PA Consulting Group, concluded that the product's main environmental impact occurs in the use phase, rather than in the production or disposal phases, and the criteria developed focus particularly on energy, water and detergent consumption.

This pragmatic use of 'streamlined' LCAs contrasts with the approach adopted in France, where the LCA for paints and varnishes was conducted by consultants ECOBILAN. The French consultants insisted on a more thorough-going investigation, including an assessment of compounds that constitute only a relatively minor part of the products. UK sources described the company as taking a more 'academic' approach that attempted an unrealistically detailed investigation of all impacts. One result of this was that two years into the development of the scheme UKEB had submitted draft criteria for four product groups to the European Commission and were well advanced with several other studies, whereas the French, after two years of study, were a long way from completing their first and had asked that industry cofinance a further six months of investigations. To UKEB, concerned to get the scheme up and running, this was evidence of the efficiency and effectiveness of its approach. To its critics, however, this disparity was taken as evidence of a rather cavalier British attitude to LCA.

The divergence between the pragmatic British approach and that taken by the French suggests that significant differences existed in their respective understandings about what should be included in an LCA and taken into account in order to decide the criteria for awarding an eco-label. These national differences are not simply obstacles to the scheme's efficiency. More importantly, they reveal tensions arising from differing scientific and policy cultures that threaten to undermine the credibility of its standards when applied on an EU-wide basis.

## THE SOCIAL CONSTRUCTION OF ENVIRONMENTAL PROBLEMS

The public controversy that erupted in 1992–3 over UKEB's proposed eco-labelling criteria for hairsprays provides a prime example of the ambiguities and tensions that can emerge when attempting to produce even a relative definition of a 'green' product that will be widely accepted. In their LCA of hairsprays, consultants Chem Systems identified the emission of volatile organic compounds (VOCs) from aerosol dispensers as a major source of environmental impact and VOC levels figured prominently in the UKEB's proposed eco-labelling criteria. As this was likely to make most aerosol-borne products ineligible for an eco-label it provoked a strong reaction from industry.[2] The proposed criteria were also challenged, however, for their failure to include animal testing of products. While wrangles over the fine detail are to be expected in the policy arena, as industries deploy technical arguments in the pursuit of their own interests, animal welfare issues introduce an explicitly moral dimension into the debate.

In the course of developing eco-labelling criteria for hairsprays UKEB's consultant, Chem Systems, records that it studied public perceptions of hairsprays' 'eco-impacts' by discussion with consumer organisations, environmental groups and manufacturers, and by reviewing articles and publications concerning hairsprays, aerosols and the environment in the press, industry publications, consumer and environmental magazines (UKEB, 1993). It reports that environmentalists, consumers and regulators expressed concern about the impacts of hairsprays in three areas: environment, human health and animal health. In order to evaluate the significance of these concerns, each was quantified very roughly according to two factors: its frequency of mention, and the level of regulatory response to it. On this basis, five individual concerns were judged by the consultants to be significant: four 'environmental' issues (the emission of ozone-depleting chlorofluorocarbon (CFC) aerosol propellants; the emission of hydrochlorofluorocarbon (HCFC) propellants; packaging waste; and emission of other propellants) and one human health issue (exposure to methylene chloride). 'Animal health' issues did not figure at all. The report observes that:

> Some concern has been expressed about animal health, because of animal testing products. This may be a concern only to a minority of the public. For instance, a referendum in the summer of 1992 to restrict animal testing in Switzerland was defeated. Animal testing of hairsprays was not considered in this study, *because it is believed to be an ethical rather than an environmental issue.* (UKEB, 1993, 12, emphasis added)

A number of observations can be made about this report and the statement regarding animal testing. First, no direct study was made of the views of consumers in the course of the consultation process; instead a mediating role was granted to various organisations, including product manufacturers:

> Manufacturers obtain a certain amount of public opinion from retailers, from market research and direct correspondence by consumers. (UKEB, 1993, 11)

Thus, public concerns were gauged solely by reference to representations constructed by actors with their own situated perceptions and interests so that, in practice, the consumer was granted only the passive role of an 'implied actor' in the ecolabelling arena (Clarke and Montini, 1993).

This does not necessarily mean that one can anticipate the views of organisational actors according to a list of predefined interests, however, as the positions of different actors and their roles and identities in relation to any particular issue are themselves contextually constructed. For example, the position of manufacturers who employ animal testing, and who are often seen as defenders of its use, is to a great extent shaped by regulatory and scientific norms and practices. The former managing director of a leading UK toiletries' manufacturer, interviewed in 1993, commented on the present product testing regime:

> There is something called the Draize test, which is an eye test in which rabbits are used, and the industry for years had been saying there must be some other better way of dealing with this *in vitro* rather than *in viva*, and actually presented quite a lot of protocols to show how this could be done. And endlessly government civil servants were saying 'I don't think that's really quite rigorous enough', you know. And yet the industry's products are not used on people's eyes, for God's sake. Of course, it's like your butane – one in a million cans blowing up – you can get some in your eyes but is it really worth while immobilising hundreds of thousands of rabbits in order to prove that. But it's not the industry that's doing that, it's governments, who set the rules and refuse to break the rules.

A second observation concerns the conclusion that animal health 'may be a concern only to a minority of the public'. The only explicit evidence offered in support of this assertion is the result of a Swiss referendum which did not support a ban on animal testing. Apart from the lack of any indication of what proportion of the Swiss actually voted against animal testing, the very fact that animal testing could become a referendum issue implies a strong current of concern in some sections of the population. Furthermore, in order to interpret the outcome of the vote one might wish to consider local structural conditions, such as the economic power of the pharmaceutical industry in Switzerland on which the livelihoods of a significant proportion of the population are dependent, which might influence voting behaviour in ways that would not apply in some other national contexts. More fundamentally, however, the consultants' interpretation of public concern fails to recognise the extent to which these issues are culturally and historically constructed and that there can be considerable cultural heterogeneity within a national context, let alone across different states. The views attributed to the 'general public' in one country on an issue such as animal testing cannot therefore be readily generalised to other populations. In the United Kingdom in particular, unlike some other EU countries, animal welfare issues are seen by many people to be part of the 'package' of 'green' concerns, just as vegetarianism is by others. Within the field of animal welfare activities and discourses, long-standing environmentalist campaigns on behalf of endangered species merge with campaigns against hunting, the fur trade and vivisection, blurring the boundaries between them as distinct issues.

Finally, and perhaps most significantly, there is the distinction that is made between 'environmental' and 'ethical' issues. This highlights the construction of 'environmental' with which the consultants and the UKEB were operating. Although the process of agreeing eco-labelling criteria is openly political, with its system of consultative mechanisms, the core concept of 'environment' to which these negotiations are anchored is tacitly decontextualised and depoliticised. The implicit construction being adopted by UKEB tends to reflect narrow technical definitions of 'environment', that have been shaped to a great extent through years of policy dialogue between scientists, industry and government, and which do not coincide with the broader moral and cultural constructions of 'environment' shared by large sections of the general population. In 1992, at the same time that the UKEB was taking this view, one of the regular *Eurobarometer* surveys conducted for the European Commission was investigating the views of Europeans on environmental issues. The results of the study suggest rather a different picture (CEC, 1992b). Rather ironically, in view of the sharp distinction made by UKEB, a question contained in the *Eurobarometer* study that explores 'concerns about various threats *to the environment*' included 'the use of animals in experiments' among the concerns listed. Whilst responses to this question did not demonstrate as high a level of concern as a number of pollution-related issues, nearly three-quarters of all those surveyed across the EU stated that they were 'worried' about animal experimentation. The assertion by UKEB's Chief Executive that 'animal testing is not in our remit on environmental concern' seems to have been at odds, therefore, with the perceptions of a significant segment of the European public.[3]

The response of the majority of concerned individuals to environmental problems is first and foremost a moral one: that the damage and destruction should not be happening, that we possess moral obligations to the living world. This is not a shortcoming, the result of a lack of rationality or objectivity, but quite the reverse: it recognises that these problems are not 'out there', somehow external to and separate from society, but rather 'in here' with us: as their originators they are *our* problems rather than those of an abstracted 'environment'. The changing constructions and appropriations of nature associated with modern societies have been mutually constitutive of new economic, social and political contradictions and conflicts. Thus 'violations of nature' turn into threats to human social, economic and physical well-being (Beck, 1992). The routine technology of environmental problems attempts to bracket off the profound moral and ontological questions that they pose, questions about human identity, about our relationships to each other and to other living things – the very stuff of cultural struggles and debates. Such questions, however, lie at the heart of 'the environment' as a social issue and regularly surface in public conflicts. It is an inherently ambiguous issue that brings together scientific and cultural discourses and reflects the intrinsic openness of the boundary between nature and culture.

It comes as no surprise, then, that UKEB's decision to exclude animal testing criteria provoked some strong reactions. Most vocal among the critics was The Body Shop, the 'natural' toiletries business that has risen to international success on the basis of its environmentalist commitment and is viewed by many as the exemplar of a 'green business'. A customer survey conducted by The Body Shop suggested that a majority expected the eco-label criteria to include the issue of animal testing. In contrast to the position taken by UKEB, a statement by The Body Shop's founder, Anita Roddick, sums up the alternative view:

We are astounded that anyone could propose an eco-label for cosmetic products which have been tested on animals, or which might use ingredients with unacceptable impacts on Third World cultures or environments. *If these issues are not 'ecological' nothing is.*[4]

The company announced that it would boycott the hairspray eco-label and lodged a formal complaint with the European Commission which maintained that UKEB had acted outside its authority by making an *a priori* exclusion of animal testing issues.

The Body Shop played a leading role in presenting the case against the distinction between 'environmental' and human or animal welfare considerations in eco-labelling policy (Wheeler, 1993a, 1993b, 1993c) but the broader ethical conception of what constituted 'ecological' considerations had much wider support. Significantly, the best-selling book that had been the 'bible' of environmentally concerned British consumers in the late 1980s, *The Green Consumer* guide (Elkington and Hailes, 1988), had already included animal welfare in its list of environmental considerations. The eco-labelling scheme was roundly criticised in the media at the time by leading environmentalists such as Jonathon Porritt, former Director of Friends of the Earth and adviser to the Prince of Wales, and subsequently was the object of detailed criticism by the editors of *Ethical Consumer* magazine (1994). The issue was also raised in parliament, in a censuring motion signed by nearly 100 MPs. Organised opposition to UKEB's decision took the form of a coalition of environmental and animal welfare groups, together with a number of environmentally concerned businesses such as The Body Shop, which was coordinated by the Women's Environmental Network, well known in Britain for its work on consumption-related environmental issues. This was followed in May 1994 by the 'Don't Give Animal Testing the Green Light' campaign, launched by the British Union for the Abolition of Vivisection with the support of 90 environmental organisations, and 'cruelty-free' businesses. Interestingly, however, environmental groups did not all see eye to eye on the issue. Some campaigners within the larger, science-based NGOs were also inclined to maintain a distinction between animal testing and 'environmental' issues, and to see the issue as being outside their remit.

The European Commission responded to Body Shop lobbying by stating that animal testing concerns did not necessarily
fall outside the scope of the eco-labelling scheme. This
opened up the possibility that they might be included in the
drafting of future labelling criteria but this did not develop.
Lobbying and public campaigning did not change UKEB's
stance on the issue and, more recently, there have been signs
that the Commission's position might well be reversed and
animal testing treated as a completely separate issue. However,
such controversies impinge upon public perceptions, and if its
implicit assumptions run counter to the views of significant
sections of the public on a given issue, the eco-labelling
scheme as a whole is vulnerable to a loss of public credibility
and legitimacy.

## PUBLIC AMBIVALENCE AND INSTITUTIONAL
## CREDIBILITY

It would be misleading, however, to suggest that members of
the public routinely hold clearly formed views on these issues
or the role of institutions and institutional actors. However,
research on the public understanding of scientific and risk
issues has shown that public concern over environmental and
other technological hazards, far from being a product of
ignorance or irrationality, can often be traced to a distrust of
the institutions claiming competence and authority, a distrust
based very often in discerning evaluations of the shortcomings
and biases of those institutions (Wynne, 1992b). More often
their feelings are expressed as ambivalence or distrust towards
institutional rhetorics and practices. The question for eco-
labelling is whether public distrust of government institutions
and industry will extend to UKEB (with its staff of civil
servants and half of its Board members from the business community) if its environmental credentials are publicly challenged by high profile actors such as The Body Shop and
environmental groups, whose environmental legitimacy is well-
established. Further, any damage to the credibility of the hairspray labels that is sustained as a result of the animal testing
issue may also undermine, by association, that of labels
awarded to other products.

Although considerable survey research has been conducted in the attempt to establish precisely what the public thinks (and, by implication, what the public will do), publics tend to demonstrate an ambivalence about these matters that is not captured by the clear-cut categories of opinion polls (Simmons, 1995). Public opinion research commissioned by UKEB was taken to demonstrate public support for an 'independent' eco-labelling body, in preference to an EU- or DoE-administered scheme. In the report on the qualitative study conducted as a preliminary to MORI's national survey for UKEB, focus group participants were described as being cautious and ambivalent about phrases such as 'less damaging', 'official' and 'impartially assessed' (MORI, 1992). The same focus group interviews found that the government, and with it the DoE, was generally viewed as having little credibility as a source of impartial information. The information that it gives out was perceived to be biased, reflecting what were seen as the vested interests of officials and government ministers, thus lending apparent support to UKEB's role as an 'independent' body.

The subsequent survey research found that 49 per cent of the respondents sampled were willing to place 'a great deal' of confidence in what 'an independent body responsible for environmental labelling' might have to say about the environmental effect of different products, placing it behind 'environmental organisations' (with 52 per cent) and ahead of 'consumer organisations' (with only 30 per cent) (MORI, 1992). These figures suggest that in comparison to government, UKEB will be in a strong position to speak with an authoritative voice and influence public perceptions. However, the answers can also be read rather differently. All the actors listed in the MORI questionnaire, which included scientists, the EU, shops, manufacturers, local government and women's institutes, had an existence and a history for various publics at the time the survey was conducted in 1992. The 'independent body', on the other hand, was a hypothetical entity of which the people surveyed had no direct or indirect knowledge. That is, the public were being asked to compare bad apples with non-existent pears. Its support for an independent eco-labelling body was therefore an endorsement *in principle* rather than *in practice*. At the same time, a roughly equivalent proportion (43 per cent) already viewed the suggestion with some ambivalence, willing to invest only 'a little' or 'not very much' trust in a disembodied body. Whether public evaluations will change once UKEB has a history, which it is rapidly acquiring in its confrontations with The Body Shop and the environmental NGOs, remains to be seen. Certainly, it seems likely that UKEB's identity and authority, far from being given, will continue to be contested as underlying cultural tensions arising from divergent and frequently incommensurable constructions of the issues continue to surface.

CONCLUSIONS

The political future of the EU eco-labelling scheme remains uncertain. Two and a half years after the Regulation was made and more than a year after the publication of the first product criteria only one manufacturer had been awarded an eco-label, and continued disagreements with industry had impeded the publication of labelling criteria for any new product groups. Meanwhile, the European Commission appeared to be distancing itself and considering divesting itself of the management of the scheme. Political concerns that eco-labelling might represent a trade barrier had also prompted moves towards global coordination and even standardisation of eco-labelling schemes in operation around the world.[5] Whatever the political outcome, eco-labelling has begun to develop its own institutional inertia and seems set to continue in some form, whether on a national or an international basis, so that the issues raised here will still need to be addressed.

The explanation of the tensions and of the controversy faced by UKEB begins from the observation that environmental problems cannot be defined exclusively in terms of objective physical processes. Just as they have their origins in particular patterns of social activity, so their significance and meaning for us is socially negotiated. The 'environment' is no longer something external to society but is, in a very real sense, implicated in the complex patterns of social and economic activity in which we engage. The public conflict over the hairspray criteria was rooted in the different constructions of 'environment' that were mobilised. The implicit construction adopted by UKEB reflected a narrow technical definition which attempted to maintain a clear distinction between spheres of value and which did not involve human relations and culture. This definition has been shaped by epistemological commitments that are shared, as a result of years of policy dialogue, by both industry and government but which do not coincide with the broader moral and cultural constructions of 'environment' which inform the views of large sections of the general population. This makes the process vulnerable to controversy, and to a consequent withdrawal of public legitimation. The alternative, acknowledging the indeterminacies inherent to environmental issues, will not produce a simpler formula for resolving them. But it can provide the basis for a more reflexive understanding of the field of environmental risk construction within which eco-labelling policy operates and of which its own activities are part.

## Notes

1.  This chapter has benefited from discussions with Robin Grove-White and Brian Wynne who, together with Phil Macnaghten and Bron Szerszynski, made detailed comments on an earlier draft. They bear no responsibility, however, for the end result. The research upon which the chapter draws was supported by the UK Economic and Social Research Council under its Global Environmental Change Initiative, grant number Y320283001.
2.  'Eco-label rules for hairsprays to rule out most aerosols', *ENDS Report*, 213 (October 1992), 22–3.
3.  Quoted in *The Guardian* (26 January 1993), 5.
4.  Quoted by Jonathon Porritt in his column in *Green Magazine* (March 1993), emphasis added.
5.  'Question mark over future of EC eco-labelling scheme', *ENDS Report*, 235 (August 1994), 25; 'Free traders put pressure on EC eco-labelling scheme', *ENDS Report*, 237 (October 1994), 24; 'Move towards international harmonisation of eco-labelling', *ENDS Report*, 231 (April 1994), 26.

## References

Abel, R., 'Risk as an Arena of Struggle', *University of Michigan Law Review*, 83(4) (1985), 712–812.
Beck, U., *Risk Society: Towards a new modernity* (London: Sage, 1992) (English translation of *Risikogesellschaft: Auf dem Weg in eine andere Moderne*, Frankfurt am Main: Suhrkamp Verlag, 1986).

Bensahel, J.-F., 'Assessing Eco-impacts', *Eco-labelling, Life Cycle Analysis and the Chemical Industry* (Brussels) (23–24 November 1992).

CEC, *Towards Sustainability. A European Community Programme of Policy and Action in Relation to the Environment and Sustainable Development*, COM(92) 23 final (Brussels: Commission of the European Communities, 1992a).

CEC, *Europeans and the Environment in 1992: Survey conducted in the context of the EUROBAROMETER 37.0* (Brussels: Commission of the European Communities, 1992b).

Clarke, A. and Montini, T., 'The Many Faces of RU486: Tales of situated knowledge and technological contestations', *Science, Technology and Human Values*, 18(1) (Winter) (1993), 42–78.

de Oude, N., 'Establishing a Common Methodology', *Eco-labelling, Life Cycle Analysis and the Chemical Industry* Brussels (23–24 November 1992).

DoE (Department of the Environment), *This Common Inheritance* (London: HMSO, 1990).

EEC, 'Council Regulation (EEC) No 880/92 of 23 March 1992 on a Community Eco-label Award Scheme', *Official Journal of the European Communities*, L 99 (11 April 1992), 1–6.

Elkington, J. and Hailes, J., *The Green Consumer: From shampoo to champagne – high-street shopping for a better environment* (London: Victor Gollancz, 1988).

Erikson, K., 'Toxic Reckoning: Business faces a new kind of fear', *Harvard Business Review* (January–February 1990), 118–26.

*Ethical Consumer*, Editorial: 'The EC Ecolabel – What's wrong with it?', (November 1994), 5–7.

Giddens, A., *The Consequences of Modernity* (Cambridge: Polity Press, 1990).

Grove-White, R., 'Environmentalism: A new moral discourse for technological society?', in Milton, K. (ed.), *Environmentalism: The View from Anthropology* (London: Routledge, 1993).

Guinée, J. B., Udo de Haes, H. A. and Huppes, G., 'Quantitative Life Cycle Assessment of Products, 1: Goal definition and inventory', *Journal of Cleaner Production*, 1(1) (1993), 3–13.

House of Commons, Session 1990–91, Environment Committee, Eighth Report, *Eco-labelling*, 1 and 2, HC 474-I and II (24 July 1991) (London: HMSO, 1991).

House of Commons, Session 1992–93, Environment Committee, *Eco-labelling*, Minutes of Evidence, Wednesday 27 January, UK Eco-Labelling Board; Department of the Environment; Department of Trade and Industry, HC 429-I (London: HMSO, 1993).

Lau, C., 'Social Conflicts About the Definition of Risks: The role of science', in Stehr, N. and Ericson, R. V. (eds), *The Culture and Power of Knowledge: Inquiries into Contemporary Societies* (Berlin and New York: De Gruyter, 1992), 235–480.

Luhmann, N., *Risk* (Berlin: De Gruyter, 1993).

MORI, *Public Attitudes towards Ecolabelling*, Research study conducted for the Department of the Environment (June–July 1992) (London: Market and Opinion Research International, 1992).

NAGEL (The National Advisory Group on Eco-labelling), *Giving Guidance to the Green Consumer – Progress on an Eco-labelling Scheme for the UK* (London: Department of the Environment, 1991).

Nelson, E., 'Ecolabelling', *Environmental Liability*, 1(1) (1993), 16–19.

Short, J. F., 'The Social Fabric at Risk: towards the social transformation of risk analysis', *American Sociological Review*, 49 (December 1984), 711–25.

Simmons, P., 'Researching Green Consumerism: Hard facts and soft identities', (unpublished paper, 1995).

UKEB, *Criteria for Hairspray Ecolabels: A proposal by the UK Ecolabelling Board* (London: UK Ecolabelling Board, 1993).

Wheeler, D., 'Eco-labels or Eco-alibis?', *Chemistry and Industry* (5 April 1993a), 260.

Wheeler, D., 'What Future for Product Life Cycle Assessment?', *Integrated Environmental Management*, 20 (1993b), 15–19.

Wheeler, D., 'Why Ecological Policy must Include Human and Animal Welfare', *Business Strategy and the Environment* (1993c), 36–8.

Wynne, B. 'Uncertainty and Environmental Learning: Reconceiving science and policy in the preventive paradigm', *Global Environmental Change*, 2(2) (1992a), 111–27.

Wynne, B., 'Misunderstood Misunderstandings: social identities and public uptake of science', *Public Understanding of Science*, 1(3) (1992b), 281–304.

# 13 Logics of Prevention: Mundane Speech and Expert Discourse on Alcohol Policy
Pekka Sulkunen

## THE PUBLIC HEALTH PREDICAMENT

A major paradox of contemporary advanced societies is that while they have reached an unforeseen degree of technical competence, people living in them are now more concerned about risks and feel more helpless before them than ever before. New risks appear as life becomes more complex and rich in consumer experiences but increasingly dependent on technology. However, the very fact that we know more about causes of troubles and about ways of dealing with them seems to arouse this worry as much as the threats to life, health, security and well-being themselves.

In the particular area of health another source of increased risk awareness is the disparity between resources and achieved levels of technical competencies in treating illness, in eliminating pain and in prolonging life.

Prevention offers itself as the obvious and reasonable societal response, and there is abundant scientific knowledge to ground high expectations of successful preventive policies in many areas of public health protection. However, prevention efforts are not growing uniformly. Most Western societies have adopted some legislation to reduce the use of drugs, abuse of pharmaceutical products and the use of tobacco. Agricultural overproduction notwithstanding, few countries now promote the consumption of animal fats in the way that was customary in Scandinavia until the late 1960s (Jensen and Kjærnes, Chapter 11 in this volume). Many harmful materials such as asbestos have been banned, and environmental programmes purport to avoid unnecessary health risks. Alcohol has become an object of preventive policies even in countries where this has for long not been possible for economic and cultural reasons. The most notable example is France, where the 1990 legislation banned almost all advertisement for alcohol and tobacco products in the name of public health.

Nevertheless, public intervention into private consumption meets resistance of a serious and fundamental kind. Scandinavian and North American preventive alcohol policies are being run down. The Commission of the European Union is driving a policy of tax harmonisation downwards, and in all of the cases where the preventive side has had the upper hand, there has been bitter conflict. To the two traditional issues over the welfare state – that of public services and that of income redistribution – a third one has been added: the conflict over consumption between different interest groups and different moral dispositions. On the one hand, consumers need protection against risks; on the other they build their identities as sovereign and independent decision makers for their own pleasure and satisfaction. Any attempts to direct consumption, on whatever grounds, will easily be interpreted as diminishing this sovereignty and therefore as unacceptable paternalism. This is what I call the 'public health predicament' of affluent societies. In this chapter, I examine this predicament, using the example of changing arguments about alcohol policy both in expert discourse and in mundane speech. Finally, I shall discuss the new role of experts and social scientists facing the public health predicament of their societies.


THE CONSUMER SOCIETY

The public health predicament is part of a profound ongoing rupture in the history of Western societies. The notion of the new consumer society is one among a large number of conceptual demarcations of the current epochal change. Like all other characterisations of contemporary affluent societies, such as postmodern or post-industrial society, risk society, experience society or information society, the notion of the consumer society is tentative and transient. But it does catch a number of important phenomena, and, most important of all, a change in the focus and locus of major social issues, better than other epochal concepts. Modern, industrialising societies have been constructed around a project, a Promethean challenge to achieve a better future through work, frugality and reason. 'Production' has been the gist in more than one sense: industrialisation in itself has been a process of accumulating the production of commodities, but production also implies a difference between action and its result.

In a parallel fashion, when we speak of the new consumer society, more than just buying and depletion of commodities is meant. In the new consumer society, the exercise of reason follows a pattern opposite to the logic of production. Action and its result – pleasure, satisfaction, fascination – coincide in the here and now, and no ultimate end, such as better performance in the future, needs to be invoked for their justification. Whereas performance in productive activity can be measured in terms of *quantities*, consummatory performance cannot be evaluated without reference to *qualities*. In affluent societies today people are faced with choice at every turn of life. Whatever promises modernity might have left unachieved, this it did not: it has broken with traditions, myths and ritual that earlier helped people to take at least some basic things for granted (Giddens, 1994). Today, everything is open for choice, and even if the selection may appear to be one of tradition, it is still a decision, a voluntary act rather than just a 'drift' (Mills, 1959).

It is in this context that the public health predicament must be placed and analysed.

THE AGE OF SUSPICION

Two factors, the loss of a progressivist time conception, and concentration on qualities – and therefore on differences – are important interpretive frames of major social issues in today's affluent societies. First, the demise of the idea of progress destroys a common value basis of moral judgements and political ideology. The instrumental and contractual nature of the social bond of classic individualistic modernity has become replaced by other kinds of ephemeral, non-instrumental and local social solidarities that Michel Maffesoli (1995) has called tribalistic. Secondly, the emphasis on differences and qualities implies another kind of moral fragmentation of society. Different paths of life, all equally valuable in the absence of common standards, or at least all contesting almost equally for legitimacy, leave little room for 'emancipation' in terms of morality, way of life and values.

The consumer society is a society of suspicion. But it is so in a very different way than in the 1960s and 1970s, when Alain Touraine (1984) scorned structural Marxists for their relentless suspicion that there is a hidden logic of capitalism which, in contrast with the appearance of benevolence, reform, democracy and affluence, denies real subjectivity and emancipation to the working class, the intellectuals or whoever it was that was glorified as the historical subject. Today, few voices demanding emancipation, reform, equality – or protection of public health – escape the suspicion of others for being a one-sided and partial advocacy for one way of life and one set of values against others.

Another kind of suspicion, emphasised by Ulrich Beck (1992), arises from the fact that our awareness of risks depends on expert knowledge. Even in obvious cases like alcohol policy, expert messages are susceptible to contradictory interpretations. The value of small quantities of alcohol in preventing cardiovascular heart disease is easily generalised to situations where only adverse effects from more drinking will follow (Edwards *et al.*, 1994). More importantly, such messages are subject to powerful particular interests. One word issued by a nutritionist may be worth thousands, maybe millions of dollars in the market of mass food products.

The suspicion of particular interest carries a contaminating effect against which even the most disinterested scientific discourse has difficulty in shielding itself. Whatever the realities, arguments for alleviating alcohol problems through public intervention into consumption, will be deflated in the public mind as the voice of the bureaucracy that is maintained by disseminating such messages.

SOVEREIGNTY

The most sensitive root of suspicion lies elsewhere, in the heart of the new consumer society. As consumers we have an image of ourselves as sovereign individuals capable of making choices on the basis of our own values and preferred ways of life. The new consumer society marks a rupture in this conception that has become a new source of suspicion.

There is one common misunderstanding about the relationship between individualistic mentality and traditional political ideologies. It is often thought that individualism has been the dividing line between liberal conservatism and the socialist labour movement, which has supported collectivism and state intervention. The issue is more complex than that, and it is related to what I call a change from a *universalistic* conception of the individual to a *particularistic* one.

Individualistic identity is characteristic of all wage labourers. As a wage earner, even the traditional working class man is his own master to the extent that he is entitled to manage his own family budget and free to sell his labour power. The social-democratic and socialist working class movements in Western Europe have undoubtedly been the leading squadrons in the construction of welfare states, and their collective organisations have given them the muscle to realise that goal. But the welfare state itself is an individualistic project: it liberates the individual and the nuclear family from economic *Gemeinschaft* ties. Social-democratic working class movements have been committed not only to the ideals of equality and security but also to a civilising project in the individualistic sense. The cult of the private home is not only a bourgeois invention; it is part of the working class ethos, charged with ideological and emotional requirements of social competence and obligation with regard to upbringing, sexuality and consumption (I. Sulkunen, 1985). Cleanliness and self-control, the physical separation of humans from nature (dirt) and from one another, are symbols of family-centred wage earners' individuality. Home, marriage and hygiene are inseparably intertwined with the individuality of the wage labourer also within the working class (Frykman and Löfgren, 1987; Åström, 1985).

Abercombie, Hill and Turner (1986) have contested the view of classical sociological theory that individualism is inevitably linked to captalism. The link is simply contingent and limited to the West; contemporary Asian capitalism proves that a capitalist economy can also be based on a collectivist culture. Furthermore, they argue that even in the West, individualism is increasingly dysfunctional with the principles of capitalist organisation, which is out of necessity collectivist, complex and large in scale. It is more a mass society than a society of free individuals.

The confusion about individualism, capitalism and mass society is partly conceptual, partly empirical. The opposition between individualism and collectivism is too crude and therefore confusing. Not only has capitalism changed and placed people in new kinds of jobs, hierarchical positions and social environments; also the cultural understandings of the individual are now different than they were for the founding fathers of sociology and they also have a different slant from those that have animated the civilising project of the labour movement.

In classic formulations, individualism had been understood as a series of *rights*: rights to possessions and acquisitions; rights before the law; rights to the satisfaction of basic needs; rights to political citizenship; rights to privacy, a private home, and a family; and rights to personal experience of emotions (Bell, 1990, 74). This is how the individual has been seen in social theory and in mainstream ethical theory (Rawls), but this is also how individualism has appeared in political discourses of legitimation. An important correlate of such a conception is that it is *universalistic* individualism: you cannot consistently argue that such rights apply only to some individuals, because they would not then be individuals but particular institutions or groups such as aristocracy, whites, men only, and so on.

The shift from the modern, production-centred society to postmodern consumer society has thrown overboard the conception of the individual as a project. What we are now experiencing is neither an apotheosis of individualism over collectivism, nor a disappearance of the individual into collective tribalism (cf. Maffesoli, Chapter 2 in this volume) or into anonymous conformity of the mass society (Mills, 1956). Egalitarian and universalistic individualism has turned into particularistic and solitary individuality; what once was a common project and a public doctrine shared by the working class and the bourgeoisie alike has now become a mentality of the privatised individual self.

To be an individual now is a *duty*, a set of responsibilities, rather than a series of rights. As an individual citizen, one is responsible for how much money one makes for the kind of work one has chosen to do; one is responsible for the choices one makes in matters of marriage and the family, in case of illness one will be evaluated for one's merits in taking care of one's own health. The irony of this is that neo-liberal appeals to entrepreneurship, freedom of choice and self-direction, which are directed against the welfare state, are themselves part of the same process of individualisation as the welfare state. In fact, we might identify here one of the processes of saturation that Maffesoli (1993) considers as the moving force behind the shift from an Apollonian to the Dionysian cycle in contemporary culture (see also Chapter 2 in this volume). The gradual decay of universal individualism as a legitimising ideology is not only in harmony with but a consequence of a culture centred on the individual; on the other hand, the pivotal place of the individual in this culture would not be possible without the universalisation of market-driven wage labour, an historical process in which the welfare state now under fire has been the indispensable midwife.

## MODERNIST ALCOHOL POLICY

The history of alcohol control in Western societies reflects the change from production-centred modernity to consumption-centred postmodern culture. Alcohol consumption increased in almost all advanced capitalist countries in the post-war period until the 1980s. This rise was related to the improved opportunities for consumption opened by material and technical progress. In cultural conceptions, new cosmopolitan ways of using alcohol, adopted from ancient European civilisations or from North American mass media, was a sign of 'modernity' (P. Sulkunen, 1983). New ways of using alcoholic beverages became a sign of distinction in the cultural battle for competence and style (Bourdieu, 1984).

In many countries the redefinition of alcohol-related problems as health hazards – or the tendency towards medicalisation (Mäkelä *et al.*, 1981) – reflected a change of moral codes in modern, individualised society but also a confidence in material and technical progress in treatment methods. At the same time, egalitarian individualism called for new, universalistic solutions to the prevention of alcohol problems. The Nordic state monopoly systems in particular were originally based on principles of social discrimination, which intended to exclude women, young people and the working class from the world of drink (Bruun, 1985; Järvinen and Stenius, 1985). As late as the 1970s there were still traces of discriminatory alcohol policy in many countries. In Belgian legislation, for example, strong drinks could not be served in public places and they were sold in retail only in vessels of 2 litres or more. The main purpose was to prevent workers from buying spirits. The well-known British rules on opening hours of public houses were also originally aimed at disciplining the working class (Harrison, 1971). French working class cafes have been subjected to similar restrictions, but here the motivation was even more explicitly political: cafes and other public drinking places have been important scenes of political agitation since the eighteenth century (Brennan, 1989), even more obviously so after the Commune (Barrows, 1991). The 'dry' history of Swedish restaurants has a very similar background (Magnusson, 1985).

The first universalistic, truly modern response to the alcohol question in the welfare state came with the theory of total consumption, originally formulated by the French demographer Sully Ledermann (1956) and later elaborated by Scandinavian, British and North American scholars (Bruun *et al.*, 1975). According to this approach alcohol control should focus on *per capita* consumption rates in whole populations rather than on individuals, particular groups, or drinking manners. Any measures such as price increases or the restrictions on availability benefit the whole population, and this justifies any inconvenience caused to moderate drinkers. The validity of this theory has recently been evaluated and its implications reaffirmed by a group of experts in collaboration with the World Health Organisation (Edwards *et al.*, 1994).

In countries with a strong temperance tradition (Canada, the United States, Scandinavian countries, Switzerland) the legitimacy of a governmental, preventive alcohol policy was for many years unchallenged by egalitarian individualism, as long as it respected the principle of universality. In these countries, and also in the World Health Organisation, the total consumption theory, or 'availability theory' as it also has been called, has been well received.

Even in many countries where the resistance to alcohol has not been part of national civil religions, preventive alcohol policy has been incorporated – on the terms of universalism – into the welfare state agenda. In France, socialist Prime Minister Mendès-France set up a governmental office to combat alcohol-related problems (Haut Comité d'Etude et d'Information sur l'Alcoolisme) in 1954; in Germany temperance organisations are quasi-governmental; and all Western capitalist countries have some sort of governmental organs to monitor the development of alcohol availability, even though they may have limited power actually to reduce overall consumption.

## ALCOHOL POLICY AND THE END OF MODERNISM

Today, in our societies of suspicion, preventive alcohol policy is facing new kinds of challenges. Particularly in the United States, Canada and the Nordic countries, the social alcohol question has gradually lost ground. Temperance movements have become bureaucratised and merged into the state apparatus. This means that the visibility and moral weight of the alcohol issue is not as great as earlier, although the alcohol problem itself is still there. The crisis of the modern welfare state has brought alcohol to the forefront in social debate in new ways. It is no longer a special issue surrounded by moral dogmas, while the shift from universal to particularistic individualism has undermined the acceptability of the total consumption theory of prevention.

The symbolic value of alcohol as a sign of taste, style and cultural competence is declining. The longevity of distinctions based on styles of consumption is proportional to the amount of economic and cultural capital they require. In this regard alcohol is steadily losing its competitive edge. It would hardly be surprising to see the French example spread to other countries (P. Sulkunen, 1989) and abstention become the most effective strategy of distinction. A comparative study of France and the United States indicates that even moderate use of alcohol among the youth predicts high absenteeism from school and poor school motivation, that is, an orientation towards lower status groups (Choquet *et al.*, 1990). Similar results have been obtained in other countries as well (Rahkonen and Ahlström, 1989). The use of alcohol may no longer be a sign of 'distinction', but rather a sign of marginalisation.

The new conception of individuality as a duty has two consequences for alcohol policy. First, the provision of services to people afflicted with drinking problems is becoming more closely related to social status. The privatisation of health care services and linking them with employment status will increase inequality in access to and in the standards of these services. Pressures are mounting to reduce the costs of public services for the most deprived people, and the political support for those services is dwindling. If the universalistic welfare state has been cruel to the most deprived alcoholics (Sulkunen and Rahkonen, 1987), it will probably be even crueller if the principles of universalism are thrown overboard.

Secondly, the debate on preventive alcohol policy has been withdrawn from traditional political agendas. Alcohol problems and other voluntary life-style hazards have come to occupy a central place in the public health predicament, but in a new way. The notions of public interest, progress and universalism suffering from a loss of credibility, these issues have turned from political into ethical ones, often blending with professional interests. Nowadays we see the flag of preventive alcohol policy being waved by doctors, social workers and bureaucrats far more often than by voluntary organisations. This is the case at least in Finland, Sweden, the United States, and France. In France, the restrictive legislation on the advertisement of alcohol and tobacco was passed in 1990 only because five leading medical experts managed to mobilise the whole medical profession to support their initiative. Voluntary organisations were far more sceptical; some were directly opposed to the new legislation.

## HETEROGENEITY OF ARGUMENTS

Epochal terms such as 'postmodernity', 'risk society' or the 'new consumer society' all carry powerful messages and are helpful in providing conceptual frameworks for interpreting the diversity of social life around us. However, one problem common to all of them must be recognised. They are ideal types rather than rigorous empirical descriptions, interpretative frameworks rather than full-fledged theories. If taken too literally, they contradict the very thesis of fragmentation that many theorists of postmodernity have held to be most characteristic of contemporary society (Featherstone, 1991). There is a great temptation to build around them excessively totalising and coherent interpretations of contemporary social reality that is in fact heterogeneous.

The weaker the binding force of commonly shared ideology and ways of life become, the more blurred will be the moral sources and guidelines accessible to us. Discursive systems – political ideologies, religious beliefs and even moral theories – have lost an important part of their coherence and structure. Nevertheless, decisions are made, action is taken and views on social issues are expressed. The less available coherent discursive systems are to us the more we have to rely on what Melvin Pollner (1987) calls 'mundane reason'. By that he means assumptions that an objective coherent world exists 'out there' and that in our practical everyday thinking we tend to adjust our fragmented experiences and observations to an image of such a world. Pollner emphasises the natural tendency of people to think coherently. It may be so; however, it is important to add that mundane reason does not exist as such, independently of relations of expressing what we believe to correspond to our images of objective reality. We are always looking at things *from a point of view*, both in relation to what we are talking about and in relation to those we are talking to. Because of such interactional elements, I prefer to speak about mundane speech rather than mundane reason. To whatever degree reason is one of its elements, it is always reason by someone to someone about something she or he is related to.

The public health predicament of contemporary affluent societies is a particular instance of such context-bound heterogeneity of discourse. Albeit strong and influential, the saturated form of individualism has no monopoly of perspective on issues of prevention and protection. Modern universalist welfare state understandings exist side by side with other and apparently less rationalistic approaches.

## LIBERALISATION OF ALCOHOL POLICY IN FINLAND

Alcohol policy in Finland is a perfect case for studying the logics of prevention in the new consumer society. Public opinion in alcohol issues has swayed, within a few years, from a relatively control-oriented position to a position where almost no public intervention into the market and private consumption is deemed to be justified. The Finnish alcohol monopoly system has been under attack by the press, and opinion polls indicate a clear shift towards 'liberalism' in demands for better availability of alcoholic beverages. At the same time individual responsibility is being emphasised in both prevention and treatment of drinking problems. In January 1995 new alcohol legislation entered into force, ending public monopoly on production, imports and wholesale of alcoholic beverages and making beverages containing less than 4.7 per cent alcohol available in any grocery stores. Also the licensing and control system was streamlined to allow more room for free competition.

However, such 'liberalisation' does not imply that preventive efforts would be completely forsworn. Drinking problems are not disappearing from the public scene. What this does imply is that alcohol control is placed in the more general but contradictory context of the public health predicament. Choice of the best way and time to die, and choice of the ills we are prepared to tolerate and spend public money on, is not only our right but also something we cannot avoid.

## THREE WORLDS OF WELFARE IDEOLOGY

The heterogeneity of mundane speech about alcohol policy was one of the most apparent results of a recent group interview study of local influentials in Lahti, a small Finnish industrial town. The study was designed to map mundane speech about alcohol policy in groups assembled on the basis of reputational scores of social influence in a snowball sample of men and women in four areas of public life: business, culture, media and politics or public administration. Group discussion on alcohol policy was prompted by showing an educational video, 'The Alcohol Roulette' by the Addiction Research Foundation (Toronto). The 'Availability Theory' approach of the Canadian research team represents what I have above described as the 'modernist' welfare state ideology of public policy. It is expert discourse, backed by theoretical argument as well as empirical data. The video presents skewed distribution curves of alcohol consumption in different countries to argue that the number of heavy drinkers depends on the average consumption rate. The video articulates the great values of modernist social policy: (a) universalism (all citizens should be treated alike); (b) solidarity (we all should cut back some on our pleasures in order to protect the weak); (c) concern about problem rates and societal costs rather than individuals; and (d) finally, the belief that rational policy is possible.

Three different approaches emerged in the group discussions: modern welfare state approach to social risks; classical conservative liberalism; and neoliberal individualism.

**Welfare State Approach**

The modern welfare state approach denies any moral superiority of the state over individuals, and therefore public intervention into private consumption needs specific justifications. Alcoholism is a disease, and should be treated as any other disease. However, efforts aimed at its prevention are legitimate, not because of the pain it causes to the diseased individual but because of the suffering it causes to others, either directly in the family, on the roads or in the workplace, or indirectly as societal costs.

The responsibility of the state to take care of alcoholics is justified on three grounds. First, alcoholism is a disease and therefore not wholly dependent on the individual's free will:

*Lauri (M)*: it's a contradiction, because you would think that alcoholism is your own fault, and if somebody gets a heart condition or something in the kidneys, well that's not of your own making. But people discriminate against alcoholism and say, is it right that enormous amounts of money is spent on that when it is your own fault. But then it is ... it is a disease and it is not up to your own will, it's up to chemical reactions or physiology, so I mean *it is right* that this problem is taken care of by society

Secondly, even if alcoholism is partly incurable and also a moral weakness, it nevertheless causes suffering to others, and these may be reduced by investing public money into treatment:

*Leena (F)*: is it any good that alcoholics have been for so long treated in this country, and it's expensive too ... but when you think of it if there is no money put into this, you'll see how there will be trouble indirectly, other people will have to suffer, maybe indirect benefits will follow [from treatment] even if the sick person would not recover.

Thirdly, alcoholism as such is a cost burden to the health care system, and should therefore be prevented or otherwise controlled:

*Jussi (M)*: there was this TV programme they talked about how much a liver transplant costs, that's 500 000 half-a-million, I don't know how many of these are made ... in this town but when the bill comes to the city, to society, well that's an expensive liver if it will be put to the same use as the old one

The welfare state approach faces a dilemma. Public intervention into private consumer behaviour is believed to be inefficient and often dysfunctional, even if justified from the public health perspective. In our groups, price policy was felt to be the most acceptable one, both on the grounds of efficacy and of justice. Taxing alcohol was considered to be just because heavy drinkers cover through them part of the cost burden they cause to society, much like in the case of environmental problems.

The problem for the welfare state approach is that consumers generally do not have a public health perspective when they are thinking about alcohol, and therefore they may not be willing to cooperate. This was willingly recognised by those representing this approach, and the contradiction between individuals' duty to control themselves and the need for public intervention caused considerable hesitation, when they talked about availability, opening hours or age limits.

## Classical Liberalism

The classical liberal stand, as formulated in the study groups, faced a different problem. This understanding of the role of public powers was individualist on the grounds that everybody should pay his or her own way rather than depend on others. The objections to treating alcoholism – which again was defined as addiction and disease – in public hospitals were quite straightforward: 'Send them to a logging camp instead! [laughter]'. This way of arguing was productivist in the sense that even alcoholics were esteemed responsible for contributing their share to the national economy. Frugality rather than pleasure and satisfaction in the here and now were cherished values and, as one man representing this approach said, 'loitering is the mother of all alcoholics'. People defending this approach did not deny moral superiority that the state might have over citizens:

> *Hannu (M)*: Finnish people have become used to obey and observe a strong central government under Swedish rule, then under Russia they picked up Russian habits like drinking, Finnish people don't seem to have the manners and even if you should give them responsibility you can't. Then of course think about young people ... if you let them decide, that's abandoning them

Even the classical individualists were in favour of liberalising wine sales moderately ('special counters in qualified grocery stores'), but then they underlined the importance of authority in the family:

> *Reijo (M)*: it became a fashion to belittle the role of the family in the alcohol question, it was some kind of socialist East German model that children were taken out of the

cradle to kindergartens, I wish we'd get back to the old safe society where the home had responsibilities. Somehow I like to be old-fashioned in this that the right ways in alcohol-related matters come from the family ... I'm against norms and strict control by society and that's why I said that the wine policy should be liberalised

The suspicion felt towards the state was not so much based on conceptions of universal sovereignty of individuals; it was rather a criticism of the idea that the modern welfare state could take over functions that in classical bourgeois society have been invested in the family.

**Neo-liberal Individualism**

The neo-liberal individualist critique of public alcohol policy has – although less willing to accept public control measures – more affinity with the modernist view than with classical liberalism. It too contests the idea that the state – or for that matter anyone or any institution – might have moral superiority over individuals. Two groups of journalists and one group of cultural personalities represented this view. They believed that alcoholism is an individual disease in the sense that it is hereditary, a disposition of the personality, but most of all a disease of the will and therefore a moral responsibility. The bottom of the problem is not signalled by loss of health or of social ties but by the loss of free will. The most serious alcoholic is the one who is not able to decide whether he or she wants to drink or not:

> *Harri (M)*: I think cirrhosis is not even a problem, like lung cancer is not either.

The thrust of this argument was that public restrictions on the availability of alcohol affect negatively individuals' competence to drink sensibly, and they are therefore harmful to society. This is a version of the 'forbidden fruit' argument but has this new line: the problem is not that interdictions attract transgression; the problem is that they detract from pleasure, convenience and habit, and therefore they disturb the civilisation process which otherwise is going on in society. In all these groups the idea of modernising drinking patterns was very strongly emphasised.

These few examples illustrate the heterogeneity of approaches to the public health predicament. Contradictory and in many ways incompatible argumentations exist in parallel, even in a society where the neo-liberal individuality of the consumer society dominates. Some take the position of a consumer, whose sovereignty is being threatened. Others look at the problem from the point of view of (lost) paternal authority; still others position themselves in the role of taxpayers or of the suffering wife.

But very few would be able to articulate their objections in terms of a coherent ideological position. In our examples, the three approaches reflected other kinds of social position, although almost all the people we interviewed were in one way or other involved in local public life. The welfare state approach was defended by local civil servants and politicians, the classical individualism by local top businessmen in private enterprises, and the neo-liberal argument was supported by journalists and young persons. The arguments were context-bound and, according to our interpretation, reflected the roles in which our interviewees saw themselves as citizens and representatives of different elites in the community. It may well be that the different arguments are not fixed to specific social groups, as classical ideological cleavages have been. The same persons could conceivably articulate different and contradictory discourses at different times, depending on from which point of view they are looking at the problem.

Whatever the point of view taken, none of the three ways of speaking about alcohol policy emphasised the drinking individuals' right to be protected from the evils of alcoholism. It is everyone's duty to exercise self-control, and this was defined in terms of competence. The classical liberal arguments were based on a moral hierarchy: youth and less competent groups should be controlled by others whereas the neo-liberals argued that such external control is dysfunctional in undermining competence and responsibility. The conception of individuality as a right appeared only in the welfare state approach, but then it was seen as the right of others not to suffer from the behaviour and problems caused by excessive drinkers.

CONCLUSIONS

From the point of view of preventive alcohol policy, the coming of the new consumer society may seem like a pessimistic conclusion to the story of modern society, with its ideals of open society, the national welfare state, rationality and progress. The new particularistic individualism will look at state interventions into consumption with great suspicion; less resources will be available to support those marginalised by the drinking problem; and treatment services will be of unequal standards.

However, alcohol-related problems will certainly not disappear, not even temporarily, from these societies. In fact they are becoming more important, albeit only as one in a bundle of problems of similar nature that can be called 'consumption risks'.

The same is true not only of lay conceptions that appear in mundane speech but also of expert discourse. The French legislation of 1990 was pressed by experts who employed traditional welfare state argumentation of universalism, solidarity, progress and scientific rationality (Dubois *et al.*, 1989). If the modernist public health point of view to prevention now suffers from a lack of credibility greater than twenty years ago, it is not because its scientific foundations are weaker or because there is less need for protection against risks. It is because its perspective represents a position in society that is not understood as a project of emancipation for the public good through a benevolent state. In their recent recapitulation of this argumentation, in the light of accumulated research, Edwards *et al.* write:

> Alcohol problems have too often been left to ebb and flow. It is the job of policy so far as possible to capture and control that tide in the public interest ... The fundamental aim of policy is to reduce alcohol problems, and all measures employed should be a means to that end. (Edwards *et al.*, 1994, 212)

The problem with this statement is that the 'should' lacks a premise. Whose obligation it is and who is imposing it for what reasons, is no longer as obvious as was the case even twenty

years ago when the same programme was formulated in Bruun
et al. (1975). If many people now find difficulty in accepting
this 'should' and the consequent recommendations, it may
not be only because they are victims of industry propaganda.
They simply do not look at the alcohol problem from a position for which such definition of goals is relevant. Something
must be done about prevention as well as about allocation of
treatment resources, and this is the core also of the contemporary social alcohol question. In a de-centred society the question and the worry about it simply disintegrate; if state
monopolies on selling alcohol are in disrepute, it is even more
difficult to maintain monopolies on combatting the drinking
problem. The definition of all social problems is increasingly
divided between the media, special interest groups and the
authorities.

Such heterogeneity of the consumer society has an important consequence for research. Quite certainly, it is and
remains the task of social science and epidemiology to carefully study and demonstrate causal effects of drinking patterns, overall consumption levels, policy measures and
treatment methods on drinking problems and on their allevia-
tion. Increasingly, however, this may not be sufficient. It is important also to identify and understand different ways of
looking at the problem, to place these views in context and to
clarify them both for elites and for the general public. Only in
this way can sociology exercise a relevant and effective
intervention in society.

## References

Abercombie, N., Hill, S. and Turner, B. S., *Sovereign Individuals of Capitalism*
  (London: Allen & Unwin, 1986).
Åström, L., 'Husmodern möter folkhemmet' (Housewife meets people's
  home), in Frykman, J., Löfgren, O., Ahlsmark, G., Johansson, E.,
  Lindqvist, M., Stigsdotter, M., Åkesson, L. och Åström, L., *Modärna tider*
  (Modern times) (Lund: Liber, 1985), 196–255.
Barrows, S., 'Parliaments of the People. The political culture of cafes in the
  early Third Republic', in Barrows, S. and Room, R. (eds), *Drinking.
  Behaviour and Belief in Modern History* (Berkeley and Los Angeles:
  University of California Press, 1991), 87–97.
Beck, U., Risk Society: Towards a new modernity (London: Sage, 1992).
Bell, D., 'Resolving the Contradictions of Modernity and Modernism – Part
  Two', *Science*, 27 (4) (1990), 66–75.

Bourdieu, P., *Distinction* (London and New York: Routledge & Kegan Paul, 1984).

Brennan, T., *Public Drinking and Popular Culture in Eighteenth Century Paris* (Princeton: Princeton University Press, 1989).

Bruun, K., 'Kön och klass' (Gender and class), in Bruun, K. and Frånberg, P. (eds), *Den svenska supen* (Drink in Sweden) (Berlings: Prisma, 1985), 298–317.

Bruun, K., Edwards, G., Lumio, M., Mäkelä K., Pan, L., Room, R., Schmidt, W., Skog, O. -J., Sulkunen, P. and Österberg, E., *Alcohol Control Policies in Public Health Perspective* (Helsinki: Finnish Foundation for Alcohol Studies, 1975).

Choquet, M., Kandel, D. and Thomas, J.-P., *Réflexions sur les critères de désocialisation au travers des résultats d'enquêtes épidémiologiques. Actes de la 1ère Biennale HCEIA* (Paris: Haut comité d'ètude et d'Information sur l'Alcoolisme, 1990).

Dubois, G., Got, C., Grémy, F., Hirsch, A. and Tubiana, M., 'Non au ministère de la maladie!', *Le Monde* (15 Novembre 1989).

Edwards, G., Anderson, P., Babor, T., Casswell, S., Ferrence, R. *et al.*, *Alcohol Policy and the Public Good* (Oxford: Oxford University Press, 1994).

Featherstone, M., *Consumer Culture and Postmodernism* (London: Sage, 1991).

Frykman, J. and Löfgren, O., *Culture Builders: A historical anthropology of middle-class life* (New Brunswick: Rutgers, 1987).

Giddens, A., 'Living in a Post-traditional Society', in Beck, U., Giddens, A. and Lash, S., *Reflexive Modernization. Politics, tradition and aesthetics in the modern social order* (Cambridge: Polity Press, 1994).

Harrison, B., *Drink and the Victorians. The temperance question in England 1815–1978* (London: Faber & Faber, 1971).

Järvinen, M. and Stenius, K., 'En karl lyder mycket bättre! Restaurang-kontrollen och kvinnan' ('A man sounds much better!' Control of public drinking places and women), *Alkoholpolitik*, 2 (1) (1985), 46–50.

Ledermann, S., *Alcool, alcoolisme, alcoolisation* (Paris: Presses Universitaires de France, 1956).

Maffesoli, M., *The Shadow of Dionysos – A contribution to the sociology of the orgy* (New York: SUNY Press, 1993).

Maffesoli, M., *The Time of the Tribes: The decline of individualism in mass societies* (London: Sage, 1995).

Magnusson, L., 'Orsaker till det förindustriella drickandet. Supandet i hantverkets Eskilstuna' (Reasons for pre-industrial drinking. The crafts-men of Eskilstuna), *Alkoholpolitik*, 2 (1985), 23–9.

Mills, C. W., *The Power Elite* (New York: Oxford University Press, 1956).

Mills, C. W., *The Sociological Imagination* (New York: Oxford University Press, 1959).

Mäkelä, K., Room, R. Single, E. and Sulkunen, P., *Alcohol, Society and the State I* (Toronto: Addiction Research Foundation, 1981).

Pollner, M., *Mundane Reason. Reality in everyday and sociological discourse* (Cambridge: Cambridge University Press, 1987).

Rahkonen, O. and Ahlström, S., 'Trends in Drinking Habits Among Finnish Youth from 1973 to 1987', *British Journal of Addiction*, 84 (1989), 1075–83.

Sulkunen, I., 'Temperance as a Civic Religion', *Contemporary Drug Problems*, 12 (1985), 267–85.

Sulkunen, P., 'Alcohol consumption and the transformation of living conditions: A comparative study', in Smart, R., Glaser, F., Israel, Y., Kalant, H., Popham, R. and Schmidt, W. (eds), *Research Advances in Alcohol and Drug Problems*, Vol. 7 (New York and London: Plenum, 1983).

Sulkunen, P., 'Drinking in France 1965–1979: An analysis of household consumption data', *British Journal of Addiction*, 84 (1989) 61–72.

Sulkunen, P. and Rahkonen, K., 'Julma hyvinvointivaltio – juopuneiden säilöönottokäytäntö Suomess' (The cruel welfare state – locking up drunken offenders in Finland), *Alkoholipolitiikka*, 52 (1987) 50–60.

Touraine, A., Le retour de l'acteur (Paris: Fayard, 1984).

# 14 Governance of Consumption
## Gary Wickham

### INTRODUCTION

Consumption is not an obvious object of sociological study. It is my contention that consumption is only available to sociology as an object of governance. I suggest that the tendency to understand consumption as a general 'other' to production is extremely misleading. This tendency is quite widespread, affecting everyday talk and social scientific work, especially Marxist accounts. In this chapter I propose a framework for understanding consumption as an object of governance. In doing this I first detail my understanding of governance, an understanding which relies on work by Foucault and by Durkheim. In the second section I define consumption as an object of governance. In the third and final section, I outline the concerns of a sociology of the governance of consumption.

### GOVERNANCE

Governance is the process of controlling or managing a known object by exercising a directing or restraining influence over it. This is a combination of dictionary definitions covering three forms: 'government', as in the rule of a nation state, region or municipal area; 'self-government', as in control of one's emotions and behaviours; and 'governor', as in the device fitted to machines to regulate their energy intake and hence their performance. Governance, by this definition, is a very widespread process. Manners can be governed, as can bathrooms, diets, company take-overs, national economies, international agreements, families, and so on. The list is potentially endless and, of course, there is a great deal of overlap between different instances of governance (for more details on this and on the other aspects of governance discussed here, see Hunt and Wickham, 1994, Chapters 4–6). Governance is never complete. It never completely succeeds, because there is always at least one criterion by which every act of governance fails (see Malpas and Wickham, forthcoming). But this is productive failure. It is because of the primacy of failure that governance continues; the incompleteness of governance is the key to its perpetuation. If governance were to succeed completely, there would be no need for governance.

Governance involves power, politics and resistance, but only in very particular senses of these terms. It involves power in terms of the imperfect operation of a machine. 'Power' is a term which is applied to particular techniques of governance. Only certain techniques of governance apply to ruling nation states or regions, and these may be labelled 'state power', but in general 'power' for this understanding of governance is similar to the way the term is used to refer to the technical process by which coal, water or nuclear fission fuels an incomplete electricity grid to drive any number of electrical appliances.

'Politics' is a summary term for those processes which have emerged and continue to emerge, in myriad form, to contest particular techniques of governance. This understanding of politics suggests that these processes of contestation are very much part of the perpetual character of governance. Whatever the object being subjected to governance – a nation–state, a friendship, a bank account, a bathroom – one technique of governance is always either being challenged by another technique, or awaiting challenge. This is the case whether a challenging technique is fully formed, half-baked or barely embryonic. It is impossible for a technique of governance to be without either challenge or potential challenge; it would not be a technique of governance if it were without either, or at least no-one would or could know it as a technique of governance. This sociological definition of politics means that the study of governance is not the study of any one set, or even any limited number of sets, of techniques of governance.

Resistance is central component of governance, reflecting the fact that governance is always subject to politics. Resistance is central to the proposition that power can only ever make a social machinery run imperfectly or incompletely. Resistance is the 'counter-stroke' to power, to use Foucault's term. Power and resistance together make up the governance machine of society, but this is not to suggest that resistance is in cohort with power, that it helps to make power work perfectly. On the contrary, power and resistance together contribute to the idea that 'things never work perfectly'.

Resistance for governance also has a darker side. James Miller's biography of Foucault (1993) helps to make sociological sense of this darker, Nietzschean side of Foucault's account of resistance. I call this darker side 'the imperative to resist'. This takes us on to the ground sociologists have traditionally called the 'irrational'. It is a ground which sociologists of consumption have more recently helped to bring back on to the sociological agenda (see Campbell, 1987; Maffesoli, 1993). The imperative to resist, in terms of the sociology of governance, is an urge to move to another level of contestation, or what others call an urge to transgress. This is the moment where the alternative governing techniques, which I described as part of politics, spontaneously urge transgression; that is, urge actions which appear irrational but which have their own rationality. A rationality of irrationality dramatically renders such techniques imperative and obviously superior for at least an instant.

Of course, Foucault was interested in this side of resistance for much of his career. His account of the case of Pierre Rivière (1975) is possibly the major single product of this interest. On a more directly sociological plane, Jack Katz's *Seductions of Crime* (1988) is exemplary. Katz pays close attention to the detail of passion killing, shoplifting, 'gang' violence, robbery and 'cold blooded' murder in an attempt to bring to the foreground of sociology a particular aspect of the imperative to resist; his book is aptly subtitled 'Moral and Sensual Attraction in Doing Evil' (see also O'Malley and Mugford, 1994). Another sociological work worth mentioning in this context concentrates on a much less dark aspect of the dark side of resistance. In his stimulating work *The Tactical Uses of Passion* (1983), F. G. Bailey addresses the imperative to resist in an organisational setting – university governance. Here the imperative does not normally push individuals to violence, but rather causes administrative mischief by, for example, taking committees in directions no single member desired or could have predicted. Therefore this mysterious aspect of the incompleteness of governance is a continuum from the mildly devilish to the wildly evil.

Foucault's work on governmentality and power touches on Machiavelli and Weber (see especially the essays and interviews, by others as well as Foucault himself, gathered in Burchell, Gordon and Miller, 1991; Gane, 1986; Gordon, 1980; Kritzman, 1988), but it has surprisingly little continuity with respect to Durkheim's conception of the social (see especially Durkheim, 1912/1965; as well as Alexander, 1988; Collins, 1985; Nisbet, 1965). When actors engage in governance, when they attempt to govern some object or other, they always address an object available via the existence of society and they always use tools made available by society. Whether the actor is an individual engaged in quiet contemplation in attempting to manage a happy romantic relationship, or an organisation like the United Nations engaged in implementing an international policy as part of an attempt to limit ethnic strife in eastern Europe, governance is completely social.

Objects like 'happy romantic relationship' and 'limited ethnic strife' are only possible as objects of governance because the prior and continuing, the always-already (to borrow a term from Althusser, 1971), intersections of actors and their spatial and temporal effects which we call society, make them available. Techniques of governance like 'quiet contemplation' and 'implementing an international policy' are also only possible as techniques because these intersections – society – make them available.

This intimate relationship between governance and society, whereby governance is always a part of society, means an intimate relationship between governance and societies' tendency to continually remake themselves, that is to produce their own binding mechanisms. Governance is about attempting to create social solidarity and attempting to recreate it as each attempt fails to some extent. Community, morality, communications and physical structures, and sacred rituals, whether formally religious or not, are direct mechanisms of social binding which are never more than partially successful and hence part of social governance. Durkheim sees 'community' as a summary term for certain techniques of intimacy, continuity and cohesion, techniques which go some way towards holding societies together. Morality, for Durkheim, is both an organising principle of whole societies and, in being this, it serves the attachment of human individuals to social groups. It only exists insofar as human individuals belong to groups; there is no such thing as asocial morality. Durkheim understands communications and physical structures as measures of social solidarity – complex forms of communication and physical structure, for example large urban centres, provide a different type of social binding than less complex forms of communication and physical structure, such that, for example, complex urban societies attempt to bind around abstract phenomena like inflation and abstract gods, while simple 'primitive' societies attempt to bind around concrete, personified phenomena and personified or totemic gods. Finally, and perhaps most importantly, Durkheim elaborates many instances of the way certain objects and processes are made sacred while others are made profane, in most aspects of life, not just in formal religions. In these elaborations, Durkheim sometimes presents sacred objects as symbols and sacred processes as rituals, both serving the function of social binding.

The study of governance, in being the study of the ways socially provided objects are subject to attempts at control and direction using socially provided techniques, is then also the study, itself always incomplete, of direct social binding mechanisms. The study of governance pays attention to the details of community activities (for example, festivals, galleries, museums, and so on) as instances of governance, the operations of moralities (for example, moralities to do with sex, driving, violence, owning, and so on) as instances of governance, and communication technologies (for example, telephone, radio, newspaper, conversation, and so on) and definite spatial phenomena (for example, parks, buildings, stadia, houses, roads or cities) as instances of governance. It also pays attention to the detail of sacred social symbols (for example religious statues, cars, houses or bodies). Of course, all rituals such as prayer, football, eating, drinking are instances of governance.

It remains to be added that the study of governance is also the study of attempts to limit or displace social binding mechanisms, usually to do with resistance, dissent or revolution. These instances are of course just as much social as those direct binding mechanisms mentioned above – they have socially provided objects and employ socially provided techniques. They are also just as much instances of governance – in these cases attempts are made to manage things so that other things do not work – with the same cycle of incompletion of failure. In this sense these supposedly anti-binding instances are ultimately and ironically binding; that is, as indirect binding mechanisms. In this, the study of governance takes its lead from a combination of Foucault's proposition, glimpsed already, that power always entails resistance, and Durkheim's insight that societies' tendency to remake themselves sometimes involves what appear at first glance to be dysfunctional instances, for example high suicide rates and high crime rates.

This convergence between Durkheim and Foucault in regard to social binding makes it possible to see how their different uses of the term 'social' can work together. Where the Durkheimian sense of 'social', as I have described it here, has a broad, always-already sweep, that which pre-exists individuals in consideration of the collective actions of individuals – the Foucauldian sense – is more limited. This sense, often given by Foucault's adherents in the noun 'the social', focuses on new questions of government (see especially Donzelot, 1988; 1991). In this usage 'the social' is a definite category of the government of nation states and regions 'invented' in the nineteenth century. The Foucauldian sense of social refers to a modern, Western phenomenon.

'The social' is a new conjunction of attempts to manage populations – their longevity, education, children, work, their health in its broadest sense. These attempts feature new governmental techniques we might now summarise in English by the term 'welfare'. These new developments were sparked by new governmental thinking around the notion of insurance. In line with some shifts in probability theory, it became possible to make very detailed calculations about, and make provision for, the health and welfare of larger and larger numbers of people. Governments before had never been able to attempt to govern the future lives of populations in such detail and on such a scale (see especially Hacking 1975, 1990; Ewald, 1991; Defert, 1991).

The two senses of 'social' come together in that the newer Foucauldian sense dovetails with the traditional, Durkheimian sense. The always-alreadyness of society is boosted by the 'invention' of 'the social' as a special, intense field of government. It is no coincidence that sociology emerged as the science of society at the time these two senses of 'social' came together. I suggest that it is neither possible nor desirable to separate the two senses in late twentieth century sociology. The always-alreadyness which is society in its traditional sense now includes those objects and techniques of government invented in the nineteenth century as 'the social' – children's welfare, infant health, mass literacy, industrial accidents, child protection legislation, special health programmes, mass compulsory schooling, industrial safety legislation and inspectorates and so on.

## CONSUMPTION AS AN OBJECT OF GOVERNANCE

As suggested on p. 277, I attempt to avoid the definition of consumption as a general 'other' to production. Consumption, as I see it, can only be defined in the particular cases of the myriad attempts to direct it. This leaves its 'itness' somewhat uncertain. I am saying, quite intentionally, that consumption has no essence for the social sciences, it is only a term given to a series of processes identified and seen to have features in common by attempts to govern them. So, just as the breathing of air can only be an object of study for the social sciences in terms of attempts to direct it in some way – attempts to provide and maintain clean air for breathing, attempts to discipline the body which concentrate on breathing techniques, and attempts to medically induce breathing are three attempts at governing the breathing of air. They are objects for social scientific study because of the involvement of governance – so the consumption of any item(s) or service(s) can only be studied by the social sciences in terms of attempts to direct it or them in some way.

I am especially inspired by Alan Hunt's project which traces various uses of sumptuary law in his *Regulating the Consuming Passions* (forthcoming). He gives several examples of the operation of sumptuary law. Here are just two:

1. An English statue of 1336 required that:

> no man, of what state or condition soever he be, shall cause himself to be served in his house or elsewhere, at dinner meal or supper, or at any other time, with more than two courses and each mess of two sort of victuals at the utmost, be it Flesh of Fish, with the common sort of pottage, with sawce or any sort of victuals ... except only on the principal feasts of the year ... on which days every man may be served with three courses at the utmost, after the manner aforesaid.

2. The preamble to a Florentine statute of 1433 reads:

> After diligent examination and mature deliberation, the Lords Priors have seen, heard and considered certain regulations issued by the magistrates ... They realise the great desire of these officials to restrain the barbarous and irrepressible bestiality of women, who, not considering the fragility of their nature, but rather with that reprobate and diabolical nature, they force their men, with their honeyed poison, to submit to them. But it is not in accordance with nature for women to be burdened by so many expensive ornaments, and on account of these unbearable expenses, men are avoiding matrimony ... But women were created to replenish this free city, and to live chastely in matrimony, and not to spend gold and silver on clothing and jewellery. For did not God himself say: 'Increase and multiply and replenish the earth'?

Hunt proposes the following working definition of sumptuary laws, or at least, of their operation: 'sumptuary laws regulate the conspicuous consumption of "citizens"; that is to say, sumptuary laws are concerned with the social manifestations of consumption'. Sumptuary law was a special area of law which attempted, always unsuccessfully, to regulate certain aspects of the behaviour of citizens across Europe and North America from about the sixth century BC to about the end of the eighteenth century, though not consistently; it seems to have almost completely died out for long periods. Roughly speaking, the aspects of behaviour which were the targets of this form of regulation were those concerned with bodily practices and rituals which had special status in terms of what Durkheim calls 'social binding'. These could be funerals, eating, dress, sex; one only need consult Norbert Elias' wonderfully rich history of manners (1978) to get an idea of the vast scope of such practices.

Consumption is an object of social scientific knowledge only because and insofar as it operates as an object of governance. However, no general definition of consumption can be constructed on this basis – not even a tentative one. To take another example, the consumption of sport is a term which covers certain 'consuming' activities around sport, identified and grouped by attempts to govern them. I define 'sport' as any activity treated as sport by historically generated sports institutions (Wickham, 1992, 220). Of course, no essence to these activities can be identified such that they can be instantly and universally recognised by students of the consumption of sport, but a working list of some of them is needed to allow sensible discussion. My list is: spectating at a sporting event; watching a television broadcast of a sporting event, or listening to a radio broadcast of a sporting event, or reading a newspaper or magazine account of an event; collecting or even perusing paraphernalia associated with a sporting event. Even conversing about a sporting event is almost by definition subject to a governing mechanism, which consists of rules and constraints regulating what can be meaningfully said about them. Shortly I discuss these activities in detail; for now, I reiterate, the list is only possible, because the items on it can be identified and can be grouped as a sensible object for social scientific discussion due to the fact that these activities are or have been governed.

## THE GOVERNANCE OF SPORTS CONSUMPTION

In line with certain methodological rules I outline elsewhere (Hunt and Wickham, 1994, Chapter 6), a sociology of the governance of consumption must involve compiling details about the various ways in which consumption is governed. Foucauldian sociology is concerned with 'how' questions, not 'why' questions. For the sociology of consumption this means a continuing concern to build detailed accounts of the techniques used in governing consumption for theoretical interpretation. Perhaps the best way to demonstrate the working of a sociology of the governance of consumption is by continuing the example of sports in more detail.

The governance of sports consumption involves governing the self, governing particular sports and governing societies, including the central issue of social binding. The governance of the self is fairly straightforward. Sports consumers are involved in the government of the self in undertaking whatever disciplines are necessary to maintain their statuses and capacities as members of a sports-consuming community or several such communities. These disciplines vary from simply turning on the television at a particular time and sitting in front of it for a few minutes, to queueing for days to obtain a ticket for an event, queueing for hours to get in to an event, putting up with extremes of weather, containing the desire to use a toilet, and submitting to the ordeals of various officialdoms. These disciplines may include participation in ritualistic violence or techniques for avoiding such violence. Every technique used in consuming any sport in any fashion must involve some discipline, some restraint and direction of the self, no matter how small an amount, perhaps no more than being in a certain place at a certain time, and hence some self-government. There is no way of knowing these instances of governance beyond their particular occurrences, as is the case for each of the three areas of governance I am discussing here; a metatheory or meta-description of the governance of sport consumption is not possible.

The governance of particular sports is more complex. Within my broad definition of sports, some involve very small numbers of participants. In these cases – say, for example, frog racing – participants are quite likely to be involved in making and carrying out decisions about the conduct and direction of their sport. They are quite likely, in their capacity as club members, or even possibly just as spectators at a live event, to help make and carry out decisions about the rules for the contest(s) involved in the event, often ad hoc, temporary rules; for example how far the frogs should race, or how each frog should be handicapped.

When larger numbers of sports consumers are involved, most consumers are unlikely to participate in the making and carrying out of decisions. Mass-consumption sports are widely recognised as important features of cultural life in many late twentieth century nations. Their governance is likely to follow patterns of the governance of other late twentieth century institutions which involve masses of citizens, including nation states themselves. British citizens do not govern Britain in the way citizens governed ancient Athens, and television-watching Olympics consumers or match-attending soccer consumers are not involved in the governing of the Olympics or of FIFA in the way participants govern frog racing at their local picnic.

This is not to say that this situation is static; that would be to leave politics out of governance. Challenges to 'official' governance are always being formulated and acted upon also in mass-consumption sports. Spectators may formulate and act upon alternatives to official techniques of governance. A good example is the supporters' magazines ('fanzines') movement in British soccer. These supporters' magazines formulate and act upon their alternative techniques for governing their particular soccer clubs outside the reach of the club's official governance mechanisms. An 'umbrella' magazine for these vehicles – *When Saturday Comes* – not only widely publicises the efforts made at club level, but also actively comments and criticises the policies of Britain's Football Associations and Football Leagues.

The huge majority of consumers of mass sports are involved in governing in only marginal ways, but in between the small-scale cases and the mass-consumption cases, there are many instances – local and regional football for example – where the degree of involvement is more equally balanced. Whether the sport in question involves a few sports consumers or a mass of them, or somewhere in between, the governance of sport is never entirely internal. Sports consumers, whatever the extent of their governing role in this area are, for instance, subject to the law of their nation state and to the laws and customs of the community they visit.

Sports consumption is part of a society and therefore part of attempts to bind this society together. Socially produced objects to do with sports consumption – the sports themselves, crowds, spectators, clubs, television sports programmes – are subject to attempts at control and direction using socially provided techniques – policing, statistics, conversation – which are themselves also objects of governance.

Sports-consuming involves techniques of intimacy, continuity and cohesion around communities: teams, clubs, regions, nations. Such communities contribute to basic moral principles, in regard to cheating or drug-taking, for instance, being unacceptable, (or, for that matter, acceptable), which help bind these communities internally and help bind them to other social communities. They act as communications devices and provide physical structures, such as grounds, club-houses or stadia, which serve, however imperfectly, in attempts to bind modern complex societies. More importantly, they provide sacred social symbols, especially teams, clubs, idols and rituals, such as attendance *per se*, watching or listening *per se*, chanting, violence, avoidance of violence, singing and collection of paraphernalia, which have very important functions of social binding (see Hornby, 1992).

Instances of the governance of sports involve instances of resistance and dissent that can be violent. Also such seemingly anti-binding instances are ultimately binding albeit indirectly. What appear at first glance to be dysfunctional phenomena like soccer hooliganism, actually serve to bind societies against the hooligans for example, or even around them, though of course never completely or perfectly.

RITUAL, RESISTANCE AND CONFLICT

The conceptual analysis presented above and its application to sports can be generalised to any field of consumption. Consumption is the site of both control and resistance, and therefore of conflict. Whatever the rationale of attempts to direct it, governance always entails an aspect of ritual and thus processes of social binding.

The chapters in this volume provide ample material for further reflection of these processes. To take a few examples, gambling in the Netherlands (Kingma, Chapter 9), the consumption of nutrition in Norway (Jensen and Kjærnes, Chapter 11), the consumption of 'environmentally friendly' products across Europe (Simmons, Chapter 12), or the consumption of alcohol in Finland (Sulkunen, Chapter 13), have been and continue to be subject to attempts to direct them in different ways. These attempts are sites of resistance and contestation; therefore they never completely succeed.

Power and the politics of contesting it have recently featured historical changes in Dutch gambling regulations, Norwegian nutrition policy and Finnish government regulation of alcohol consumption. The traditional welfare state regime of power-governance has come under attack by techniques which urge more self-regulation. It is my suggestion here that the recent success of these latter does not signify less governance; instead it should be understood as a change in the regime and kind of governance. As the Dutch example shows, when authorities have deregulated gaming they find that this has led to a need for more regulations to govern gambling addictions and other troublesome behaviours.

Furthermore, new kinds of conflicts could be expected to emerge. If resistance has earlier taken the form of publicly defying various interdictions or recommended diets, could at least part of the addictive behaviours in such areas be interpreted as half-conscious private resistance through self-destructive behaviour? In such instances, governance continues to work incompletely, the resistance contributing to both their governing and the incompleteness of this governing. The result is marginalisation and unnecessary suffering for a minority of consumers, but somehow the society must face the fact that their pain is an ill and a burden for others and the society as a whole. This leads to new kinds of conflicts over the governance of consumption.

This situation is part of a larger picture of social binding in the countries concerned. Both the objects of governance – gambling, alcohol and food – and its techniques – government regulations, moral and physical constraints – are only available as social constructions through the always-already-ness of society. The consumption of alcohol, gambling and nutrition and their governance involve techniques of intimacy, continuity and cohesion to the extent that we can say that different communities of consumers are formed. These communities in turn are the ground for the operation of certain moral codes, in favour of healthy bodies, healthy diets and an healthy environment, against the emotional and physical excesses of drunkenness and gambling. These moral codes operate in incomplete ways to produce binding both for and against them by making some objects and processes sacred, like individual pleasure for some, good health and reasonable life for others.

The emotional commitment to such codes can be interpreted as a result of the ritual aspect of the attempts to govern and resistance to such attempts. Such an interpretation entails the ironic situation whereby even supposedly anti-binding practices like resistance to government regulation and to self-discipline, the spontaneous desire for excess, and so on, contribute to social binding, always incomplete of course, always perpetuating governance. But also the more obvious binding practices, like government regulations and consumer organisations, represent ritual and not only rational or instrumental forces of social binding.

This interpretation exemplifies the way the Foucauldian sense of 'social' dovetails with the traditional, always-already Durkheimian sense. The always-alreadyness of governing the consumption of gambling, nutrition or alcohol includes objects and techniques invented as part of 'the social' in the nineteenth and twentieth centuries. Public health programmes, welfare legislation and programmes, environmental legislation and inspectors, mass education and mass literacy are all important conditions of existence for governing drinking practices, nutrition or gambling. It may be that the nature of these structures is changing in the new consumer society but even the new techniques of governance of consumption depend on their always-alreadyness and to socially constructed existence of their objects.

## References

Alexander, J. C. (ed.), *Durkheimian Sociology: Cultural studies* (Cambridge: Cambridge University Press, 1988).

Althusser, L., 'Ideology and Ideological State Apparatuses', in Althusser, L., *Lenin and Philosophy and Other Essays* (London: New Left Books, 1971).

Bailey, F. G., *The Tactical Uses of Passion: An essay on power, reason and reality* (Ithaca: Cornell University Press, 1983).

Burchell, G., Gordon, C. and Miller, P. (eds), *The Foucault Effect: Studies in governmentality* (London: Harvester Wheatsheaf, 1991).

Campbell, C., *The Romantic Ethic and the Spirit of Modern Consumerism* (New York and Oxford: Basil Blackwell, 1987).

Collins, R., 'The Durkheimian Tradition', in Collins, R., *Three Sociological Traditions* (Oxford: Oxford University Press, 1985).

Defert, D., '"Popular Life" and Insurance Technology', in G. Burchell *et al.* (eds), *The Foucault Effect: Studies in governmentality* (London: Harvester Wheatsheaf, 1991).

Donzelot, J., 'The Promotion of the Social', *Economy and Society*, 17 (3) (1988), 395–427.

Donzelot, J., 'The Mobilisation of Society', in G. Burchell *et al.* (eds), *The Foucault Effect: Studies in governmentality* (London: Harvester Wheatsheaf, 1991).

Durkheim, E., *The Elementary Forms of Religious Life* (New York: Free Press, 1912/1965).

Elias, N., *The Civilising Process, Volume One: The History of Manners* (Oxford: Blackwell, 1978).

Ewald, F., 'Insurance and Risk', in G. Burchell *et al.* (eds), *The Foucault Effect: Studies in governmentality* (London, Harvester Wheatsheaf, 1991).

Foucault, M., *I Pierre Rivire, Having Slaughtered My Mother, My Sister and My Brother: A case of parricide in the nineteenth century* (New York: Pantheon, 1975).

Gane, M. (ed.), *Towards a Critique of Foucault* (London: Routledge & Kegan Paul, 1986).

Gordon, C. (ed.), *Michel Foucault: Power-knowledge* (New York: Pantheon, 1980).

Hacking, I., *The Emergence of Probability* (Cambridge: Cambridge University Press, 1975).

Hacking, I., *The Taming of Chance* (Cambridge: Cambridge University Press, 1990).

Hornby, N., *Fever Pitch: A fan's life* (London: Victor Gollancz, 1992).

Hunt, A., *Regulating the Consuming Passions* (forthcoming).

Hunt, A. and Wickham, G., *Foucault and Law: Towards a sociology of law as governance* (London: Pluto Press, 1994).

Katz, J., *Seductions of Crime: Moral and sensual attractions in doing evil* (New York: Basic Books, 1988).

Kritzman, L. (ed.), *Michel Foucault: Politics, philosophy, culture* (New York: Routledge, 1988).

Maffesoli, M., *The Shadow of Dionysus – A contribution to the sociology of the orgy* (New York: SUNY Press, 1993).

Malpas, J. and Wickham, G., 'Foucault, Sociology and the Importance of Failure' (forthcoming)

Miller, J., *The Passion of Michel Foucault* (New York: HarperCollins, 1993).

Nisbet, R., *Emile Durkheim* (Englewood Cliffs, NJ: Prentice-Hall, 1965).

O'Malley, P. and Mugford, S., 'Crime, Excitement and Modernity', in Barak, G. (ed.), *Varieties of Criminology* (New York: Praeger, 1994).

Wickham, G., 'Sport, Manners, Persons, Government: Sport, Elias, Mauss, Foucault', *Cultural Studies*, 6 (2) (1992), 219–31.

# Index